D1330244

'You need this book on your shelf.'
LONDONIST

'A fascinating look at a fascinating part of London.'
ROBERT ELMS, BBC LONDON

'A charming addition to the canon. The "Lives" in the
subtitle – a colourful cast of rock stars, bohemians,
hustlers and slum landlords – are brought to life in
such detail, you can almost smell the jerk chicken.'
EASYJET TRAVELLER

'I've published two novels about Notting Hill,
but after reading Julian Mash's *Portobello Road*
I realise: THIS is the book I wish I'd written.'
RACHEL JOHNSON

'Julian Mash lets the people tell their own stories of obsession,
creativity, challenge and community. Let's just hope this
work of vitality and energy doesn't turn out to be an elegy.'
CATHI UNSWORTH

'A wonderful paean to a district that remains home to genuine
local characters and retains a uniquely Bohemian air.'
TRAVIS ELBOROUGH

12670760

PORTOBELLO ROAD

Lives of a Neighbourhood

Julian Mash

F

FRANCES LINCOLN LIMITED
PUBLISHERS

Frances Lincoln Ltd
74–77 White Lion Street
London N1 9PF
www.franceslincoln.com

Portobello Road
Copyright © Frances Lincoln Ltd 2014
Text copyright © Julian Mash 2014
Illustrations copyright © Alice Smith 2014
Picture acknowledgements as listed on page 308

First Frances Lincoln edition 2014
First paperback edition 2015

All rights reserved. No part of this publication may be reproduced,
stored in a retrieval system or transmitted in any form, or by any
means, electronic, mechanical, photocopying, recording or otherwise, without either prior permission in writing from the publisher
or a licence permitting restricted copying. In the United Kingdom
such licences are issued by the Copyright Licensing Agency,
Saffron House 6–10 Kirkby Street, London ECIN 8TS.

A catalogue record for this book is available
from the British Library

ISBN 978-0-7112-3744-5

Set in Monotype Perpetua
Typesetting by Bracketpress

Printed and bound by CPI Group (UK) Ltd, Croydon, CR0 4YY

9 8 7 6 5 4 3 2 1

Contents

PART ONE
INTO THE MARKET

PART TWO
LORD, DON'T STOP THE CARNIVAL

For Gudrun

Beyond the Blue Door

Living and working around Portobello Road, one soon grows accustomed to the hordes of tourists who descend on the street at weekends. They spill out of Notting Hill Gate Tube from early on Saturday morning, emerging blinking into the daylight in couples and small groups. Whatever corner of the globe they may have come from, one common goal unites them: they are here to find the Blue Door, and the bookshop from Richard Curtis's 1999 film *Notting Hill*. Dressed in pac-a-macs and puffa jackets and clutching phones and maps close to their chests, they ask passers by and shopkeepers for directions. Nosing their way to the top of Portobello Road they descend its hilly incline and, if successful, find themselves outside 13–15 Blenheim Crescent where the sign marking the Travel Bookshop hung between 1980 and 2011.

I had begun working at the bookshop almost by accident when one day in February 2007, I spotted a sign taped to the window advertising for staff required. At the time I was in a struggling indie band, on the look out for a part-time job to help pay the rent, and the Travel Bookshop seemed like the ideal environment. For the first few months it worked perfectly – the bookish peace of the shop provided the ideal foil to my life of rehearsing and writing songs, making flyers and posters for gigs or traipsing across the country on trains, buses and in cars. We would play in pubs and clubs to whomever would listen, lugging our amps and guitars up and down stairs, selling our 7-inch singles and chasing down money from unscrupulous promoters.

Incrementally, though, the bookshop took over from the band, where tensions were beginning to show and tempers were fraying. I would look forward to unpacking deliveries and ordering books more than working on new songs and playing gigs. Events came to a head with a post-gig fight in a Parisian hotel room, a stolen taxi, a trashed dressing room and a run-in with the local gendarme. A long, stuffy, silent coach journey home the following day left us pondering our future. One thing was certain: I now knew it was not advisable to be in a band with your girlfriend. It might have worked for Fleetwood Mac, but it certainly did not work for me.

Now I was a full-time bookseller, the *Notting Hill* film was part of my daily existence, and I adopted the mantra of, 'No, it was filmed in a studio but this was the inspiration,' chanted back by staff in response to the query of whether this was indeed the 'shop from the film'. I remained stunned at how popular and far-reaching the film remained, its idealized version of life in the capital resonating with people from as far afield as Beijing and Sydney. It was more than a love story to its fans – it was a vision of London life to aspire to and seek out.

Day after day, I would see the same scene played out on the shop floor – a group of tourists would enter with a look of amazed excitement on their faces, some shrieking with delight, grabbing on to one another as if to steady themselves from the shock of finding The Shop. Lines from the film would be recited, photos snapped and songs hummed. Some would be so intent on recording the moment on their phone or camera that they would barely look up from the screen before leaving, experiencing the whole episode digitally. Excited Japanese girls would ask to have their photo taken with me, standing next to me flicking their double V-for-victory signs, some even asking for my autograph – this had never happened to me in the band.

In their quest for the Blue Door and The Shop these tourists were unwittingly honing in on one of the vital elements at play in the changing make-up of any neighbourhood: the desire for the authentic experience. Sharon Zukin, who made a recent study of the New York suburb of Brooklyn, cites authenticity as a key factor as neighbourhoods are reshaped: 'Authenticity in this sense is not a stage set of historic buildings.... it's a continuous process of living and working, a gradual build up of everyday experience, the expectation that neighbours and buildings that are here today will be here tomorrow. A city loses its soul when this continuity is broken.'[1]

Of course, a city is by its nature a constantly renewing space shaped by layers of migration, but the changes that were occurring in and around Portobello over recent years were happening with such speed that it was stripping away the origins at an alarmingly fast rate and intrinsically altering the manner in which the community interacted with the place. Shops that had been a feature of the street for decades were being forced out by huge rent hikes, replaced by impersonal high street chains.

With the sudden closure of the Travel Bookshop in September 2011, I found myself cast within this narrative, part of the disappearing neighbourhood I had been observing. During the final week, as we sold off the remaining stock at a 50 per cent discount, I was struck by the very real sense of loss felt not just by locals and regular customers but also by the media, who jumped on the story. Reporters and television crews from around the world camped outside, local writers gave interviews plugging the importance of the shop and a group of poets clubbed together, trying desperately to prevent its closure. It seemed that people cared about the origins of the place, about the past, about continuity.

It was more than simply a place to buy the latest Lonely Planet or replace a lost Patrick Leigh Fermor paperback; it was some-

Portobello Road

where to drop in, have a chat, ask for a book recommendation, book a ticket for an author reading or leaf through a new hardback. For many, the shop was the first port of call when planning huge life-changing journeys across continents, or even just a weekend away in Stockholm. Customers would always enquire about where I was going next. What great trip did I have up my sleeve? Now that I no longer had the shop to anchor my days to the area I was free to think about where I was headed. But I already knew where I was going, my journey had already started and now I had the chance to lose myself in it, unhindered by lack of time – my journey would be in search of the origins of the neighbourhood.

What follows is a series of snapshots of the recent past, made up of interviews with residents, shopkeepers, writers, artists, musicians and market traders. It is a beating of the bounds, an update on the ancient custom whereby the community would walk the boundaries of the parish and pray for protection and blessings for the lands. Using Portobello Road as my geographical spine, and confining my roaming to the post-war era, I will be using buildings and people as signposts along the way, walking the length of the street from leafy Notting Hill Gate in the south to gritty Golborne Road in the north, standing in the shadow of Trellick Tower, I will be unravelling some of the lives of the neighbourhood.

PART ONE

INTO THE MARKET

Early morning Portobello Road, 2014

There is nothing more enjoyable than to walk the length of Portobello Road on Fridays and Saturdays with the market in full swing, admiring the stalls that have appeared overnight, which transform it into an eclectic fair selling everything from records and vintage clothes to spicy street food and fruit and veg. I agree with Iain Sinclair's assertion that 'walking is the best way to explore and exploit the city', as each section of the road reveals its own distinct character, its own sights, sounds, smells and atmosphere – from the rough and ready bric-a-brac at its northern end around Golborne Road to the more expensive antiques on offer the closer you get to Notting Hill Gate.

My flat is full of Portobello Road finds, from the 1950s standard lamp to the Danish coffee table and Philips record player. These bargains were picked up on the strip between Chesterton Road and Oxford Gardens, where I often stop and chat to stall-holders, like Irish Brendan who is always smiling and tells me about his adventures the night before as he eagerly anticipates the football results later that day – or Gareth the dealer next door in his old blue transit van. When I enquired about his recent absence from the market, he informed me he had been away on tour with Bruce Springsteen, where he is employed as his tour chef, looking after The Boss's culinary requirements.

The canopy under the Westway houses the vintage fashion stalls. If you arrive early enough you will see the stallholders setting up for the day ahead, unloading shopping trolleys and

Tony and his tiger are regulars

carts laden with laundry bags full of clothes. Metal poles clang and clatter as they are slotted together to form the stall frames, soon to be turned into individual clothing emporiums.

Further along Portobello, the enticing smells of street food begin to mingle in the air. A truly global cuisine is on offer, from Ethiopian and Moroccan through to burger and chips and falafels. Past the Afghan shop – which seems to sell everything one could need for the home, from mousetraps to curtain rods – the costermongers stand behind their stalls, dusting down their fruit and veg while hollering out the prices of apples and potatoes as they try to woo the passing shoppers with their deals. Peeling off Portobello onto Talbot Road I often look into Rough Trade Records and flick through the new releases, passing the time of day with Nigel, the long-serving manager. Just around the corner I grab my caffeine fix in the Coffee Plant, where the whole neighbourhood seems to queue up for a takeaway cup of their aromatic brew. Then it is on and up past the

Portobello Road on a busy market day

antiques arcades, where you can find stalls specializing in every-thing from silver plates and pocket watches to antiquarian books and Persian rugs. There are far fewer antique shops than there used to be on this stretch, though some of the originals remain, such as Judy Fox at number 81 and Barhams at 83.

The following chapters contain interviews and encounters I have had with some of Portobello's shopkeepers and market traders. They include conversations with those currently work-ing in the neighbourhood, as well as with some who moved on long ago, but whose memories of Portobello offer a unique insight into the history of the area. I have tried to capture the spirit of a street where unexpected meetings occur and you never quite know what you will end up carrying home.

In recent years Portobello has lost some of its best-loved shops. These include the Kingsland Edwardian Butchers at 140 Portobello (which was forced to close after 163 years of trading after a massive rent increase), the famous Travel Bookshop

Rummaging for bargains on Golborne Road

(which shut its doors in 2011), and most recently Intoxica Records (closed in 2013). There are an increasing number of stalls selling tacky T-shirts and key rings and high street shops such as Kurt Geiger and Whittard. The recent closure of Lipka's Arcade, with the loss of 150 stalls, in exchange for a branch of the high street retailer All Saints, does not bode well. But it has been heartening to see the Save Portobello campaign spring into action and garner so much local support demanding that the council protect this stretch of the city from more development.

Guiding my journey through the neighbourhood have been the words of Jane Jacobs, the American journalist, author and activist, who highlighted the importance of street life and street contact in her seminal 1961 work *The Death and Life of Great American Cities*:

The trust of a city street is formed over time from many,

many little public sidewalk contacts. It grows out of people stopping by at the bar for a beer, getting advice from the grocer and giving advice to the newsstand man, comparing opinions with other customers at the bakery and nodding hello to the two young boys drinking pop on the stoop, eyeing the girls while waiting to be called for dinner, admonishing the children, hearing about a job from the hardware man and borrowing a dollar from the druggist, admiring the new babies and sympathizing over the way a coat faded. Customs vary, in some neighbourhoods people compare notes on their dogs; in others they compare notes on their landlords.[2]

The next time you are strolling down Portobello Road, look out for some of the people included here. You too can buy some apples from Peter Cain or refuel with a falafel from Mustafa's 'Happy Vegetarian' van. Because in spite of the slow encroachment of chain shops and super wealth that has so changed the community over the last fifty years, there remains a unique spirit running through these streets. You just have to know where to look.

Out of the Barrow and
into the Ring

Throughout the 1960s, audiences at Odeon and Gaumont cinemas were treated to one of the *Look at Life* mini-documentaries screened before the main feature of the evening. Designed to replace newsreels, whose format felt increasingly outdated in the television age, the look and feel of the series reflected the new jet age of modern Britain. They tackled subjects as diverse as motorways, airports and space travel, alongside domestic news stories such as the rise of the coffee bar, the scooter craze and swinging London. In the spring of 1965 an instalment called 'Market Place' hit the screen: a short film looking at the relevance of street markets versus the new breed of supermarkets which were cropping up in increasing numbers across Britain.

One of the markets that the Rank Organisation's small three-man film crew had spent time filming in was Portobello Road. It features heavily in the finished film and the footage they shot is remarkable – the street is bursting with life, people jostle to get a spot at the front of the queue as stallholders scream and holler at the top of their lungs about the quality of their wares. The jaunty script, full of pithy one-liners and amusing anecdotes, is narrated by Sid James, whose chuckling delivery gives one a sense of warm familiarity. As the camera lingers on a group of people crowding around an antiques stall full of silverware, sharp elbows ready to edge out the competition, we are told, 'This is the chief market in London for new and second-hand silver goods. Some of the stallholders standing here are carrying on a tradition started by their grandfathers and great-grandfathers.'

While this is true, and Portobello is of course famous for its antiques and bric-a-brac stalls, it is wrong to attribute the origins of the market to antiques; rather, Portobello is built on vegetables. Its position today is underpinned by the trade that sprang up over a hundred years ago, when certain enterprising individuals loaded up their barrows with fresh fruit and vegetables, hauled them down to the Lane, as Portobello was then known, and sold them to the local population. The market was founded in order to feed the poor of the neighbourhood with good, cheap food.

There are still a handful of fruit and veg stalls whose families have been here for several generations, trading long before the council licensed the pitches and the police would spend their days trundling up and down the street clearing away the illegal traders. But the number is dwindling fast. In autumn 2011 the street lost two families who had held pitches here for over a hundred years, quietly admitting defeat in the face of supermarket dominance and the area's changing landscape.

I knew that I would come up against resistance from some who would question why I was writing and what my credentials were. As welcoming and village-like as Portobello is, it also displays that village mentality of distrusting the newcomer. Even people who have lived here for ten or twenty years are viewed with a certain level of suspicion. The success of the film *Notting Hill* and the notoriety that it has bestowed on the street has not helped this, hardening attitudes, making people wary and media shy. And who can blame them? This media fascination with the street is in danger of killing off the thing that made it so unique in the first place – its identity.

Being a creature of habit I had tended to frequent one particular fruit and veg stall over the years. If I needed a few potatoes for that night's supper, or some fruit to snack on in the afternoon, I would go to the stall at the corner of Talbot Road and pick something up. I had a bond, a loyalty to the stallholder, and we would have a quick chat about the football or the weather and I would be on my way.

One morning I outlined my project to him and asked him if he could spare me some time. 'Sorry mate, I never talk to anybody. Nothing personal, just the way I've always been. Keep it all inside, know what I mean?' I did understand, and was prepared for his rebuttal, but the disappointment still stung. Turning away he called back, 'Why don't you try my nephew, Peter Cain, just down the street?'

I did just that and, after sussing out my intentions, Peter agreed to meet up and discuss his life and experiences in the market. It was then that things took a turn for the frustrating. Peter is one of a dwindling band of people who have resisted the encroachment of the mobile phone, so rather than exchanging numbers we agreed to meet the following Monday at the pub opposite his stall. How refreshing, I thought. This is what the market is all about: connecting with real people, an antidote to the digital 3G age. Who needs a mobile anyway? Just make an arrangement and turn up, easy.

On the scheduled day I arrived a little early with my tape machine and notebook at the ready, found a seat in the corner and waited. Fifteen minutes went by, then half an hour. I polished off my first Guinness, and read and re-read the *Metro*. Soon it became obvious he wasn't going to turn up. He must have forgotten. I kept checking my phone, half expecting a text to pop up on the screen announcing that he was running late. But of course there was no message. How frustrating. Why didn't he have a phone? Who doesn't have a phone nowadays? This was just the sort of situation when a mobile comes into its own, when it is essential, in fact. The next day I popped by his stall and as I drew up on my bike I saw his face registering his mistake – he was very apologetic and we rearranged for the following week, same time, same place.

Sadly it was not only same time and same place but also same outcome as the previous week. This was getting tiresome now. And so it went on. The more the arrangement was broken the more determined I became. Several meetings came and went. I began to doubt myself. Was there something I was doing wrong? My girlfriend thought I should forget him – it was too difficult; I should concentrate on something else; it wasn't as if I was pushed for material, quite the reverse in fact. But with every broken, non-meeting and my subsequent chat with Peter we were forging a close bond; in a funny kind of way, through these non-meetings I felt I was getting to know him better than ever.

My perseverance paid off when we finally met at the pub in mid-December, amid the lunchtime drinkers and raucous office Christmas outings. As the afternoon went by, and one Guinness turned into another, Peter proved to be the most charming and interesting of characters. There can't be many fruit and vegetable sellers who are also former middleweight boxing champions with 165 fights to their name, as well as having starred in Pier Paolo Pasolini's *The Canterbury Tales* in 1972. But I am getting ahead of myself here, for above all Peter Cain is a Portobello man through and through. If anyone can claim to be a local then he can.

There have been Cains selling fruit and veg on this street for three generations, ever since his great-grandmother Dolly Cain moved west from Paddington after the First World War. One of the founders of the market, she would sell from the back of her barrow wherever and whenever she could and was one of the first stallholders to be granted a fully licensed pitch in the late 1920s. She would entertain young Peter with stories of how she had served notorious mass murderer and local resident John

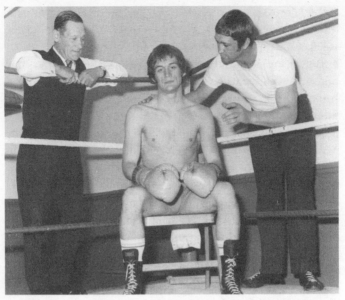

Peter Cain with trainer Len Cain, and grandfather Jack, October 1973

Christie, insisting that she never trusted him. During the
Second World War they worked on in spite of the Blitz, taking
cover in the shelter on Blenheim Crescent during the raids and
opening up again as soon as the all clear sounded.

Peter's father joined the trade when he returned from the
Second World War broke and jobless, borrowing a flat barrow
that he would wheel down to Covent Garden every morning,
and 'buy ten boxes of cauliflower 'cos he didn't have a lot of
money, put them on it, wheel it all the way back down here,
trim the cauliflowers up and try and sell 'em'.

Peter was born in the winter of 1951 in a small room in
Dunworth Mews, just off Portobello Road, a few feet from his
current pitch. 'There was a little tiny kitchen, toilet downstairs,
a little front room and two small bedrooms. Running water

coming down the walls rather than out of the taps, the zinc bath would be bought out once a week and whoever was dirtiest got in it last.' He attended the Colville School before going on to Holland Park Comprehensive. It wasn't long before Peter was being taken on the daily trip to Covent Garden Market or even down to the docks where his father would buy produce directly from the ships as they unloaded their cargo.

Talking to Peter is like plugging into the soul of the market. He is a big man, over six foot, lean and fit looking, with piercing blue eyes that hold your gaze. He is not prone to nostalgia but over the course of the time I spent with him it becomes obvious that he feels a deep sense of loss and regret at the position that the fruit and vegetable market finds itself in today. 'The supermarkets have not only ruined the small businessman, they have broken down communities,' he states, remembering when Tesco first opened on Portobello in the early 1960s and his father pointed it out to him saying, '"That's no good, they wont be happy until they have it all," and he wasn't wrong was he?'

Looking at the market today one would have to agree with him. Where once the street was packed with fresh produce, and stalls selling bread, fish, meat, fruit, vegetables and salad, now only a handful stand, holding out until the bitter end. It really does feel more like a film set dressed with a few stalls rather than the working, bustling market depicted in celluloid in the *Look at Life* film forty-five years ago.

The market used to be the hub of the community and Peter saw his job as much as a social enabler as a fruit and veg man. 'People would communicate and have a chat at the stall, have a bit on tick. If they needed to find a plumber they might ask you and you would try and help and suggest someone they speak to. It was a whole network of people, a community.' Not surprisingly, Peter reveals that the last three to four years have been the quickest in terms of the decline of the stalls, with some of his oldest friends and fellow traders leaving the street for good.

It is a far cry from the 1970s, when there would be more than seventy stalls all doing a roaring trade, packed in one after another along the street. His father would arrive back from Covent Garden in the truck filled with new produce, and a queue would form next to his pitch full of people eager to purchase from them. His mother would regularly sell '9 tonnes of potatoes a week, in the fifties and sixties – now you wouldn't sell four bags of potatoes in a week!'

He is proud of the role that he and his family have played in the history of the market. Although he was only a young child at the time, he can clearly remember his great-grandmother Dolly Cain's funeral in the late 1950s, which involved a procession through the market as all the stallholders and residents paid their respects. This is a tradition that has been upheld to the present day, though as fewer and fewer traders live in the area it has become a rare occurrence.

As we leave, Peter retrieves a large canvas bag from under the table with a couple of boxing gloves bulging out of the top. He is off to train some young boxers, to keep his hand in he says, as his fighting days are long behind him. He knew it was time to call it a day in in the late 1970s when he wasn't recovering as quickly after each fight.

There is a glint in his eye when he recalls some of his finest moments in front of packed houses at the Royal Albert Hall and York Hall in Bethnal Green, including his 1974 fight against Henry Cooper. His training regime was strict, rising at dawn to run up and down Parliament Hill before a day on the stall. Perhaps it was his peak physical shape that attracted the eyes of one of Pasolini's film scouts when in early 1970 he was accosted as he strode down Regent Street and asked if he would be interested in acting in a film. With nothing to lose he found himself summoned before the great director, who was holding court at the Piccadilly Hotel, having booked out the entire top floor. Pasolini liked Peter's face and he was given the role of Absalom in *The Canterbury Tales*. He spent the next few months ensconced on location in Canterbury and Somerset, grappling with his lines and rubbing shoulders with a whole new set of thespian friends.

But it is to Portobello that Peter has always returned, and where he will play out the remainder of his working life on the pitch that has seen so much change and in such a short burst of time. A few weeks ago, as he was setting the stall up, pulling his barrow out of the lock up in the mews where he was born, someone opened a window above him and shouted out . . .

'Excuse me could you please not make so much noise. Me and my girlfriend can't sleep.' So I looked up at him and I said, 'Mate, this is still Portobello Road Market, these stalls were here before you. If you don't want any noise then I suggest you bugger off to Berkeley Square.'

Laughing to himself, he heads off into the December night, bag under his arm, shouting a greeting to an old friend across the street.

Cheryl Collins
Costermonger

Cheryl is the third generation of her family to have traded on
Portobello Road. I spoke to her from her pitch outside the
Oxfam shop about her time on the market and her thoughts
over its future.

I started when I was eight, helping my parents on
Saturdays. I used to sell lemons from a little box on the
corner five for a shilling. I left school at sixteen and I'm
fifty-five now so it's quite a few years, every day. No
holidays – I don't do holidays because my body clock takes
too long to get used to a break, then I'm back here again,
no point. I get up at 3.30AM every morning. It takes me
half an hour to put my make-up on and wake up, then half
an hour to get to market. I take around four hours to run
around and choose my goods and I get back here at half
eight. I go to the Western International Market, near
Heathrow. I like it better there – my dad used to go there
so I followed on. You have to be on it – for example, this
morning I bought some strawberries. He charged me 80p.
Exactly the same strawberries were down the road for
70p. I went to cancel them but the porter had very quickly
put them on my van so I couldn't take them back – little
things like that, you gotta be wise! My dad had done it
since he was eleven, and died when he was seventy-three,
and his dad had done it, right back to my great-grandad.
All along here the Collinses have always been here as far as
I can remember. I don't know whether my kids will take it
on – this generation are too damn lazy. Trade is terrible
now, look around you. I am blocked in by clothes for
tourists; there is nothing here for locals. The tourists just
take pictures and ask questions. They are hard work, they
are not really here to buy, they want the cooked food.

Cheryl Collins serving a customer

You come here on a Saturday it's all cooked food – it's absolutely destroyed the market, it's finished. There is only about ten original families left on Portobello and I think when we give it in that will be the end of this market. When I was sixteen this was all family-orientated shops; now there is nothing, it's all corporates, look around. There is only one family-orientated place left and that is the Coffee Plant, and that is the only place I would ever go here. All the rest are big stores who don't pay their taxes. [Shouting a hello to a customer] You just don't get this with Tesco [motioning to a couple who have walked past]. I seen their children grow up and now they have their children, it's just so nice. But the market won't last. Cooked food will take over – slops I call them – the stink of them makes me heave. I'm so anti, I'm old school. I've got people who live above these shops here, all bankers now, the only people who can afford these rents. They go on the Internet and have Ocado delivered – you see it in the morning.

The Cock and Bottle
17 Needham Road

The neighbourhood pubs have mostly moved on from the kind of dingy and dangerous places that Martin Amis used as inspiration for The Black Cross, the pub situated on Portobello Road frequented by Keith Talent in *London Fields*. Most of them have become gastropubs and been given a makeover of stripped floorboards and flea market furniture. This has even happened to the Kensington Park Hotel (or KPH) on the corner of Ladbroke Grove and Lancaster Road, where mass murderer John Christie used to drink in the 1940s and which had remained a dimly lit spit and sawdust place until its overhaul.

There are still a few local pubs that resist the inevitable change, like The Portobello Gold, where Motörhead's Lemmy would hold court, and The Cock and Bottle on Artesian Road, just off Westbourne Grove, which attracts a small bunch of regulars, men in late middle age from artists and actors to builders. I spoke to the landlord Richard, a genial Northern Irishman in his late fifties, who has been serving pints in Notting Hill since the 1970s. He started out at The Alma on Westbourne Grove, which is now the hugely popular and trendy Grangers restaurant. He worked there from 1975 to 1990, and when the lease came up on The Cock and Bottle he moved here. He tells me, 'Prior to 1987 this pub was called The Swan. It has been a pub for over 160 years. I know that because I have seen a map from that period that shows the Catholic church on one side and pub on the other.' He proudly tells me that they haven't changed the decor 'one bit', explaining that 'We have redecorated but we have always put it back exactly the same way.'

He has seen the shift from pubs to restaurants in this area. 'Down the road at 202, which is now a restaurant – that was The Duke of Norfolk; what is now The Ledbury restaurant used to be a pub called The Duke of Cornwall; and Bumpkin

The bar at the Cock and Bottle

restaurant used to be a pub. That is four pubs just off the top of my head that have shut in the last twenty years.' The shift from bedsits to single occupancy houses and the influx of money saw trade drop: 'The gentry round here don't use the pubs like the flats and bedsits people used to.' This, combined with the sale of cheap alcohol in supermarkets, has left Richard feeling pessimistic about the future of small establishments like his. 'People don't want these places any more. For years I thought they would make a comeback, but now I am not so sure.' But he loves his job. 'I wouldn't have been doing it for over forty years if I didn't. It's the fun industry, it should be the fun industry.' The old pre-Internet idea that if you need to contact someone then you should head to the pub still holds sway here, as Richard explains:

> We have all sorts here. If you need someone to direct a film we've got somebody – in fact, we have probably got two or three. If you want somebody to sing a song for you we've got plenty because there are so many music people coming in here. If you want somebody to demolish something or build something for you we have got them all here. If you ever do anything wrong and you need a top barrister just come down here, alongside the guy that sweeps the streets and empties the bins.

Vinyl Habit: Minus Zero and the Life and Death of the Record Shop

I know one thing for sure: vinyl is not a convenient format. Carting my ever-growing record collection from flat to flat in my twenties was not a pleasurable experience. During one move, as I made my way up and down the stairs to my room located on the top floor of a house on Ladbroke Grove, one of my new housemates stood and stared at my antics in astonishment. 'Why don't you just convert them to mp3 and get rid of the records?' he helpfully suggested. 'You'd still have the music and wouldn't have the hassle of shifting them.' Standing in front of him gently perspiring as I buckled under the weight of my Motown and Girl Groups section, I could tell it would be useless to try and explain the magic of vinyl, so I just nodded and agreed that yes, that was a great idea, it had never occurred to me before.

While it was, and still is, the music that is contained in the dusty grooves of these slabs of plastic that first caught my imagination, the collecting and acquiring of them is equally important. I have spent months of my life in record shops, becoming attuned to their eccentricities and rhythms. I have made lifelong friends and been turned on to music I would never have otherwise listened to. Over the years I have learnt to use record shops as signposts, acting as urban markers that say more to me about the usefulness of an area than any guidebook could.

When I was on tour with my band I had become adept at

Flicking through the racks in Rough Trade, 2014

nosing out record shops in the dead hours between arriving at a venue for the sound check and the gig. For example, while I would be next to useless as a tour guide to Cardiff, oblivious of the locations of its historic monuments and sites of interest, I could lead you with authority to Spillers, one of the city's oldest and best record shops, tucked away behind the main high street.

It was in this spirit that I began to explore Portobello when I moved into a flat on Chesterton Road at the dawn of the new millennium. I was pleased to discover that I was living among some of the capital's best record emporiums – Honest Jon's, Rough Trade, Dub Vendor, People's Sound, The Record and Tape Exchange and Intoxica were all on my doorstep. However, it was Minus Zero/Stand Out!! on Blenheim Crescent that fast became my favourite, and the place where I would invariably be found on a Saturday afternoon.

Upon first entering the shop I knew I was onto something special. As I pushed open the heavy wooden stable-style door, it was like entering a Narnia for record collectors. I was greeted by a dimly lit interior, there was a distinctly musty smell – part damp, part stale cigarette smoke – and the walls were festooned with picture discs, foreign issue EPs and original gig posters. The racks overflowed with vinyl as the first 13th Floor Elevators LP blasted out of the shop speakers at full blast. I fell instantly in love with the place.

Over the course of my first few visits I noticed something odd. Rather than a single record shop I was in fact entering two shops, one was called Minus Zero and the other Stand Out!! They both stocked similar records (psychedelia, folk and soul) and to make matters even more confusing the proprietors were both called Bill. On the right hand side was Bill Allerton and on the left was Bill Forsyth.

Things had not always been this way. They had started the shop as a joint venture in 1984 under the name Plastic Passion, but a falling out in the late 1980s led them to this compromise, quite literally dividing the shop down the middle and trading as two separate businesses, creating a sort 38th parallel that had endured ever since.

It was amazing how quickly as a customer you accepted this situation and before long it seemed perfectly normal. Having more in common with Bill Forsyth's musical tastes I found myself chatting to him about obscure Dylan bootlegs and early REM albums. Sometimes I would just idly flick through the racks and earwig on other customers' conversations. Takeaway coffees would be bought in from the Coffee Plant and drunk by customers and the two Bills. It was more like a social club than a shop. On any given Saturday there was usually a customer at the counter umming and ahhing over a pile of records or trading in some discs from their own collection. I learnt to trust Bill Forsyth's recommendations – through him I became acquainted with the privately pressed early 1970s folk albums of Agincourt and Ithaca, and I came to appreciate the genius of Robert Wyatt.

On one of my usual Saturday visits in autumn 2009, Bill Forsyth broke the news to me that the shop would be shutting the following spring. I was stunned. A combination of a sharp rise in the council's rates, a migration of record shopping online and a further irreparable breakdown in relations between the two Bills had led to the decision. Perhaps this news should not have come as a surprise; it was simply another statistic to factor into the huge numbers of record shops going to the wall.

In the space of a just over a decade the number of independent record shops in the UK plummeted from 1,064 in 1998 to just 269 in 2009. In the era of digital downloads and cut-price CDs, perhaps this decline in their numbers was a natural development. Whatever the reasons, it filled me with sadness to think that the current generation of music lovers would be turned on to new sounds by clicking on YouTube links and scouring blogs rather than trawling record shops and chatting to their staff.

Over the next six months visiting the shop became akin to visiting a sick relative, and as the date loomed ever closer my visits increased along with my purchases. In spring 2010 a huge sale was held as lifelong customers made their final pilgrimage to the shop they had been visiting for decades. Following its closure Bill Forsyth and his wife Anne decided the time was right to move out of London, settling in the Sussex town of Bexhill-on-Sea. They had been part of the Portobello community for forty years and had watched the neighbourhood change year by year. Packing my Dictaphone and notepad in my bag I took the train down to Bexhill on a chilly winter's day to hear their story and capture their memories of Portobello.

Tucked away in his upstairs record room Bill recalled how he got into the record dealing world, with Anne chipping in to correct dates and gently remind him of people and places. Bill is a baby boomer, born in Paddington in 1951 and part of that enviable generation who came of age just as London became the swinging capital of the universe. Failing his O-levels, thanks to an unhealthy obsession with John Peel's 'Perfumed Garden' radio show, and unable to play an instrument, working in a record shop seemed like the next best thing. He frequented the happening folk clubs of the time, such as Les Cousins and Bunjies, before graduating to the Roundhouse, witnessing seminal concerts by the likes of Pink Floyd and Family.

His first job was at Soho Records, a small chain of shops that were partly funded by the Pye label. Stationed at their Ludgate Hill branch, which specialized in classical music, he was their token long-haired member of staff and given the job of curating their brand new rock'n'roll section. He remembers the lunchtime rush, when the shop would be filled with bowler-hatted gents flipping through the latest classical acquisitions, propping their umbrellas up against the counter as they read the composers note on the back of the LP. Bill would use this moment as his opportunity to test out the first Black Sabbath LP, gingerly unwrapping it from its plastic sleeve before blasting it from the shop speakers, waking the aged City gents from their lunchtime reveries and proving that the new generation were a noise that couldn't be ignored.

Moving from Soho Records to stints at seminal shops Musicland and One Stop Records, Bill was witness to the beginning of the golden age of the record shop. In the wake of *Sgt. Pepper*, albums had replaced singles as the countercultural currency of choice and the record shop was the only place to get them. Every week an incredible new LP would be released by the likes of Led Zeppelin or Pink Floyd and customers would flock down to pick up their copy.

By this time Bill and Anne had a young daughter and were living in a flat on Blenheim Crescent. They would spend most Saturday mornings nosing around the Portobello and Golborne

Bill and Anne Forsyth, 1970

Road markets picking up bargains for their flat or looking at second hand clothes and records. Bill became friendly with a local hippy known as Canadian John, who had a record stall on Golborne Road. Flicking through his boxes one day Bill noticed that some of them were priced much higher than the rest, commanding up to £10 instead of the usual pound or two. What's more, he owned some of these expensive LPs, but had never thought of them as valuable items. Canadian John explained that some were worth more because they were a certain issue or a deleted album, and in that instant Bill became initiated into the world of record dealing.

It is easy for today's collectors, who use the Rare Record Price Guide and Popsike, to forget that things were not always this way. Back then collecting was mainly the preserve of the 1950s rock'n'roll fanatics, as Bill recalls: 'It was an open field at this point. There were no price guides, only a few collectors' shops specializing predominantly in rock'n'roll.'

It wasn't long before Bill started to trade in records on the market, sharing a stall with Canadian John before securing his own pitch. Punk brought a whole new generation of record buyers, and Bill remembers one day on the stall in 1977 particularly well. He had been doing a good trade in a Sex Pistols bootleg called *Spunk*. *Spunk* essentially consisted of high-quality demos of their album *Never Mind the Bollocks, Here's the Sex Pistols* recorded with the original line up (including bassist Glen Matlock), which many fans consider to be a superior version. It certainly sold well and generated considerable publicity, leading to speculation that manager Malcolm McLaren was involved in its leaking and distribution.

Bill was selling these bootlegs on Golborne Road in the autumn of 1977. 'They were selling really well for five or six quid when this old school friend of mine called John Tiberi showed up. I would run into him sporadically and we had a chat. He looked at my records and said, "Have you got anything good in, what's selling?" and I said, "I've got this new Pistols bootleg, selling really well actually," and pulled it out to show him. He inspected it as I enquired as to what he was doing these days. He looked up and replied, "I'm road manager for the Sex Pistols." Trading in bootlegs was a highly illegal activity and Bill did not want to get on the wrong side of the law so early on in his record dealing career. 'But John did not mind at all and even bought a copy.'

After a spell working at one of the first Virgin Megastores on Oxford Street, which he ultimately found 'vast and soulless . . . so impersonal', Bill found himself back on the market and setting up a mail order business. There was no grand plan to find a shop; rather it happened almost by accident when, one day in 1984, Anne spotted a 'To Rent' sign hanging outside number 2 Blenheim Crescent and the idea took hold. They called the number written in black marker pen on the sign and were promptly shown around the shop. Bill knew instantly it was the right move and invited his record dealer friend Bill Allerton to share the premises with him. They opened up that autumn.

The shop went on to become one of the most well known and well loved record shops in the capital, trading first as Plastic Passion before splitting down the middle in 1989 and continuing as Minus Zero and Stand Out!! A stream of regulars would visit alongside the rock royalty like REM, Courtney Love and Bobby Gillespie.

Over the course of writing this book Portobello has lost another of its most revered record shops: Intoxica. Intoxica had traded at 231 Portobello Road since 1994 before finally succumbing to an insurmountable rent rise, closing its doors for good in January 2013. I had become a regular customer over the years, picking up singles and trading in records when money was tight. The staff were friendly and knowledgeable and manager Nick Brown could be relied upon to play you a killer garage single you just had to buy. Like Minus Zero, it had deep roots in the area, having grown out of Vinyl Solution (a legendary shop that traded first on Hereford Road before moving to 231 Portobello in 1989). Nick took over the shop in 1994 and renamed it Intoxica. 'I thought that at the time all record shops were just boring. It was the same old Van Morrison and Hollies albums for sale with a load of old Beatles rubbish. I just thought all these rock record shops were really dull – the ethos of Intoxica was to stock records that we loved. So we started selling jazz, soundtracks, soul, R&B, funk and easy listening, as well as rock music and punk stuff and new wave.'

That was exactly what Intoxica set about doing for the next nineteen years, picking up a loyal customer base. One of those customers was Mark Lamarr, who now owns the ultimate memento of the shop – the Intoxica sign, as Nick explained: 'I was due to hand the keys back to the landlord on the last Thursday in January. On the Wednesday night I had a phone call

Two shops in one: Minus Zero/Stand Out!! Records in 2005

from Mark Lamarr, who I have known for years and years. He said, "I just drove past your shop and the sign is still up. Can I have it?" I said, "Yeah, if you want," but explained how big and heavy it was.' Expecting this flight of fancy to go no further Nick returned the keys to the landlord and a few days later spoke to Mark and was astonished to discover that he had indeed taken the sign, enlisting the help of Bill Bailey. 'They had showed up at about 3AM with a pair of stepladders and some screwdrivers, getting it off the wall and loading it into the back of the van. He has since cleaned it up and it now sits in his record basement.'

With these record shop stories swirling around in my head and the recent closures on the street I was beginning to feel downhearted about the future of the record shop. Were we heading for a world where eBay and Discogs.com ruled? Were the days of the independent record shop numbered? As if the gods of the record shop could sense my despair, I was met with a heartening sight on a bright sunny day in April 2013. I had arranged to meet a friend at Rough Trade on Talbot Road on Record Store Day, an annual celebration of independent record shops, when in-store gigs took place and special edition records were pressed up by labels and made exclusively available. Having not participated in it before, I did not know what to expect.

Arriving soon after lunch I was astonished to find hordes of people gathered on the pavement outside the shop watching bands perform through a makeshift PA. Not only that but a long queue snaked around the corner as customers waited their turn to enter the shop before emerging, smiling and happy, into the sunshine clutching bags of vinyl. Nigel House, the long-standing manager of the shop, was in his element, chatting to new and old customers with his infectious enthusiasm. Locating my friend among the crowd of hipsters, we watched a mod-looking Japanese singer belt out a few numbers on an acoustic guitar.

Seeing Rough Trade buzzing like this, I felt a wave of relief wash over me. It was clear evidence that vinyl still has a place in the post-digital world.

The Coffee Plant,
180 Portobello Road

Portobello Road is not short of places to cure your caffeine craving: from market stalwart Mike's Café on Blenheim Crescent, which has been serving strong builders' tea and hearty fry-ups for decades, to Café Lisboa further north on Golborne Road, which is invariably thronged with customers drinking *bica* (Portuguese espresso) and sampling the delicious *pastel de nata* (egg pastries), undoubtedly the best in West London. But the place that unites everyone from market traders through to David Cameron is the Coffee Plant at 180 Portobello Road.

It has been at its present location for twelve years and operates in the grand tradition of the London coffee house as somewhere to meet friends, gossip and disseminate news. It is a no-nonsense sort of place opting for metal utilitarian chairs and tables rather than upholstered armchairs or sofas. They invariably blast out music on weekends – anything from banging techno to the Band. On weekends the queue can often stretch out of the door at mid-morning peak coffee-drinking hour, but as the owner Ian Henshall told me, they specialize in dealing with it quickly. 'Our biggest problem is that people who don't know us see the queue and think they are going to have to wait 20 minutes when actually they will get their drink in about 5 minutes.' The Coffee Plant sells around 200 kilos of coffee a week and serves 3,500 hot drinks, so it is always busy.

Specializing in gourmet, organic and Fairtrade coffee, Ian started out by roasting coffee on a Portobello Road forecourt in 1985. 'I got some green coffee from Kenya but found it was almost impossible to get it roasted. Then I realized that this problem offered an opportunity, and me and my friend built our own homemade coffee roaster and started roasting it right on the street. It made quite a lot of smoke, leading the *Evening Standard* to describe it as "the best smell in London".' From

The Coffee Plant at 180 Portobello Road

these makeshift beginnings Ian built a business that has thrived despite several chain coffee shops popping up all along the street – in addition to a branch of Whittard setting up camp right next door. But with coffee and an atmosphere this good I certainly won't be switching – mine's a flat white.

The Notting Hill Bookshop now trades on the site of the Travel Bookshop and the tourists still flock to take photos

The Travel Bookshop
1979—2011

When I first started working at the Travel Bookshop I was astonished at the number of tourists who flooded the shop at the weekend keen to experience 'the shop from the Notting Hill film'. Most of them were so excited to be entering the hallowed interior that they overlooked the fact that they were standing in one of the best independent bookshops in the city. As if blinded by the glitz and glare of Hollywood, they would video and photograph everything and ask the dreaded question: 'Is this the shop from the movie?'

The answer was both yes and no. It was the inspiration for the film's setting but it was shot on a set at Shepperton Studios. Moreover, the exteriors were filmed just around the corner at 142 Portobello Road, now a shoe shop rather fittingly called Notting Hill. But when any of us attempted to explain this situation to our foreign visitors we were met by blank expressions, making it sometimes easier to just nod and say, 'Yes, this is the shop from the movie.'

The obsession with the film obscured the fact that the Travel Bookshop was a neighbourhood institution that had, over the course of its thirty years on Blenheim Crescent, carved out a unique reputation as a pioneering bookshop presided over by knowledgeable staff. Established in 1979, it differed from other bookshops in the way it was arranged: geographically rather than A–Z by author; here novels, non-fiction and guidebooks shared the same shelf-space. That might not sound particularly noteworthy today in the Internet age, but thirty-five years ago it was a ground-breaking idea.

Founder of the shop Sarah Anderson explained how it came to her following a frustrating visit to Hatchards in the late 1970s. 'I was going on a trip to China and I went in and asked the staff "What novels do you have set in China?" And they pointed me to the fiction section and I said, "Well, I don't know!" I suddenly thought to myself, "Gosh, how wonderful it would be to have everything about a country gathered together on the same shelf." And it was a unique idea, I mean, no one had done that before.'

When she was back in London the idea had solidified into a plan. She was certain that this was not only a good idea, but also a gap in the bookselling market. With that in mind she set about acquiring stock, enlisting the help of renowned travel writer and journalist Peter Hopkirk, whom she credits as being 'terrifically helpful' in passing on his extensive knowledge of Central Asian and Middle Eastern books to her and advising her on what to purchase. 'Every weekend he would take me off to second hand bookshops that were near-ish to London and advise me about what to buy.'

Sarah explained that she initially opened the shop on Abingdon Road in Kensington, where it traded for two years before she moved to Blenheim Crescent in 1982. Notting Hill was still a relatively down-at-heel area, but she had 'a hunch' and felt that there was a community here that would support a bookshop such as hers. Her family and friends could not understand her decision to move. 'I faced enormous opposition from everyone saying, literally, "Notting Hill? Who's heard of Notting Hill?", but I was just determined, I just knew.' Her uncle, who was helping to finance the business, was very unsure and needed persuading, but in the end Sarah's determination won out and he came around to the idea.

Buying the building, she set up shop at 13 Blenheim Crescent and with money being tight she didn't have much to spend on the interior, fitting it out with simple wooden bookshelves. She remembers that at one stage someone suggested they hire an elephant to walk down Portobello Road to publicize the re-launch of the shop – sadly this proved too difficult to organize.

Over the next few years she put in long hours, manning the shop with the help of just one part-time member of staff. She was practically tied to the building, an irony not lost on her. 'I was meeting all these people going off on these wonderful trips but I couldn't go away at all.' But business was brisk and her timing could not have been better with the early 1980s witnessing a boom in travel writing, as writers like Jonathan Raban, Paul Theroux and V. S. Naipaul sold in their thousands. 'It really was the Golden Age. And travel reprints began to appear at that time, something which had never been done before – there was Eland, Century Travellers, and then Penguin started doing it too.'

Travel guides, too, were just starting to take off, catering for this new generation of globetrotters. 'At that time, guides hardly existed. I mean, Rough Guide were just beginning, and Lonely Planet had only been going for a bit. There was just one guide to Czechoslovakia and I think today at the last count there were about thirty-five to Prague alone!'

Sarah sold the business in 1990 while remaining as shop manager, freeing her up to travel again. It is testament to the brilliance of Sarah's idea that the Travel Bookshop's model of laying out the shop country by country was adopted by James Daunt, who has a chain of renowned independent bookshops across London named Daunt Books.

We come to the question that follows Sarah everywhere when people find out she is the founder of the Travel Bookshop – was her shop really the inspiration for the film? 'It was all very mundane really,' she explains. 'Richard Curtis, who lived around the corner and was a customer anyway, came in and said he was thinking of writing a film set in a bookshop, and could he sit and take some notes? So I said yes and that is exactly what he did. So for a couple of mornings he sat and took notes, looking at the type of people that came in and the telephone calls that would be taken and so on. And I never really thought it would happen, because a lot of people say they are planning to do things and they never really happen.'

But it certainly did happen. In fact, the filmmakers came back and photographed the interior of the shop, modelling the set on what they saw, right down to the flickering black and white CCTV monitor next to the till. Sarah was not working when they made this visit. 'The next thing I knew was that they were filming in Portobello Road!' During the shoot both Julia Roberts and Hugh Grant came into the shop. Julia Roberts bought some Rumi, Sarah tells me, rolling her eyes. Were there any of the moments in the film she recognized from the time Richard Curtis spent in the shop with his notepad? 'I think possibly the scene where there is a customer persisting in asking for a book they don't stock and the guy is saying, "No, it's a travel bookshop." I think that happened.'

Sarah has mixed feelings about the film. On the one hand it put the place on the map, but hadn't she already done that through creating a respected and pioneering independent book-shop? The hordes of tourists arrived 'almost instantly' in the film's wake. 'It was on the Japanese bus tour of London and the bus used to stop outside and disgorge, and they would all troop in. Eventually we had to stop them because it just flooded the shop. Everyone imagines it must have increased business, but I don't think it did particularly, because those kind of people don't buy books.'

And it hasn't stopped. 'Rarely do I go out of my front door

without seeing somebody taking a photograph.' It is ironic, I think, that despite all this publicity the shop still could not fight off the dramatic downturn for independent bookshops in recent years. The factors are myriad but one of the key turning points was the collapse of the NET book agreement in March 1997, which meant that books could now be sold for less than the publishers' recommended cover price. She describes that decision as 'a disaster, a disaster. It was quite obvious that it would be, because bestsellers used to be the bread and butter for small bookshops. It didn't used to matter where one got them, but of course it is completely different now with the Internet. I mean Tesco are selling Harry Potter for £2.'

In the rush to secure the cheapest price we are taking our trade online to Amazon, and combined with the recent and ongoing recession, the bookshop is an endangered breed. In 2012 independent bookshop numbers in the UK sank to a new low of 1,028 compared to 1,535 in 2005. But those figures only tell part of the story, for we won't know what is truly lost for some time to come. Independent bookshops are not just about buying and selling books – they are places where likeminded people can interact and debate, and without them the street will be a poorer place.

Lutyens & Rubinstein,
21 Kensington Park Road

In October 2009 the neighbourhood gained a wonderful new
addition to its literary heritage when bookshop Lutyens &
Rubinstein opened for business at 21 Kensington Park Road.
Founded by Sarah Lutyens and Felicity Rubinstein, the shop
grew out of the literary agency of the same name that the pair
had been running since 1993 from an office on nearby
Westbourne Grove. It had long been an ambition of theirs to
open a bookshop, and ever since the closure of the beloved
local Elgin Books they felt that there was a need for a general
bookshop to compliment the specialist booksellers in the area.
When the lease on number 21 came up they jumped at the
chance and moved their agency into the basement of the building where it operates from an office behind a secret bookcase
doorway. On the other side of the sliding shelves the shop is
beautifully designed. Handmade shelves display a stock of
around 6,000 titles, fiction and non-fiction, plus a wonderful
children's section. Felicity describes the stock as 'heavily
curated', offering a 'bespoke service' to the local community.
The staff are always ready with a recommendation whenever
I pop in and they regularly host events in the evening that
have seen authors like Jennifer Egan and Geoff Dyer reading
from and discussing their latest work. It seems that despite
these tough times for independent bookshops, Lutyens &
Rubenstein are proving that there is still a need for a well run,
expertly stocked independent local bookshop. Felicity is
upbeat describing their first four years as 'better than we even
dared hope. I think although people enjoy shopping online
they are now remembering why they enjoy shopping in
bookshops again.' Having grown up in the area and lived on
Westbourne Park Road for the past twenty-three years, she
describes the community as 'incredibly literate, full of film
makers, writers and dramatists'. She has been heartened to see

Felicity and Sarah in the doorway of Lutyens & Rubinstein,
the heart of literary Notting Hill, 21 Kensington Park Road

local people using the shop on a regular basis. 'There has been
an amazing amount of local support, which is really fantastic.'

Alice's Antiques, 86 Portobello Road

Homeless Bones:
Antiques

Director Dick Clement had high hopes for *Otley*, the 1968 film he adapted for the big screen with Ian La Frenais. It starred Tom Courtenay as Gerald Arthur Otley, a hapless drifter and general layabout, who dabbles in antiques and lives and works around Portobello Road. But it did not prove a box office success and watching it today it is easy to see why – it is an uneven mix of comedy spy caper and swinging London film that doesn't quite gel and is saved only by brilliant performances from Tom Courtenay, Romy Schneider and Leonard Rossiter. However, it is worth seeking out for the opening five minutes, which feature some superb footage of Portobello Road. We follow Courtenay as he walks down the street on a busy market day from its junction with Chepstow Villas past its intersection with Westbourne Grove. It is particularly interesting because it shows us how this stretch of the street looked when it was dominated by antique shops. The market is in full swing all around Courtenay as he strides down the middle of the road, waving to friends and acquaintances, pausing for a moment when something catches his eye on a stall before resuming his pace. Children race past as couples walk arm in arm and locals scurry past carrying baskets filled with their weekly shop. A Don Partridge song titled 'Homeless Bones' soundtracks his progress before we lose him in the crowds as the camera pans back from an upstairs window.

I am discussing the film with Michael Barham, proprietor of Barham Antiques at 83 Portobello Road, one of the shops clearly visible in those opening frames. His father had bought the building in 1962 and transformed it from a Welsh dairy that had been there for at least one hundred years into the antique shop that it remains today. Although he was just a young boy at the time he tells me he has distinct memory of the filmmakers asking his dad to hang something from the doorway of the shop.

Michael started working here as a thirteen-year-old on Saturdays in 1969 and now runs the business with his brother. The shop is crammed with beautiful little wooden boxes with mother of pearl inlays polished to perfection, along with small clocks, silver toast racks, plates, candlesticks and trays. I am careful not to knock anything over as I chat to Michael, now in his mid-fifties and one of only a handful of the original antiques dealers left on Portobello Road. He tells me that his dad was happy to have found suitable premises, having traded from a market stall on Portobello since the 1950s. He had originally taken to antique dealing when he was demobbed from the army and was looking for a way to earn some money. Michael explains that back in the 1960s many of the dealers on the street were part-time traders, picking up stock during their travels in the week and selling at the weekend. 'A lot of them claimed to be actors,' he says, 'but how many of them were I don't know – permanently resting actors, perhaps.'

He describes it as an intriguing place to work, 'full of interesting characters that you can't imagine doing anything else for a living because they were not particularly employable. It was laid back; there were a lot of people jostling to make money, but it wasn't frantic. Even in those days you could have times when it was very quiet, a bit like now,' he says, gesturing around the empty shop, 'but Saturday was always busy.'

In the old days, he would accompany his father on buying trips to small antique shops outside London, but as these have dwindled in number he now acquires most of his stock from big antique fairs that that take place up and down the country throughout the year, augmented by bits and pieces picked up at auction. Up until the 1990s they specialized in Victorian furniture, supplying a buoyant Spanish market, but when their economy went 'belly up' they shifted their focus to the sort of thing that people can carry away with them easily or stow in a suitcase, catering to the crowds who descend on the street on Saturday and nowadays Sundays as well. 'So I went into boxes, and as luck would have it Americans bought them, and the American market has always been strong with antiques.'

I ask him if he has ever had something slip through his fingers or been sold a fake. 'One day a chap came in with a skeleton clock. Now I never buy anything from people who just turn up and bring it in. But he seemed quite respectable and he wanted £200 for this clock. I looked at it, but I wasn't sure, so I didn't buy it just to be safe.' He watched the man leave and go around the corner onto Ledbury Road, later learning that he took it to a clock specialist who immediately identified as a Daniel Quare worth in the region £50,000–£60,000. The clock dealer assumed it must have been stolen, and turned the gentleman away before calling the police. He was apprehended further along Ledbury Road and after some questioning the police ascertained that he was indeed the owner of the clock. Michael wryly notes: 'So the dealer did him a favour, because he didn't know what it was or what it was worth!'

The main difference today is that the number of antique shops in the neighbourhood has plummeted. 'This whole block here was antiques. Over the crossroads there were more arcades, but those would have been mostly shut during the week. If you went down Westbourne Grove, that was all antiques, including all along Ledbury Road. That was the way throughout the 1970s and 1980s, right up until the early 1990s.' Dealers and customers would flock to the area specifically to buy or trade, whereas

Some beautiful wooden boxes in Barham Antiques

nowadays he regularly hears people walking past saying things like 'Why are there so many antique shops down here?' or 'Oh look, an antiques shop!' There is a hint of sadness in his voice when he says, 'They think Notting Hill is a whole different thing, where they will find fashion shops and they might see somebody famous, or they are looking for the Blue Door.'

He talks with pride of the old days.

There was very much a community spirit among the dealers. Everybody knew everybody else, and you were always in somebody's shop to borrow something. If you were carting bits of furniture around, everybody would chip in and give you a lift. The ones of us who are still old school still do that; for example, I have been with Judy Fox this morning to deliver something of mine and something of hers to a place in Park Lane.

'What's your best price?'

He doesn't see this community spirit in evidence with the new crop of market stalls selling mobile phone covers and cheap T-shirts. In fact, he has seen several arguments and fights break out in recent years. He is quite rightly concerned that this shift to tourist-oriented tat will damage the area in the long term.

If you are a tourist and you are travelling around, you don't want to see the same stuff that you see everywhere else. You go somewhere for a reason, to see what is peculiar to that place. And to fill it with all the same generic stuff just doesn't make sense. It makes me angry because we are Portobello Road, we are what it is, and everyone else, like property developers, is living off it. That's what makes me angry because they are selling what we created. We are helping to draw the crowds and they are being sold T-shirts.

You know we will stick here for as long as we can, but I wouldn't want my kids to do this. Most of the dealers here are past fifty, and if their kids don't carry it on then I can't see them staying. Most of the shops here command rents that the dealers can't afford, so it'll just end up as a tacky tourist area, really.

At that moment a delivery arrives that requires Michael's attention, so I take this as my cue to leave. Thanking him for his time, I turn left out of the shop and go three doors down to 89 Portobello, looking in at Portobello China and Woollens Ltd, where Delia Holt has been selling beautiful Scottish cashmere and English-made porcelain for over forty years. I knew her son Matt, a musician who still occasionally helps out at the shop, and his mother proved just as chatty as him. She explained that she never imagined she would spend her working life on Portobello Road when she was dispatched in 1970 to look after the shop we are standing in today. The company was owned by a pair of Canadian businessmen, who had a concession in Harrods selling antiques and glass paintings. Portobello was their West London branch, run by Delia. She didn't enjoy selling the antiques because she didn't feel she knew enough about them and 'it really upset me to make things up'.

The landlord, 'a rather drunken artist', lived upstairs. 'He was called Olaf Blayney Barnett. He used to sit upstairs at the window, drinking and smoking and watching the girls go by, trying to entice them in to be painted. And I was down here trying to be an antiques expert and selling glass paintings. The Spanish used to come in and say, "Roll them up for us", and of course I'd say, "They are glass so I can't!"'

Despite her reluctance, Delia was doing a great job and her Canadian bosses instructed her to go and source some new stock. She tells me how she and her husband went down to Brighton and bought 'a big stack of hunting scene plates, all brand new and put them on a table in the corner of the shop.

The Spanish just loved them and they flew out!' It seemed she had hit upon a lucrative market. Their next port of call was Stoke-on-Trent, famous for its ceramics, where they bought a whole load of seconds that at the time were being thrown away because nobody wanted them.

With business booming, they expanded into number 103 and 101 just down the road when they came up for sale. 'I put a huge tea chest stuffed full of china in the back garden,' and the stock stretched over two floors. She commissioned an architect to redesign the whole building along with the teapot that you can still see hanging from outside number 101. She tells me that there was a certain amount of resentment among the older antiques dealers that she was dealing in new stock. 'But it was fine, you know. Nobody was nasty to me, or threw eggs at me, or anything like that! The older people who were here just didn't like it, like Barham's dad and the guy next door. But even so I used to go out drinking every Saturday night with them.'

In 1987, she set up on her own after the Canadians moved their business into Covent Garden. Rather fittingly, she was able to rent number 89, where she had started out, and where she remains to this day, still selling the stock she pioneered all those years ago. Folding a new delivery of scarves into a neat pile as a stream of German tourists come in, she tells me, 'It has been a challenge but I've enjoyed it. I have dealt with some of my suppliers now for thirty-five years.' With the small interior of the shop getting busier I head out into the market, strolling northwards past the antique arcades that are shut up today. I try to imagine what it must have been like in the 1960s or 1970s, before the Hummingbird Bakery and Ben Sherman moved in. Some tourists on the corner of Westbourne Grove are grappling with a map, and stop me as I pass, asking me for directions to the Blue Door.

Nadi Antiques
Red Lion Arcade

The antiques arcades have been an important feature of Portobello Road for decades. The majority of them open only on Saturdays, when the street market is in full flow. In 2010 the much-loved Lipka's Arcade on the corner of Portobello Road and Westbourne Grove hit the headlines when it was closed with the loss of 150 stalls, and the property was rented out to All Saints, who have filled the 15,000-square-foot shop with rails of clothes commonly found on the high street. However, there are still over half a dozen arcades, where small stalls trade in a wonderful variety of antiques, including pocket watches, candlesticks, cigarette cards, nineteenth-century prints and engravings, Russian dolls and old telephones. I spoke to Muhammed Fuheid outside the Red Lion Arcade, the oldest arcade on the street, which was founded in 1951 by Susan Garth.

'I started first of all with jewellery, then moved to specializing in English silver and silver plates. I do tableware, cutlery, and I do teapots and decorative items as well. I taught myself. I started out working part time in an antiques shop first. I came from an education background – I have a Masters degree in diplomacy from the Diplomatic Academy of London – but I fell in love with antiques and I decided to carry on with it.' His stall is packed with spoons and candelabras. 'I don't have very expensive stuff. For example, a set of six silver teaspoons is roughly £70–£75. I concentrate on the portable, especially for the tourists – they don't like to buy something too bulky.'

Right now, in the run up to Christmas, people are buying wine decanters and cutlery for their Christmas lunch. We pause our conversation as Muhammed fields a query from a customer who is looking for a silver butter dish. A gentleman then approaches him and whips out a small silver spoon from his pocket, hoping to sell it to Muhammed, but after a brief

Muhammed behind his silver stall

exchange he walks away. Muhammed explains: 'These days we have to be careful. I pick and choose who I buy from because there are so many things stolen and I have been in the business twenty-seven years and I have never had the police come to my stall. This business is all about reputation.'

Like Michael Barham and Delia Holt he laments the recent changes, with stalls being rented out to traders selling 'I Love London' shirts and tourist tat made in China. 'The council, I think, should play a role in preserving the character, because if you look at the antiques markets in London they are diminishing by the day. Bermondsey has gone down now to about ten stalls, but it used to be a very good antique market. Camden Passage in Islington has come down to a quarter of what it used to be. This affected us, the people who love antiques and who deal in it.'

Tomorrow's You:
The Health Food Revolutionaries

One of my first memories of Portobello Road was a lunchtime visit to the Grain Shop, a dedicated vegetarian takeaway housed at 269, where you can choose from a variety of main dishes and salads that are then piled high in one of a range of different-sized trays. Everything about the place harked back to the 1970s, from the exterior signage that depicted sacks of overflowing grain to the utilitarian interior with shelves displaying a selection of wholemeal bread. It offered a reminder of the old, hippy spirit of the neighbourhood, a heartening sight among the swish new boutiques, restaurants and nail bars. In fact, the Grain Shop stands on the site of Ceres Grain Shop, one of the first health food shops in the country, and an integral part of the early health food movement.

It all began in February 1968 at 36A Westbourne Terrace in the basement of the Gloucester Hotel when Seed – the first macrobiotic restaurant in the country – opened for business. 1968 is well remembered as the year when radical politics and revolution gripped the world, but it seems a quieter revolution, concerned with changing the way we eat, was under way beneath the streets of West London, led by Craig and Greg Sams, two California-born brothers.

Seed soon became the hippest place to eat in the capital, and anyone venturing down the flight of stone steps that led to the restaurant would have found themselves in a large room enveloped by a tent-like structure, pinned at the centre, giving it the feeling of a Bedouin tent. Wooden chairs and tables were arranged across the room, seating around thirty diners, and it was connected by a doorway to a smaller room with a more laid back air – in here cushions were scattered around low-slung tables (actually old electrical cable drums). A soundtrack of psychedelic rock and mellow blues played constantly on the reel-to-reel tape machine set up in the corner of the larger room. On any given night you might have seen regulars John and Yoko holding court, or various members of the Stones with girlfriends in tow, or actor Terence Stamp flushed with the recent success of *Far from the Madding Crowd*. Perhaps your eye would have been drawn to the curly-haired young man helping himself to the free menu of brown rice, vegetables and green tea: this was Marc Bolan, a struggling musician who had walked from his flat on Blenheim Crescent.

Seed was the first venture the Sams brothers made into the health food market, and their empire would soon expand to include a natural food shop, bakery, bookshop, café and distribution centre. They were instrumental in kick-starting the natural food boom that is still in full flow today. Nowadays all the major supermarkets stock a wide range of natural food products and dedicated health food shops are a common sight in towns up and down the country. But until the late 1960s healthy eating, vegetarianism and organic foods were the preserve of a few sandal-wearing radicals.

Greg still lives in the area, just up the hill in Kensal Rise, and was happy to talk to me about those early days in the area. Opening the front door, he greets me from the wheelchair he has been using since he fell from a tree and broke his back during his first term at Berkeley in 1967, aged eighteen. He is a charismatic and charming individual, who betrays his roots as a Californian hippy with plenty of 'oh mans' peppering his speech. He has not had anything to do with the food industry since 1988, having spent the last twenty-five years writing about chaos theory, authoring several influential books on the subject and speaking at events across the world. But I want to discuss his first passion of bringing natural foods to the masses, those pioneering days with his brother Craig, and how it all happened just down the road in and around Portobello.

Sitting in his kitchen one could almost believe we were in a house nestled halfway up Laurel Canyon in California – the back door opens up to a beautifully wild and verdant garden, where waist-height plants and apple trees populate the lawn. The kitchen looks like something from a 1970s handmade homes book, a vision of natural wood cupboards and furniture. Sitting at his kitchen table, I can see cuttings pinned to the noticeboard on the wall next to me concerning chaos theory along with articles and news on the Reclaim the Streets movement. A series of cardboard stars, painted in psychedelic colours hang suspended from the ceiling.

As Greg makes me a cup of tea I ask how he became interested in health foods and healthy eating in the first place. He explains that it grew out of circumstance rather than study. His father had become very ill after returning home from fighting in the Second World War. At that time the family were living in Los Angeles, and the doctors had given up on him, they couldn't diagnose what was wrong or, more to the point, offer a treatment. 'It could have been some sort of post-traumatic stress, we really don't know. But what was clear was that he was wasting away – he had lost half of his bodyweight and his skin had turned black. He was on the way out.'

It was at this point that someone suggested they go and see a local Japanese doctor called Dr Nakadadi, who took one look at him and immediately put him on a strict diet. He was only allowed to eat whole cereals, beans, wholemeal bread, no frozen or tinned food (about the only convenience food then),

GREGORY SAMS, WHO IS
CO-DIRECTOR OF THE
MACROBIOTIC MINI-EMPIRE
IN ENGLAND, WHICH
INCLUDES HARMONY FOODS,
CERES GRAIN SHOPS AND
THE GREEN GENES CAFE.
HE IS SHOWN ABOUT TO
RAVISH A TYPICAL MACRO-
BIOTIC MEAL OF ORGANIC
RICE, BUCKWHEAT
CROQUETTES, VEGETABLES
NITUKE, UNLEAVENED
BREAD, SOY SAUCE AND
APPLE CRUMBLE.

Greg in *Fiesta* magazine, 1971

no sugar and no meat. Looking back Greg realizes it represented the core of a macrobiotic diet, and after a few weeks of following it his father 'almost immediately started getting better'.

That was enough to convince the Sams family that there was something in this, and from then on they stuck to the new healthy eating regime. Greg stresses that 'we weren't extreme, we would eat meat sometimes and Mum would put a little bit of sugar in your apple pie. And Craig and I were allowed one teaspoon of sugar every day, which we would put on our breakfast cereal in the morning. We ate really well.'

The family moved to England in 1951 and his mother Margaret would bake their own wholemeal bread because, as Greg reminds me, you couldn't buy it back then. He tells me that by the time he was aged ten he had stopped eating meat, mainly because he didn't like the taste, and when he discovered there was a thing called vegetarianism, that was it. Smiling, he says he decided, 'Right, that's me then!' He was the only vegetarian he knew all through primary and secondary school.

It was his older brother Craig, four years his senior, who turned him on to the history and significance of the macrobiotic diet when he returned to the family home in London in 1966 following his degree at the University of Pennsylvania. Craig had spent some time in New York where he had visited the Paradox, the first macrobiotic restaurant in the country, and later the bookshop of the same name, which specialized in titles explaining the theory behind the diet and its history. The very next day after Craig had visited, the bookshop was raided by the FBI, who seized the stock pending an investigation into their content. Greg laughs and says, 'Well, we both have this contrarian streak and we said, "Hey, let's find out about these books they are burning – there must be something there." Because here was a book that was telling people that a diet of Coca Cola, hamburgers and French fries was not good for your health – and that was the whole American diet, so to say it wasn't good was tantamount to heresy.' The books were burnt and an article in *Reader's Digest* written shortly afterwards dubbed the diet the 'Hippie Death Diet'.

Reading anything he could lay his hand on about the macrobiotic diet, Greg felt an immediate affinity with it. 'I had, after all, been vegetarian since I was ten and now I was being handed a diet that was based on what I ate, not what I didn't eat. I just thought that was great. I knew what I was eating then – it wasn't just "is there meat in it or not?" so I really embraced it and immediately felt so much better. Suddenly, teenage angst went away, I had lots more energy, lots more focus, never even thought about getting sick. So it went from there.'

With Greg bound for the University of California in Berkeley, it was Craig who set about bringing this new diet to London. Throughout 1967 at the hip underground UFO Club he sold macrobiotic food he had prepared at home, and arranged for pamphlets published by the Ohsawa Foundation to be stocked at the Indica bookshop. Indica Books was the influential basement shop underneath the gallery of the same name, run by Barry Miles and John Dunbar with strong links to the Beatles, each pamphlet had an insert with Craig's telephone number printed on it. In this manner he gradually gathered a group of like-minded individuals together.

By February 1967 he felt ready to launch the first incarnation of Seed, which opened at Centre House, 10A Airlie Gardens, just off Campden Hill Road in Notting Hill Gate. In today's parlance it would be dubbed a 'pop up' but back then it was simply illegal, situated as it was in the basement of a residential building. It proved instantly popular, with queues around the block and Graham Bond installed as the in-house entertainer, thumping away at his organ every night. Chuckling, Greg recalls that 'the whole of the top of the hill was vibrating'. Needless to say their neighbours were none too happy about finding themselves at the centre of the health food revolution, especially when it was this noisy, and duly complained to the council who promptly shut them down. The whole venture had lasted only three months.

During this time, Greg had returned to England following his accident at Berkeley to undergo rehabilitation at Stoke Mandeville Hospital. His rehabilitation was to take an unexpected turn when Craig was forced to return to the US leaving Greg in charge. He wasted no time in finding a new, legal location for Seed in the basement of the George Hotel on Westbourne Terrace. Enlisting his mother's help with the cooking, he came up with a menu he christened 'Tomorrow's You'.

Once again the people flocked in, despite the fact that it was located well off the beaten track. 'Theoretically, it was in the worst location imaginable – zero passing trade, no one walked past there, there were no other businesses nearby. You had to know that we were around a corner and down in a basement. And yet it was filled every night.'

The groovy vibes did lead the police to come knocking one night, alerted to Seed's existence by the long-haired denizens coming and going into the once-quiet basement. Greg laughs, a twinkle in his eye: 'When we first opened they did come down ready to bust the hippies in their drug den, but when they came down all they found were smiling hippies chopping vegetables and sautéing shit, and they just left looking confused, thinking they had got the wrong place, you know!'

They would hold impromptu parties every few months and Marc Bolan would bring his guitar along and play for the regulars. It was at Seed that Marc was introduced to the drummer Mickey Finn, who went on to join him in T. Rex and make some of the biggest hits of the 1970s. Another friend from the music world, Jeff Dexter, one of the promoters at the UFO Club, would bring bands down to eat and soak up the atmosphere. John Lennon would sometimes hand Greg a tape, still warm from the studio, of early demos to try out on the restaurant sound system.

It was an inclusive atmosphere and, in keeping with the communal vibe, Greg instigated a free menu. 'We had free food, so if you couldn't afford it we had a bowl of rice and vegetables and a cup of tea. But you couldn't have your run of the menu and have puddings. It worked well. Very occasionally it was abused: sometimes if you told someone dessert wasn't included in the free meal, they would pull out a £5 note, the equivalent of a £50 note today!'

Greg was soon being quizzed by customers asking where they

could buy the food they found on the menu. They wanted to experiment and try cooking it up at home. The problem was there was no single shop to recommend – Greg spent much of his time traipsing across the city sourcing the food from a variety of different locations. He would go to a Greek shop, a Polish shop, a Japanese shop and a Chinese shop in order to source ingredients such as millet, tahini and seaweed. He began to sell produce from the restaurant from time to time, but this was not a long-term solution. The next logical step was to open a health food shop where they could stock all this food under one roof, and that is exactly what he did, opening up the Ceres Grain Shop in March 1969 at 8A All Saints Road.

Greg proudly informs me that it was 'the first ever natural food store in the country'. Up until the arrival of Ceres, if you went to a health food shop, 'you could buy red kidney beans, rolled oats and wholewheat flour – about the only three food-stuffs they sold. Everything else was herbs, pills potions, mixes and elixirs – food wasn't part of it and my brother and I really got into food.'

This first address for Ceres was a few doors down from the Mangrove restaurant, a hotbed of political activity that was forever being raided by the police. It was an interesting coincidence that the Black Power revolution was taking place next door to the natural food revolution:

Frank Crichlow would sit in his Jaguar outside with his Black Power friends, because they assumed everything else was bugged and they would talk revolution. Meanwhile I'd be in the back of my shop talking drugs and music with my friends. They were constantly getting raided, man, it was just total harassment. Once we had some trading standards official in giving me a going over in the shop about fire precautions or something, and when I complained they said,

Ceres and Ceres Bakery shops, 1971

you know, we are really sorry and we wouldn't be bothering you only we have just been next door at the Mangrove and if we don't give you the same treatment they will think we are being prejudiced! They were being that open about it, like we would understand!

After a year and a half, Ceres moved to larger premises at 269 Portobello Road. By this time Craig had rejoined his brother, and when the lease came up on what had been a pie and eel shop next door, the brothers moved in, jumping at the opportunity to expand, and Craig established a wholemeal bakery. 'That was the first dedicated wholemeal bakery in the UK. One or two people would bake wholemeal bread in their repertoire but this was the first wholemeal bakery, period.' The upstairs was turned into a bookshop selling cookery, yoga and other assorted esoteric titles. In March 1971 the old premises on All Saints

Road were turned into what Greg reckons was the first and only working men's health food café ever. The Green Genes Café sold simple food at cheap prices. You ordered at the counter and helped yourself, and it was only open during the daytime. The only flaw in the business plan, as Greg notes ruefully, was that 'everyone just gave away shit to their friends', so this arm of their burgeoning empire had to be abandoned fairly quickly. What proved more successful was their travelling kitchen, which provided food for the masses at the Isle of Wight Festival and the first Glastonbury Fayre in 1971.

In addition to running the restaurant and shop, the brothers had begun to branch out into distribution, having noticed that a number of other people were following their lead and opening up health food shops around the country. Infinity in Brighton, Suma in Leeds, Real Foods in Edinburgh and On The 8th Day in Manchester. They would often see the proprietors in Ceres Shop, noting down how they did things and buying up stock. People from as far afield as the Findhorn Foundation in Scotland would make special trips down with a van and load up on provisions designed to last them a few months until their next visit.

Economically it also made sense to move into distribution, since they were forced to import a minimum order of 5 tonnes of organic brown rice at a time. They rented a building at 10 St Luke's Road (300 yards or so from the shop) and began to import enough products to start a range. The company was christened Harmony Foods with a yin-yang symbol as its logo. 'That was the first time ever that small amounts of branded brown rice were sold in a packet – along with a whole load of other things, probably about 150 other things, like buckwheat, pumpkin seeds, sunflower seeds – all things that had never been on the market in the UK before. We even had patchouli oil on our first price list!' Greg made branded labels using Letraset lettering sheets on coloured paper, which he would then duplicate and heat seal onto plastic bags, in which they'd package the foodstuffs.

Greg talks so fast it is sometimes difficult to keep pace with him, his mind working so fast his mouth struggles to keep up. It is easy to see how he and his brother must have been an unstoppable force back in late 1960s and early 1970s and achieved so much in such a short space of time. Greg seems as incredulous as I am, noting how a year back then seems like ten now. Perhaps they inherited this tremendous drive and zeal from their father, Ken Sams, famed for his forward-thinking ideas and energetic manner. He too got involved in the business when he returned from Vietnam in 1972, where he had held a high-level civilian position as an employee of the Air Force in Saigon. He took on the editorship of the newly founded magazine *Seed: The Journal of Organic Living*, a monthly publication that grew from *Harmony* magazine, which Greg had produced single-handedly for three issues, enlisting the help of John Lennon, who supplied a cartoon for the cover of the first instalment.

It was apt that he should take on this role having been responsible for founding *Grunt* magazine in Vietnam. *Grunt* (slang for GI) was the most widely read countercultural publication read among serving GIs from its inception in 1968 until Ken returned to London in 1972. It featured a mixture of poetry and stories alongside irreverent humour and sly jokes reflecting the regular GI's disenchantment with the war. Ken took to his new role immediately and *Seed* magazine ran monthly from November 1971 to March 1977, covering all aspects of the organic and health food movement. A glance through the archives reveals a wonderfully eclectic and informative magazine, full of recipes and cartoons, mixed with readers' letters and articles on wind energy and how big business was starting to muscle in on the organic market.

Listening to Greg describe their work back then is inspiring.

It is incredible to think that in a six-year period the Sams brothers went from selling macrobiotic food at UFO to distributing it countrywide via Harmony, alongside running a restaurant, café, bookshop, magazine and bakery. Though some of these projects were more successful than others, they were undoubtedly well ahead of their time in terms of the scope of the ideas at play. It can certainly be argued that Portobello was the crucible of the health food revolution.

John Lennon cartoon for the cover
of *Harmony* magazine, 1968

The Happy Vegetarian,
288 Portobello Road

The street food revolution has hit Portobello Road in a big way in recent years. There are now more food stalls along the road at weekends than fruit and veg. Gone are the days of soggy sausage rolls and chips. Nowadays, street food can compete with the best restaurants and the range on offer is astounding. You can sample everything from Middle Eastern, African, German, Caribbean, Mexican, French and Spanish, all within a short walk of one another. In fact, a popular stall on Golborne Road serving homemade Moroccan soups presided over by Mohammed and Ibrahim Siteri, using ingredients sourced from the market, won the Best Takeaway award at the BBC Food and Farming Awards in 2012. The whole area has become a foodie heaven, with the Acklam Village Market under the Westway housing stalls selling everything from cheeses and fresh bread to cupcakes and olives.

My favourite destination is a falafel stall outside the Tesco supermarket on Portobello Road. It may not sound like the most exciting choice, but it is so delicious and tasty you see the same faces queuing up day after day. The man behind this enterprise is the most generous and kind of men, named Mustafa, who prides himself on knowing his customers by name and always has a word of encouragement or wisdom. Standing in line I often think he must be the most well connected man on the market. He trained in catering at Westminster College in the early 1990s and, after working at the catering department at the Royal Brompton Hospital for almost ten years, he finally secured a pitch on Portobello in 2004, having been on the waiting list for three years. He decided to focus on vegetarian food after noticing a lack of options for vegetarians on the street. 'I tried a few things that didn't work, like roast vegetables with humus, wraps and some vegetable samosas, but we ended up doing falafel because

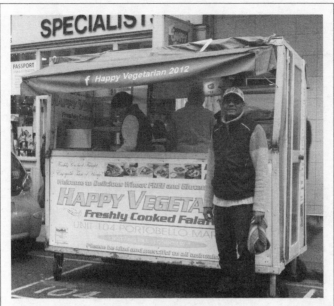

The ever-smiling Mustafa

it's less demanding and easy and quick and fresh.' Trade is still brisk but not as busy as it used to be and interestingly he ascribes this to there being 'too much hot food' on the market, which has had the effect of 'putting the customer off from coming. Since the Olympics in 2012, when many more people started to sell hot food it has been the case. Before then you saw more vegetables and fruit; now it is all hot food.'

Cleo outside Sunset Boulevard in 1972. Note Terry de Havilland
shoes accompanying 1940s dress and cardy

Sunset Boulevard
and the Birth of Vintage Fashion

Two closely guarded warehouses in the middle of the Devon countryside house what is regarded as the most comprehensive vintage clothes archive in the world. Inside stretch rail after rail in all directions, and you can find everything from beautiful Victorian ball gowns through to immaculately kept Biba blouses and Alexander McQueen jackets. It is regularly visited by designers, stylists and celebrities eager for inspiration with their next look or collection. The only catch is that nothing here is for sale; it can only be hired out for a stipulated time period. Archives like this have become increasingly common over the last ten to fifteen years as quality vintage clothes have become more and more difficult to source. The couple behind this hoard are Cleo and Mark Butterfield, regularly cited as two of the most powerful people in the fashion world, counting Kate Moss, Ralph Lauren, Burberry and Louis Vuitton as regular clients. Cleo's love and knowledge of vintage fashion has its roots in Portobello Road, where she started out with a stall in the late 1960s, before opening a shop on the street in the early 1970s. She has been at the forefront of a revolution in the fashion world, helping to inspire the birth of vintage fashion and the fascination with retro-inspired looks that grip the industry today.

I arranged to meet them when they were next in London, envisaging an interview in some swish West End hotel suite. But on the evening in question I headed to the rather more modest surroundings of the bar of the Premier Inn on Haverstock Hill where Cleo quickly proves to be one of the most inspirational people I have met over the course of writing this book. Sparkling with wit and intelligence, it is easy to see why she has made such a success of her career in vintage. Flanked by her husband Mark, who manages the archive with her, it is obvious from their chemistry that they make a great team, he finishes sentences for her and reminds her of dates and people to mention.

Cleo is a youthful sixty-six and met fifty-three year old Mark eighteen years ago at French country dancing lessons. She explains that in the 1990s she had moved from buying and selling vintage into hiring out clothes for film and television, so the idea of establishing a vintage archive was the logical next step. Their move from London to Devon twelve years ago was prompted by Cleo's diagnosis with breast cancer, and it seems to have worked well as she's since recovered. The country air keeps them fit and healthy and their archive has plenty of space to grow.

Cleo began to experiment with clothes as a teenager growing up in suburban Edmonton. It was 1966 and, with miniskirts and the Mary Quant look in all the magazines, Cleo preferred to dress in 'weird 1940s dresses from charity shops. Nobody else I knew did that.' It wasn't until she moved into London to study linguistics at LSE in the autumn of that year that she began to spot other similarly dressed people when she ventured over to Portobello Road Market, and she began to realize she was not alone. She attributes this initial urge to wear second-hand clothes bought from jumble sales to an anti-consumerist stance. 'At the beginning of the 1960s there weren't a lot of consumer goods and then suddenly there was a plethora of them, but they were mostly shoddily made. So I think I was reacting against that, coupled with the "can do" spirit.'

She started to trade from a stall on Golborne Road Market in 1967 when she found herself with a surplus of clothes. Laughing, she tells me she used to buy so much that the only thing to do was to have a stall and try and get rid of some of it. But she quickly discovered that she loved working in the market, enjoying the camaraderie and banter between the stall-holders, and of course meeting and chatting to customers, as well as it being a fun way to make money.

A hitchhiking trip to Turkey later that year resulted in some exotic items appearing on the stall. She recalls some 'amazing vintage brocade silk coat lined with fur, incredible things, and proper Afghan coats before they became widely available in the shops here.'

By 1971 Cleo had graduated from the LSE and despite embarking on a PhD, her heart wasn't really in it. When her partner at the time suggested she open a shop, it sounded like an exciting move and, on finding vacant premises at 306 Portobello Road, she got in touch with the landlord. 'It was a bit hairy trying to persuade him that I could afford it, but I don't think anyone else wanted it so that was all right in the end.' She set about transforming the interior with a huge Indian rug that 'we got out of a skip' and the big double room was filled with rails of clothes. The counter was topped off with 'one of those old fashioned cash registers', and the shop was christened Sunset Boulevard and specialized in clothes from the Victorian era through to the 1950s. She tells me that the basement was decked out in silver: 'I part painted and part foiled the walls so it was like Warhol's Factory and we often had parties down there.' Though she lived in the East End of London, she would sleep in the basement of the shop over the weekend on a specially installed waterbed.

Listening to Cleo talk about those days it sounds like great fun. 'Everybody was our mate down there. It was fabulous. If

Cleo in Sunset Boulevard, 1972

there was anybody else with long hair you were their friend immediately. You could just go up to someone and say, "Hey, man, where is the crash pad?" and they would put you up. It was like the masonic handshake of the time, because there were so few people like that.'

When they opened, their stock reflected the trend for all things 1940s and art deco, popularized in music by the likes of Roxy Music and David Bowie. Interestingly, Cleo believes that the 1930s and 1940s films shown at the Electric Cinema helped inspire these looks, and she recalls how they would spend many an evening in a fug of dope smoke. 'It was a wonderful place. There was a cat that used to come and sit on your lap. If somebody had a joint they would pass it along the row even if they didn't know you. There was a little hatch where you could buy sandwiches and tea at the back. I think that was where we got that love for that look, by seeing all those 1940s dresses. Playing at being a film star, that was and still is very important, and I think Barbara Hulanicki said the same thing about Biba: it was all about playing at being a 1940s glamour star. I mean, later on we dressed up for real. I would put on my Terry de Havilland shoes and we would go to the Rainbow Rooms at Biba.'

For Cleo and others like her growing up in the bomb-damaged grey streets of London, dressing up was part of their attempt to build a new world, in which experimentation was encouraged. Cleo is keen to make the point that it wasn't only women who would shop at Sunset Boulevard. 'My partner at the time, along with many other men, used to wear 1940s satin blouses and shrunken Fair Isle jumpers with perhaps a women's fur coat. I'm sure that was the start of glam: men decked out like that topped off with feather boas.'

Throughout this time she would go on regular buying trips to rag yards, mostly in the East End of London. She describes them as filthy places, but filled with interesting clothes from the

Victorian era through to the 1930s and 1940s. She recalls an early bestseller:

> Those long scarves, called torpedo scarves, from the 1930s, with very deco patterns. All the rock stars of the time, like the Stones and the Beatles have a photo somewhere of them wearing one. They were really trendy at that time and very expensive. I used to get them from a rag yard out east. The guy sold them for £1 each, which was a lot of money then, and he told me that he bought his E-type Jag with the money he made from selling those scarves.

As soon as the shop first opened, she noticed designers would come in and buy garments for inspiration. 'I used to have somebody called Rae Spencer-Cullen coming into my shop. She designed for Mr Freedom and was "Miss Mouse" as her own label. She used to come in and buy 1940s prints to copy. I think that was the moment it started, because that is what I do now, and I think we can say that is where it began. It marked the beginning of retro fashion, the absolute beginning of it.' Nowadays, we are used to old styles being co-opted by the mainstream and made available on the high street, but this marked the start of that phenomenon. Cleo also became aware of designers taking note of what people on the street were wearing and incorporating those looks into their own designs – the start of street fashion.

One colourful group of customers who made quite an impression on Cleo were a group of gay men known as the Rad Fems. 'I guess it was part of early gay liberation. They used to come in dressed up as Monty Python women and they were hilarious – headscarves and handbags and pinafore dresses – and they would parade down Portobello in a big group.' Rock stars would swing by too, such as Paul Kossoff, the guitarist from Free, who lived only around the corner and would come in and buy jackets, 'always completely stoned out of his mind on mandies – he never used to be able to get the jackets on so you would have to help him'.

In 1973 Cleo moved from Portobello Road to a stall in the Antiquarius Antiques Centre on the King's Road, but she would still visit the market every weekend to source clothes and see her friends. She is clearly as in love with clothes and dressing up as she was as a teenager in Edmonton, and she tells me that if someone had told her forty-five years ago that she would trade in vintage clothes her whole life, she would not have believed them. She feels privileged to have made a career out of doing what she loves.

The Electric Cinema
191 Portobello Road

The Electric Cinema opened for business on 27 February 1911 at 191 Portobello Road. Designed by Gerald Seymour Valentin, it could seat up to 600. In 1919, in an effort to keep pace with the times, the Electric changed its name to the Imperial and operated a classic repertory programme of three double bills a week. By the 1950s its popularity was dwindling, as the new Odeon on Westbourne Grove provided stiff competition with its more comfortable seats and plush interior. The Imperial became better known to locals as the 'Bughole', offering cheap entry and all-night shows.

From 1969, a group of enterprising young hippies led by John McWilliams, began hiring the cinema on Saturday nights, showing alternative cinema under the name The Electric Cinema Club. It proved such a success that they soon took over the place, with Peter Howden installed at the helm as chief programmer. I spoke to Dave Hucker, who was the general manager from 1972 to 1980. He described the state of the building when he took it on. 'Nobody had spent any money on it in fifty years. It was a complete dump with no heating and no proper cinema seats, just rows of wooden bench seats. A 78 rpm record player provided the sound for the interval music and the projectors were completely old and wrecked.' The first thing Dave and Co. set about doing was to put in some decent seats and new projectors that came from an unlikely source. 'They used to belong to Winston Churchill, who had them in his projection room at Chartwell. He had died a few years before and they had come on the market – they were pretty much brand new.' The cinema flourished under its new leadership, Dave proudly explained. 'We were the leading arts rep cinema in England at the time, and many people copied it, from the Ritzy in Brixton to the Oxford Playhouse and Birmingham Arts Lab.' They would run seasons

The Electric Cinema, 191 Portobello Road

such as film noir, music films, gangster movies and musicals. 'We showed *Pat Garrett and Billy the Kid* in its uncut form and twinned it with Boorman's *Point Blank*. That was a killer one; there were queues down the road every time we showed it.' They championed the work of Michael Powell and took particular delight in showing his films on Churchill's old projector – the Conservative leader had famously loathed his work. Other staples in their programme included *Performance*, *Pink Floyd: Live at Pompeii* and the work of Kenneth Anger. Dave left in 1980 and the cinema had a difficult decade with locals campaigning to keep it as a cinema in the face of plans to build a supermarket on the site. It is now part of the Soho House group. Hearing Dave's stories of how it used to operate in the 1970s, I can't help but feel a twinge of envy. Expensive ticket prices mean that it is now the preserve of the wealthier residents of the street; the bar advertises champagne, and you can choose from sitting in a sofa, an armchair or even a bed.

The immaculately turned out Paul Breuer at his stall

From Rogue to Vogue:
Paul Breuer Vintage Clothes

At the northern end of Portobello Road, where the street meets the Westway flyover, underneath a specially designed tent-like structure, a vintage clothes market takes place every Friday and Saturday. Over the years, picking up coats, shirts and jackets, I have come to know many of the dealers, and my girlfriend is always rooting around looking for Bus Stop dresses or obscure boutique labels from the 1970s. On Fridays, stylists and fashion designers mill around looking for inspiration pieces from the thirty or so stalls that are packed tightly in. As Paul Breuer, one of the longest standing traders here, explained: 'I would say that this is far and away the best market in the world, in terms of cutting-edge fashion or street fashion or whatever you want to call it. Because, to be honest, I think most of the people who have got a stall down here on a Friday know more than the designers that they are selling to, in terms of general knowledge, understanding and ideas, which is why they come – because their work has been done for them.'

I have been buying clothes from Paul for over ten years. He specializes in vintage American clothes, from coats and jackets to shirts and T-shirts. We had become friends, bonding over a shared love of the Byrds and Buffalo Springfield, and when I discovered Paul was a musician we swapped CDs of our respective bands. Relaxing over a glass of wine after a bitterly cold day in the market, Paul explained how he ended up making a living out of vintage clothes.

'It was kind of accidental, probably the same as most people that work here on a Friday. You start it as a semi hobby to fund whatever else you are doing – whether you are a musician, an actress or a writer or an artist. And then for better or worse it ends up being what you do.' Paul found he could fit in his market days with his touring and gigging schedule, but gradually the market took over and now it is his full-time job. In fact, he just opened up a shop in Margate where he lives.

He recently turned fifty and is always immaculately turned out, today being no exception. He tells me that, growing up in the North East, his love of clothes grew out of his love of punk during his teenage years. 'I grew up listening to Bowie and punk rock and you couldn't buy the clothes that you saw them wearing at that time, so it was a question of making your own or adapting them.' He would buy suits in local charity shops and take in the legs and the arms in an attempt to emulate the rock stars he saw in magazines. He was particularly fond of the Clash. 'They were one of the first bands to wear these American clothes. They went off on tour there dressed as punks and came back dressed as Jimmy Cagney, basically, from punk rock to American vintage. I was like, "What the fuck? Where do you get this stuff?" Obviously they were just going round thrift stores and it was just everywhere, but here it wasn't.'

Ten years later he was on tour in America himself with his band Cotton Mouth, and he tracked down some of these rag yards and second-hand clothes shops. He figured out that you could buy these clothes by the weight and have them shipped back to the UK and that is exactly what he started to do, scouring the town for suitable vintage clothes before each gig. When he started out in the early 1990s it wasn't called 'vintage'. 'The average person in the street is now much more aware of vintage clothing. It is a valid thing to wear, whereas when I started out it used to be thought of as dead men's clothes. But now the terminology has changed. It's the same old stuff but now it's classed as "vintage" clothing so there isn't a stigma attached to it.' He is passionate about clothes, and explains that apart from anything else the quality of vintage garments is far better. 'If I am selling original US Navy pea coats from the 1940s or 1950s for £100, you cannot buy that quality on the high street for twice or even three times the money.'

What he stocks has evolved over the years. He started out selling American vintage from the 1940s through to the 1960s,

> but you can't fill your stall with 1950s American clothes any more because it's not out there, you just can't get it. As the decades go on you can't find that stuff. Twenty-five years ago you could get good American vintage clothing a lot easier. For example you could get great old Levi's shirts and jackets and jeans, with the capital 'E'. 1971 is the key year because after that Levi changed their manufacturing, the dye and the weight of the denim and all sorts of technical things. If you are in the trade it is very easy to spot pre-71 Levi's from the colour and the style of the jeans. So back then you would always find one or two great pieces like that. But now, forget it, you don't see them. And you could say the same with nice old biker jackets, the Brando horse-hides, 1950s rock'n'roll gabardine jackets – none of them you see any more.

Fridays see stylists, fashion designers, pop stars, fashion bloggers and students descend on the stalls, looking for inspiration and the new look for the upcoming season. Paul explains that every designer from Paul Smith to Ralph Lauren to Donna Karan and J. Crew have all bought from him over the years. He tells me how one famous big name American designer would come down every Friday and buy 'twenty T-shirts off me, pay me whatever I asked, money no object. These would then be tweaked and used as "inspiration", stamped up with their

Fancy brogues await new owners

company name and put out in the shops the following season'. He smiles when I seem surprised, explaining that this process is 'the same principle as song writing really. With a great designer you won't be able to tell exactly where they got their inspiration from, just like with a great songwriter you won't be able to tell exactly where they got that sound or melody from. It sounds familiar but fresh, making you think, "I know that from somewhere but I don't know exactly where".'

He neatly sums up the journey. 'A better man than me once said that clothing and fashion go through stages of rogue, vogue and mainstream, and it is a really good way of looking at an article of clothing.' When a stylist or pop star wears something that might look ridiculous or stupid it is at the rogue stage. It becomes vogue when that musician or celebrity is photographed wearing it in the style pages or in magazines. Finally it is co-opted by the mainstream when you can find copies being sold in Topshop. Paul has seen this happen time and again, telling me, 'There is no way that will stop, it always continues.'

Paul sells to numerous stars and celebrities, and over the years he has built up a special relationship with Damon Albarn. He has kitted out the Blur and Gorillaz man in all sorts over the years.

'It's got to the stage now where if I have something that I think he will like I'll set it aside and give his PA a ring and he will come and have a look.' When Blur did their run of shows in 2012, around the time of the Olympic-sponsored Hyde Park show, Paul was chatting to Damon at his stall and suggested they come and do a warm up in his home in Margate, and that is exactly what happened. The band played the Winter Gardens on August 1st 2012 and during the afternoon paid him a visit at his shop, stocking up on clothes. During the gig itself, Paul proudly tells me, 'he gave me a big announcement, and it brought a tear to my eye. My kids were looking at me shocked, saying, "Is he talking about you, Dad?" Stuff like that is really cool.'

His Portobello routine has 'basically stayed the same for the whole twenty-five years – I am a real creature of habit. I have always got down here for 5 AM, so now I wake up at 3 AM and drive in, park the van and then I am buying. I'm walking up and down Portobello Road and Golborne Road looking for things. I start setting the stall out at 8 AM and trade until 5 PM. Saturday there is not as much buying to be done so I start setting up the stall at about 7 AM.' He tells me that nowadays there is less trading going on among the dealers so early. 'It used to be the situation that at 5 AM this was a real buzzing market with a lot of people open and the trade was all done by 7 AM.' it is all a little later now.

He has sniffed out some real bargains over the years by being there so early. He laughs as he tells me that it is musical equipment that has proven to be the rarest stuff he has found. 'I used to have a guy on Golborne Road who did house clearances. He is dead now, God rest his soul, but he used to have a contact at one of the tips in South London and would get all the stuff that people were chucking out and over the years. From him I had amazing AC30S AC15S, really early Marshall 50 watt heads and Hiwatt heads.' Paul would pick these guitar amps up for twenty quid a time, but that has dried up now. 'You don't see it so much now. There are very few house clearance people and the tips have changed their rules. It used to be really good and worked for everyone. The house clearance boys would go around the tips and come down to Portobello and sell it on for a bit of cash in hand. There was all sorts ... stereos, amps, guitars, furniture, anything; then down to the Portobello Road where it would be sold on.'

Despite these less-than-sociable hours, Paul clearly loves the market, and though he has never lived in the neighbourhood, he feels a great affection and connection to it. 'I am part of the fixtures and fittings, everybody knows me.' But what is the future for vintage? It seems to be getting harder and harder to find with the rise of archives in the last ten years. People are hanging on to vintage clothes rather than selling them, and if they do they are very expensive. Paul is optimistic though.

I think vintage is a constantly evolving thing. People tend to say, 'It's terrible; it's over; you can't get good clothes any more', but you know what? They were saying that twenty-five years ago. Back then they were saying, 'You can't get Victorian stuff or Edwardian stuff.' That was true, but you could get 1950s and 1960s stuff. It just evolves. Now I am buying 1980s and 1990s stuff that ten years ago I would never have bothered with. If you know what you are doing, then it's fun. Things that before you didn't look twice at, you can now look at and say: that is a good example of that particular genre. That is how it evolves.

I ask whether he has let anything slip through his fingers over the years, and he instantly replies, 'I really regret not buying a pair of Max Miller's shoes and one of Screaming Lord Sutch's drapes. Those are the two things that I really regret not buying, and I could have for no money. I was in a bad mood or hungover or something, and I missed them both, I passed them by.' He explains that he was offered Max Miller's shoes about twenty years ago from an old woman who would occasionally trade on the market and who had a background in theatre and musical hall. The shoes were a pair of his black-and-white correspond-ent shoes, signed on the inside. 'She only wanted about £60 for them and first thing in the morning I didn't have the money. Afterwards I kicked myself, I was so stupid.'

Screaming Lord Sutch used to live near by, and was a regular presence on the market, where he could be found visiting his girlfriend who had a stall there.

He was always wandering around in his drapes and stuff, and you would say, 'All right, Sutch?' and have a chat with him. He was just a local character, and when he died she sold a load of his stuff off from her stall. All his stage stuff was there and nobody bought it – it just got picked off by local dickheads wanting to dress up. I mean, that guy was an English rock'n'roll legend!

Some of the other vintage traders have joined us at the table and are ordering another bottle of wine. Paul continues:

Even after twenty-five years, I love clothes. I feel privileged to be working here – this is a fantastic market. The atmos-phere is second to none; you don't see it anywhere else. The stallholders might change but the camaraderie is the same. You get a real disparate group who are all drawn together, almost like being misfits that nobody would employ any-where else, but we all have this love of clothes that unites everyone. It's almost like being in a family. There are rows and fallings out and people fucking somebody or fighting with somebody else. It's a pretty unique work environment and very exciting.

I Was Lord Kitchener's Valet,
293 Portobello Road

One of the most influential fashion boutiques of Swinging
London opened at 293 Portobello Road in early 1966. I Was
Lord Kitchener's Valet grew out of a market stall with the
same name and helped to popularise antique military uniforms
as fashion items. Owners Ian Fisk and John Paul saw their shop
shoot to fame on Friday 27 May 1966, when Mick Jagger purchased a red grenadier guardsman's jacket, which he sported
on *Ready Steady Go!* that evening, when the Stones performed
'Play with Fire'. The following day there was a queue snaking
down Portobello Road full of kids keen to emulate Mick's
look. By the end of the day they had sold through all the stock
in the shop. It proved a popular look as other rock stars of
the time, such as Eric Clapton of Cream and Jimi Hendrix, got
in on the action, with Hendrix famously wearing the Hussars
jacket he had picked up at the shop during his set at the
Monterey Pop Festival.

Fashion historian N. J. Stevenson believes that the appro-
priation of military wear by the counterculture was a
'tongue-in-cheek recognition of the patriotism of the country
that they had taken over'. It is claimed that pop artist Peter
Blake got the idea for the *Sgt. Pepper* artwork while walking
past the shop in 1967 – the same year that the owners split the
business. John Paul moved to Soho, where he opened two
branches of IWLKV, leaving Ian Fisk with the Portobello shop
that he promptly renamed the Injun Dog Shop. The military
look has weathered the years well, with bands such as The
Libertines sporting them in the early 2000s. As Stevenson
notes: 'The red and black close-cut jackets with brass buttons
and gold frogging that looked particularly fine on the emaci-
ated post-war youth have passed into fashion history. In 2002
Marc Jacobs, the American designer known for repackaging
pop culture, elevated the military tunic into high fashion and it

Where military chic was born, I Was Lord Kitchener's Valet,
December 1966, 293 Portobello Road

became the jacket that spawned thousands of imitations, from
GapKids to Primark.' There is still a stall under the Westway
specializing in military wear, including replicas of the Victorian
guards jackets, just like I W L K V did all those years ago.

An Appointment with
the Dentist

I am in a thoroughly good mood as I sit in the waiting room of the dentist's surgery at 42 Pembridge Road, close to Notting Hill Gate. I have a few minutes to spare before my appointment but, unlike most dental practices, where all you will find are well-thumbed copies of *Marie Claire*, here I can while away the time admiring the artwork on the walls. There are a number of large photographs of artists and craftspeople going about their work. I can see a violinmaker in his workshop holding aloft a piece of wood, alongside an illustrator with her pen poised. A small blurb informs me that these photographs form part of a project called 'The Makers' by London-based photographer Nicola Tree. I smile at the girl sitting opposite me in an armchair, but she seems less happy than I am, perhaps because I am not here to have any root canal treatment or even a check-up. Rather, I am here to talk to Simon Godley and hear how his dental practice has become a popular exhibition and performance space, hosting impromptu gigs by the likes of Robyn Hitchcock, KT Tunstall and Green Gartside over the last ten years.

I had first become aware of the practice's use an art gallery when I looked in to see an exhibition of portraits of Portobello locals by Gill Bradley, and was so charmed by the idea that I decided I must find out more. When Simon appears in the doorway he reminds me of a cool supply teacher, in his chunky cable-knit zip-up cardigan and bushy beard. He suggests we head over the road to the tiny café squeezed in next to the Gate Cinema that he cheerfully informs me does terrible coffee and provides even worse service.

Settling into a corner of the minuscule café the story that unfolds is even more unusual than I had imagined. It transpires that Simon, now in his early fifties, is not only a qualified dentist but has a parallel career as a stand-up comic, writer and actor, who looks after the teeth of the cream of British comedy. After training at King's College he hit the stand-up circuit with his childhood friend Phil Clarke, who has risen to become Head of Comedy at Channel 4. Simon tells me, 'He was my best friend at school and from fifteen we decided we were going to change the face of British comedy!'

Despite touring and writing success, he always returned to dentistry to help pay the bills, and ironically it was through the intervention of some of his comic friends that he ended up setting up a practice in Notting Hill. Tucking into a slice of toast he explains that in 2001 he was working out of a practice in Hampstead Garden Suburb, and one afternoon both Eddie Izzard and Griff Rhys Jones were booked in to see him.

The practice was a bit rough around the edges, and Griff had not met Eddie before. Sometimes when comedians meet it can turn into a competitive-joke-telling kind of thing. Well, it wasn't quite that bad but at some point Griff started saying very loudly to me, 'Look at this place – it's a shit hole, it looks like Beirut, it's like a tribute to the 1970s – I can't believe you still work in this shithole!' My boss was next door and despite my trying to signal to Griff to shut up he just wouldn't. Unfortunately my boss heard every word of it!

Shortly afterwards Simon was informed that there would be a

The waiting room of 42 Pembridge Road

significant rent hike, but it turned out to be a good thing. It was
the push he needed. He sold his flat and moved into his friend
Mark Lamarr's place for three months while Mark was away on
a road trip. Scouring the city aboard his moped looking for suitable premises he stumbled upon 42 Pembridge Road.

It had previously been home to a Dr Ibrahim, a GP who had
been there for around twenty-five years. 'He grew up in Sri
Lanka, the son of a farmer, and was taken to Moscow to study
medicine. This was at the height of Communism when they had
various outreach programmes for Third World nations. Well, he
studied hard and learnt to speak fluent Russian, but encountered such racism that he left as soon as he could and came to
London, setting up a practice here.' Simon managed to raise the
necessary funds and moved in. He lives in a flat at the top of the
building and explains that they are a unique practice in that they
offer experienced specialists in all major areas of dentistry
under one roof.

Simon began hosting the art exhibitions pretty much straight
away. 'I heard that in a past life in the 1960s this had been an
Islamic art gallery, and I thought it was such a nice space it

Simon (right) and 'the rock 'n' roll doctor' and
country music legend Hank Wangford

would be good to introduce art again. Plus I thought it would
humanize the place as well as giving artists the chance to
exhibit, because they need people to see and hopefully buy their
stuff.' They hold three or four exhibitions a year, ranging from
photography and painting to small sculptures – with just one
condition on the exhibitors. 'It can't be disturbing, shocking or
upsetting. I didn't mind if it is confronting or confusing. And it
can't have anything to do with teeth – that is very important!'
The only thing that he asks for in return is a painting or a
photograph. 'It is a relaxed thing, not a commercial venture.'
The events and performances grew out of the exhibitions.
Recently Laura Del-Rivo gave a reading from her new book,
alongside a screening of the Michael Winner film *West 11*, to a
small group squashed into Simon's tiny flat.

It sounds like the most inappropriate place to do that but it works. We have had poetry readings and storytelling. We've had Robyn Hitchcock doing a few songs, as well as KT Tunstall and Green Gartside from Scritti Politti and Hank Wangford. They are quite unplanned. They normally happen if someone turns up with a violin, a kazoo or a guitar. I get a lot out of it, as it's the best way of diving into a community without having them lying on their backs with their mouth open. I also think it's the most positive way I can demonstrate the humanistic side of dentistry, something that some people have huge fears about. By having these exhibitions it allows people to wander in and see stuff.

Simon tells me a wonderful story of how, at a private view for a recent exhibition, an *Evening Standard* journalist had commented on the incongruity of being served a drink by Simon in his surgery, which had been turned into a makeshift bar for the evening. 'I told her a story about a doctor who had worked in the same building in the 1940s and 1950s, called Dr Dempsey, who was an old-fashioned Irish doctor. Now, if you went to see Dr Dempsey he might say at the end of the appointment, "Would you like a little drop of Jameson?" and he would prepare a couple of little medicinal shots and it was all very friendly. I told this reporter that I was just following on in that tradition.' The journalist duly mentioned Dr Dempsey in the paper and Simon immediately began to worry that perhaps he had got the story wrong, and he didn't want to upset a former patient or even family of the doctor. But months passed and he forgot all about it, until one morning an email appeared in his inbox saying, 'Dear Simon, my name is Yvette Dempsey, daughter of the late Dr Dempsey. Imagine my surprise when I saw our father's name in the *Evening Standard*. What memories it brought back of Pembridge Road, and it is true there was always a little Jameson around in those days.' Simon was thrilled, and he tells me that Dr Dempsey's three surviving daughters came to the surgery two Christmases ago and toasted the late doctor with a bottle of Jameson. 'So I feel I have got permission to be there. I feel that Dr Dempsey would approve of what I am doing, especially in an age of over-regulation and lack of humanity.'

We quickly finish our drinks as Simon has an appointment looming and head back over the road to the surgery. As we cross the street I tell him I think these exhibitions and performances chime with the old, bohemian spirit of Notting Hill and he nods in agreement, saying. 'I think that despite the huge amount of money that has poured into the neighbourhood, and the aspirational groups with their underground car parks and swimming pools, there is another level of stuff that exists, almost against the laws of nature in this tough economic climate. But it is there if you just peel back the layers and you will find this incredible subculture just below the surface.'

Gill Bradley
Portobello Portraits

I heard about Gill and her Portobello Portraits project long before I met her. Many of the people I interviewed told me that they had sat for her, and it seemed our respective endeavours covered similar terrain. She explained that the idea of painting those around her dated from her earliest days in the neighbourhood in the late 1970s, when she was still a student at Camberwell Art School. Inspired by her tutor Linda Kitson, who urged her students to go out and draw what they saw, she did just that. 'I would go out every Saturday and do drawings of the stallholders.' Following a successful career in animation she only returned to the project in 2010, and she explains that the portraits that have grown out of it are a mixture of friends, acquaintances and people she has only met for the first time through drawing them. 'Sometimes you get to know people and then you lose touch and reconnect years later. It's not that you know somebody and know them for ever, you just drop out of that circle and then it gradually comes back around again.' She explains that she likes to spend time with her subjects before painting them and prefers to work from life rather than from photographs. Her portrait of legendary steel-pan player Russell Henderson came about when she was contacted over plans to mount a blue plaque on the side of her house commemorating his work for the Carnival. She agreed on the condition that she could paint him, spending several memorable afternoons in his company at his home in Kensal Rise. She has created a wonderful visual document of an area she is still clearly besotted with.

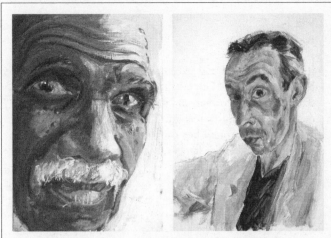

Gill Bradley portraits of Russell Henderson and Tom Vague

Gill Bradley portrait of Laura Del-Rivo

PART TWO

LORD, DON'T STOP
THE CARNIVAL

Expectant Carnival crowds gather on the corner of Elgin Crescent
and Ladbroke Grove, 2013

The history of the annual Notting Hill Carnival is a complicated and at times troubled one that has seen it grow from humble beginnings to become the biggest street party in Western Europe, attracting crowds of upwards of 1 million people over two days. It is a story that is inextricably linked to the neighbourhood, reflecting its changing identity and celebrating the diversity of its inhabitants. Its origins can be traced back to the race riots that rocked the area in August 1958, which culminated in violent clashes between the newly arrived West Indian community and the predominantly white, working-class local residents. With similarly violent race-related incidents shaking Nottingham earlier that month, civil rights activist Claudia Jones sought to address this racial tension by staging the first indoor carnival event, held in January 1959 at St Pancras Town Hall near Kings Cross. Designed to showcase the positive elements of Caribbean culture, it proved such a great success that it was staged on a further four occasions until her death in December 1964.

The Carnival did not make an appearance on the streets of the neighbourhood until September 1966, when the determination of local community activist Rhaune Laslett combined with the idealism of the London Free School to stage a week-long festival dubbed the Notting Hill Fayre. With a steel band parade, along with poetry, jazz and theatre at the local church hall, Rhaune succeeded in showing the world that 'from our ghetto there was a wealth of culture waiting to express itself'.

The work of local teacher Leslie Palmer at the 1973 Carnival marked the start of its transformation from a local party to a nationally recognized event. With its fast-growing popularity came some troubled years, signalled by the riots at the 1976 event, which ushered in years of hostility and difficulty, as the police learnt how best to regulate such a sprawling festival. The debate continues over whether it has become too big and unwieldy to be held in the streets and should be moved to another venue such as Hyde Park. One thing is certain, though: Carnival is big business, generating a reported £93 million a year, a sum unimaginable all those years ago when local residents and friends donated their time and energy for free, and the emphasis was on giving the poor and deprived a day to remember.

Whatever your feelings about Carnival – whether you spend the weekend in the thick of the crowds dancing to your favourite sound system or whether you are a local resident who heads for the hills, vacating the area for the weekend – you cannot dispute that it is the ultimate street party. For two days the neighbourhood is reclaimed for the purposes of hedonistic partying in a celebration of the unique diversity of this corner of the capital. It is a completely democratic occasion, with free entry guaranteed to all comers, blurring the boundary between observer and participant.

The following chapters examine some of the key years in Carnival history, alongside interviews with some of those involved in it today. Treat it as a series of snapshots, and the next time you venture this way for Carnival weekend perhaps you will spot the Mangrove Steelband performing, or the Fox Carnival Band decked out in their costumes. Perhaps it will spur you on to further reading and investigation into the event, or inspire you to join a band or learn the steelpan. I have learnt so

Carnival in full swing, 2013

much through my journey into the world of the Carnival. Before these interviews and experiences my knowledge of the event was limited to rolling around the streets with a can or two of lager, enjoying the sights, sounds and smells on offer. I had little idea of the Carnival pioneers of the past or the present, who devote their time and energy to help create such a unique experience.

Raymond and Maj-Britt Morrison, the couple who inflamed the riots

There's a Riot Going On:
1958 and the Notting Hill Race Riots

Today, 9 Blenheim Crescent could not look more inconspicuous if it tried. Painted a non-descript shade of brown, it sits sandwiched between an upmarket glassware shop on one side and a boutique gallery on the other. The streams of tourists who flock past it every day *en route* to its more famous neighbour, The Bookshop from The Film, barely give it a second glance. Yet it was here on the night of Monday 1 September 1958, that the worst race riots in post-war British history culminated as some 300 black men clashed with a mob of white locals and Teddy Boys.

The violence that erupted with such ferocity that night had been simmering throughout the preceding summer. The Metropolitan Police arrested over 140 people during the two weeks of disturbances, and 108 people were charged with crimes ranging from grievous bodily harm, affray, riot and possessing offensive weapons. The underlying causes have been much debated in the years that followed, with Edward Pilkington writing the definitive account in *Beyond the Mother Country: West Indians and the Notting Hill White Riots*. What is undoubtedly clear is that it was triggered in large part by the lack of suitable housing and by the slum conditions that prevailed in swathes of the neighbourhood. Feelings of animosity and distrust were stirred up by a number of fascist groups active in the area at the time, who blamed the newly arrived West Indian community for the problems.

In the decade that had passed since the *Empire Windrush* had deposited its first cargo of West Indian immigrants at Tilbury docks, a total of 125,000 had made the journey from the Caribbean to start a new life in the 'Mother Country'. Of these, some 7,000 had settled in Notting Hill. That they should end up in Notting Hill was down to necessity rather than choice. They soon discovered that the majority of landlords in London were unwilling to rent to them. This is evidenced by a survey conducted in 1956, which found that 90 per cent of landlords would not accept black lodgers. However, one area where rooms could be found was in the dilapidated and seedier parts of Notting Hill.

The first landlady prepared to take in black tenants was a Mrs Fisher, who owned a property on Tavistock Road. Soon other landlords followed, realizing they could make easy money from these would-be tenants, who were desperate for somewhere to live and who could be charged extravagant rents, with as many as four or five people per room, paying per head.

The Colville area including Powis Square and Colville Square as well as Colville Terrace, a street that intersects with Portobello Road in the heart of the market, fanning out eastwards to Ledbury Road, became a popular destination, so much so that it was nicknamed 'Brown Town' by the locals. The large five-storey houses that occupy this stretch had been built in the 1860s by property developers hoping to attract middle class families to the neighbourhood. When this demographic failed to materialize, the houses were immediately split up into multi-occupancy blocks, rented first by transient individuals and groups like the Irish immigrants drawn to the area through their work on the railways.

The passing of the 1957 Rent Act deregulated the amount that could be charged for a furnished room, inadvertently helping slum landlords like the notorious Peter Rachman. It was a move designed to increase housing stock, but in Notting Hill it simply allowed landlords to remove tenants, who were more often than not white, and let their properties to West Indians, who would be charged per head.

Bill Richardson, a West Indian who moved to Notting Hill aged twenty-seven in 1947, witnessed first hand the appalling housing conditions from his home on Colville Square.

As every fresh boat of West Indians came in, they were naturally orienting themselves towards Notting Hill because it was already set up as a black ghetto area. Their friends were here. By that time, Rachman had done his utmost to get many of the white tenants out by various diabolical means, in order to crowd West Indians in. There were as many as eight to ten men sleeping in one room. In fact, we discovered rooms in the area where there were ten men sleeping there each night, then ten night workers sleeping there by day. The beds were never empty.[3]

The West Indian immigrants were finding London to be a very different place to the one they had been taught about back home. They were treated with suspicion or outright hostility, as an unofficial colour bar operated all around them. The climate was cold, damp and grey. Jobs were few and far between, with many forced to take menial, under-paid positions for which they were vastly overqualified. Edward Pilkington notes that 'Of the West Indians who came in the 1950s, only 22 per cent had worked in the Caribbean in unskilled or semi-skilled jobs, yet once they arrived in Britain that figure rose to 63 per cent.'[4]

Coupled with this, the economy was stalling in the wake of the oil shortages caused by the Suez Crisis. The Conservative government's policy of squeezing credit in an attempt to cut inflation had exacerbated the problem and raised unemployment for the first time in a decade. By 1958 half a million were jobless in the UK, a little over 2 per cent of the workforce. When Loftus Burton arrived in Notting Hill from Dominica that year, his first impressions of the country were far from unusual:

It was completely confusing: the fog, snow, trains, buses. And the coldness of the people was apparent. I was coming from home to the local shops and a car passed me and one of the occupants wound down the window and spat at me. They said the usual words: 'You're a black bastard, go back to your country.'[5]

Basil Jarvis, born in Antigua in 1946 came to London in 1959 and became one of Rachman's tenants. He went on to become a prominent community activist and recalled what he encountered when he first arrived.

I found this country to be a nightmare. It was not what I was told it would be like when I left Antigua. Everyone who was leaving various parts of the Caribbean was given a brochure: 'You are coming to England, the mother country. The doors of opportunity are open to you.' But when we arrived here we saw notice boards outside paper shops with 'Room to let. Sorry, no coloureds, no wogs, no coons, no Irish, no dogs,' as we were known in those days. In those days I didn't know it was racism – only later in life, because we never knew of racism back in the Caribbean till we arrived here.[6]

Into this volatile mix entered a number of fascist groups who sensed this could be fertile ground upon which to disseminate their views. The White Defence League, led by Colin Jordan, acquired a property at 74 Princedale Road, west of Ladbroke Grove near Holland Park, which they duly set about turning into their headquarters. A swastika flag was hung from the roof as military music blared out of loudspeakers positioned near open windows.

Alongside the White Defence League, Oswald Mosley's Union Movement moved in. His party members were soon to be found on street corners and outside Ladbroke Grove and Latimer Road stations, distributing leaflets promoting the repatriation of the West Indian immigrants. They would also frequent the neighbourhood pubs, where they would buy rounds of drinks and ingratiate themselves with the locals. In 1959 Mosley attempted to get back into frontline politics when he stood for the Kensington North seat in the general election. He failed miserably, losing his deposit.

The weekend before the riots, a group of Teddy Boys had spent the evening cruising the streets in their car, 'nigger hunting', as they described it. From midnight until 5AM on 23 August they wreaked a trail of violence across the neighbourhood, leaving four men in hospital with serious injuries and a further two with minor wounds. Shops, restaurants and cafés that did business with the West Indian community also found themselves targeted, with bricks hurled through their windows and staff intimidated. Teddy Boys were only too happy to spread thuggery and intimidation. Local resident and writer Mo Foster described them wonderfully in her book *Teddy Boys Picnic*: 'The Teds move in packs round our way in west London. Flocks might be a better word, they are very birdlike. They strut with skinny drainpipe legs, big chicken feet crepes, chests thrown out and hair a coxcomb. They chirp out insults from the sides of their beaks.'

It was an incident at Latimer Road Tube on Friday 31 August that is considered crucial in explaining the ratcheting up of violence later that weekend. An argument between a Jamaican man and his Swedish wife spiralled out of hand as they left the

September 1958 race riots in Blenheim Crescent

Tube station. As they spilled out onto the street, screaming and shouting, a group of white locals tried to intervene and a scuffle ensued. In itself this was a minor clash but its repercussions were to be widely felt.

That evening the local pubs seethed with news of what had happened, and as the alcohol flowed, views hardened and words grew harsher. A collective desire to 'teach the schwartzers a lesson' took hold. It was not the altercation itself that had so angered the white locals, rather that the couple represented all that they feared and hated – that a white woman should form a relationship with a black man. The stylish glamour that the West Indian men possessed intimidated them, and they were jealous of the admiration it elicited from white women, who found these exotic black men highly attractive. (A Gallup poll conducted among the white community after the riots found that 71 per cent of respondents were opposed to racial inter-

2 September 1958: Teddy Boys and girls run through Blenheim Crescent

marriage.) Ben Bousquet arrived in Notting Hill from St Lucia in 1957 aged eighteen. He recalled:

> We added colour. I remember everyone dressed very dully, but we came with our bright colour and we wore colourful things. I remember wearing a pair of dungarees and yellow shirt in Oxford Street – that must have been about 1959 – and I turned everybody's heads. They had never seen anything like this.[7]

On Saturday and Sunday 1–2 September the pubs were packed until closing time each night as renditions of black baiting songs like 'Bye Bye Blackbird' were bashed out at the piano, audible through the open doors and windows. Notting Hill was fast becoming one of the centres of the post-war fascist revival, with Edward Pilkington noting that 'By providing an organized forum, and urging white people to take action, the fascists helped to translate racial hatred from its passive to its active voice – from pub gossip to street violence.'[8] This is borne out by Eddie Adams, a white local resident, born in North Kensington in 1936, who went on to become a leading community activist and local historian. He recalled:

There were groups of white youths going round at that time, looking for black people to beat up. But the thing I noticed most was there were these characters in the crowd who were stirring things up, wandering round saying, 'Let's get the black bastards.' They weren't working class. They seemed to be a bit from somewhere else – not from the area.[9]

By Monday, the black community had had enough, and a tipping point had been reached. Enough was enough. Augmented by friends from Brixton local residents gathered at 9 Blenheim Crescent, home of Totobags Café. Totobags was an important community hub for the West Indian community, where customers would sit and play dominoes, chatting and exchanging news, as early sound system selectors like King Dick, Baron Backer and Count Suckle entertained them. It became known for its edgy bohemian atmosphere, attracting musicians and writers such as Georgie Fame and Colin MacInnes, alongside daring aristocrats like Winston Churchill's youngest daughter Sarah – all keen to soak up the excitement, no doubt hoping that some of its exotic danger would rub off on them. However, that night it was a violent rather than a bohemian atmosphere that hung in the air.

Crammed inside the small café the black men were armed with meat cleavers, machetes and Molotov cocktails. The white rioters outside began to shout, 'Burn the niggers out', and that was all the encouragement that was needed. The upstairs windows of number 9 were flung open and a barrage of missiles including milk bottles and bricks rained down on the white men below. The front door was then opened up as the black men charged out to confront their tormentors. Around the corner, Portobello Road was awash with reporters eager to get a glimpse of the trouble. Teddy Boys were photographed in front of the Electric Cinema striking aggressive poses for the assembled press photographers, images that would be splashed over the next day's editions. As the violence began to escalate, the ringing of police sirens broke though the din, as six Black Maria's sped into Blenheim Crescent. The most vocal white men and some West Indians were arrested as the crowd was dispersed. Mercifully, no one had been killed, but the fallout was evident, with broken glass and bottles littering the street. Heavy rain on the Tuesday evening certainly helped dampen spirits as people stayed indoors. The worst of the rioting was over.

Watching these scenes unfold was Claudia Jones, a forty-three-year-old Trinidadian woman, who had recently been deported to Britain from the United States. As a prominent member of the Communist Party, she had already been imprisoned several times, becoming a victim of the McCarthyite witch-hunts. She had moved to Harlem aged nine with her family, growing up in its notorious slums, watching her mother die of overwork and reportedly too poor to afford a gown for her graduation ceremony. Joining the Communist Party in her twenties, Claudia quickly established herself as an intellectual force and a popular speaker, appearing at rallies in Japan and China and rising to become an editor of the *Daily Worker*.

Upon arrival in Britain in April 1958, she founded the *West Indian Gazette* above a shop in Brixton, the first black daily newspaper in this country. In the aftermath of the riots, Claudia found herself called upon for ideas on how best to mend race relations, with visits from the prominent members of the black community. Shortly afterwards she organised a meeting with community activists and concerned residents to discuss possible ways to move forward and mend relations. Donald Hinds, who worked on the *West Indian Gazette*, remembered how Claudia asked those present for ideas on how to 'do something to wash the taste of Notting Hill and Nottingham out of our mouths'. Someone piped up with the idea of holding a carnival. But it was deep in the English winter – how could they hold a carnival? Claudia was not one to be put off by the British climate and duly booked up St Pancras Town Hall for the first indoor carnival, held on 30 January 1959.

The event proved to be a huge success, with 1,000 people turning up, far more than could be accommodated in the hall. The BBC covered the action, which included a beauty contest, calypso music and limbo dancing. The following year, the event was moved to the bigger Seymour Hall in Marylebone where 2,000 people attended and in 1962 a carnival masquerade costume competition replaced the beauty contest. Claudia was thrilled with its success, and it would surely have continued if not for her ill health returning, which sadly saw her pass away on Christmas Eve 1964. In 2008, a plaque was unveiled on Tavistock Square commemorating the life of Claudia Jones, describing her as 'the mother of Caribbean Carnival in Britain'.

There were no further indoor carnival events, and it would take almost two years before carnival was again used to bring a community together, with the 1966 London Free School Fayre, due in large part to the work of another strong-willed and intelligent woman, Rhaune Laslett.

Pageant, Fireworks, Music, Plays and Poetry: The London Free School and the 1966 Carnival

On the morning of Wednesday 9 March 1966, in Flat 6, 115 Queensway, twenty-nine-year-old John Hopkins, Hoppy to his friends, sat down at his desk in front of his Olivetti typewriter to compose a letter to the members of the recently formed London Free School. They were a loose-knit group who had been meeting twice a month at his flat since the previous November, with the intention of pooling their skills and offering classes to the poor and disadvantaged of Notting Hill. The roll call of names involved reads like a who's who of the London underground: record producer Joe Boyd, Pink Floyd manager Peter Jenner, black activist Michael de Freitas, radical writer John Michell, folk singer Julie Felix, Beat poet Michael Horovitz and psychedelic artist Nigel Waymouth, to name a few.

Hoppy was proving to be an influential figure in the counter-cultural scene, displaying a natural gift for bringing the right people together and making things happen ... except not a lot seemed to be happening with the London Free School, a project he had been keen to explore since witnessing the Free University movement on a trip to the United States in 1963. They had finally held their first public meeting the previous evening at St Peter's Church Hall on Elgin Avenue, and he saw this letter as an opportunity to jolt the members into further action. Under the instructive heading, written in capitals – 'IMPORTANT THAT YOU READ THIS CAREFULLY' – he wrote: 'I feel we have reached a point where we have either to stop and forget the whole project, or go forward with a more purposeful attitude, collectively, than we have done so far. I know that any sort of move in any specified direction will cause friction and dissention, but I think it is absolutely necessary if this is going to work, whatever it is.'[10]

'Whatever it is' is a telling description, and hit at their core problem: as a group they were yet to define exactly what they were trying to achieve. There was a general consensus that they wanted to offer classes in a range of subjects, such as photography, music, mental health, race relations and housing problems, but just how they were to organize themselves and achieve these aims remained unclear. Reading through the minutes of these early meetings is a frustrating experience, for despite the enthusiasm and intellect in the room, they seem to be unable to make decisions and move forward. This is not helped by the revolving cast of members at each session, forcing them to backtrack and recap each time. The topics under discussion range from methods of fundraising, canvassing techniques, what subjects they should cover, finding suitable premises and whether or not they should have a clearly defined manifesto. As late as January 1966 they were still discussing their aims and objectives, as the minutes note:

A long discussion ensued on motives and aims. Is it a school/ experiment/help the poor group? Is it an attempt at communication, in the first place, of information people need to know and don't have? It might be wrong to think in terms of starting anything permanent. The Free School, if it worked, might have to be superseded after a few years, like all present institutions. We hope however to give the system a shock.'[11]

In keeping with the mood of the times there was a distrust of formal organization, and they shied away from assigning roles within the group. When a suggestion was made to look into the possibility of registering as a charity, at their sixth meeting on 8 February 1966, the minutes noted: 'Michael de Freitas said registering as a charity would be a drag, it created too many ties.'[12]

Despite this shaky start, 120 people turned out to their meeting on 8 March, with at least fifty expressing an interest in signing up for classes, keen to find out what this experiment was all about. Over the spring and summer months, classes got under way at their newly acquired headquarters, the basement flat of 26 Powis Terrace, the home of radical writer and expert on the occult, John Michell. John had donated the space rent-free, and after some initial scepticism at its suitability – it was dark, full of rubbish, and had no heat or light – the group had accepted, sprucing the place up as much as they could.

A newspaper, christened *The Gate*, later changed to *The Grove*, was set up to broadcast their news and views to the community. In the first issue we learn of the progress of some of the classes: 'The music group is already working on two different projects. The photography group was last seen at a "Happening" at the Marquee Club, surrounded by people dancing around in cardboard boxes. The Teenage Group have been playing folk music and listening to Dylan records.'[13]

One local resident who spent a lot of time there was fifteen-year-old schoolgirl Emily Young, who has since become a world-renowned sculptor, living and working in Tuscany. I was keen to speak to someone who had experienced the Free School first hand, and we arranged to meet when she was next in

London. We met in the Great Western Studios complex, tucked under the Westway motorway and next to the railway line leading into Paddington station.

In March 1966 Emily was a pupil at Holland Park Comprehensive, the famous flagship institution for comprehensive education, which opened in 1958 with a student population numbering well over 2,000. One morning during an otherwise dull assembly, sandwiched between news of the school's upcoming football fixtures and an update on work to the new art department, Hoppy shuffled out on to the stage. He had somehow managed to persuade the headmaster, Mr Allen-Clarke, into giving him a slot to plug the Free School's activities. Emily's ears immediately pricked up. She smiles today and tells me that his description of the classes on offer sounded almost too good to be true, she was 'like a moth to the flame'.

The very next day, along with her school friend Anjelica Huston, daughter of renowned American director John Huston, she did just as Hoppy had suggested, leaving her home in Holland Park and descending into the heart of the dilapidated and dirty end of Notting Hill, which she describes as 'rough and tough'. Peter Rachman owned most of the houses on Powis Terrace, with Michael de Freitas acting as his 'letting agent'. Descending the stone steps to the basement she describes what she encountered:

It was this filthy old basement with magnificent old brocade furniture, gilt thrones and things from the Portobello Market. We would go gathering firewood for the heating – there wasn't a lot of money around and we would go and get vegetables from the market at the end of the day, taking the old boxes of fruit and veg that the traders had left behind, and make soup. There were no real classes to speak of – it was more like a bunch of people sitting around smoking dope and drinking tea. We would talk about poetry, art and philosophy, but didn't do very much, partly because everyone was too stoned. There was real poverty and a lot of drugs – there were junkies around and all sorts of people passing through. There would be this very high level of activity when Hoppy was around. He would have all these intellectuals coming in from Amsterdam, New York, Los Angeles and Paris, when there would be lots of interesting conversations and activity. But then it would soon go back to playing music and smoking dope again.

Emily began to spend more time at the Free School than at Holland Park Comprehensive – a situation that did not sit well at home. Her father, Wayland Hilton Young, 2nd Baron Kennet, sat in the House of Lords, and was unnerved to see his young daughter socializing with drug-taking hippies. 'After that I was sent away to a Quaker boarding school in the countryside.' But her time at the Free School was deeply important to her. Fixing me with her sparkling eyes she says, 'It was this visionary opening up of human consciousness to new possibilities and potential.'

In the intervening decades the reputation of the Free School has not weathered well, and it has largely been written off as a failed experiment by both commentators and those directly involved. Joe Boyd has played down his role, saying, 'I was more of a fly on the wall than a contributor,' adding that his vague commitment to teach never came to anything. Hoppy went further, describing it as 'a scam', adding, 'It never really worked out. It never really got off the ground and it's an idea that really shouldn't be inflated with too much content, 'cos there really wasn't too much content.'[14]

Were the story of the Free School to end there I would be inclined to agree. But it was through their work with local

resident Rhaune Laslett in helping to organize the Notting Hill
Fayre, a precursor to the annual Carnival event, that their place
in local history has been assured. Joe Boyd was right when he
described the Free School as being 'a galvanization of certain
forces and energy'.[15]

Those forces certainly came together when Rhaune Laslett
intersected with the Free School. She had been working along
similar lines to Hoppy and Co. for a number of years, helping to
establish a children's nursery from her home at 34 Tavistock
Crescent. A trained nurse, of Native American and Russian lineage, she had moved into the neighbourhood in 1958, in her late
thirties, and soon became a well-liked figure in the community.
She lived with her husband Jim O'Brien and her young son
Mike, and her door was always open to those in need of help
with housing issues or medical problems. The nursery, which by
1966 had grown to include an adventure playground on some
scrap land near by, including a mini zoo with hamsters, guinea
pigs and tropical birds, received a rather well known visitor on
Sunday 22 May in the form of world heavyweight champion
Muhammad Ali. *The Grove* newsletter described his visit with
barely concealed excitement:

> Muhammad gently sat down on the floor and talked with
> the children, signing countless autographs. Half an hour
> passed quickly, and party dresses got crumpled and care-
> fully brushed hair got wildly ruffled. But no one minded,
> least of all Muhammad himself. It is not often you have
> the chance to climb all over the World Heavyweight
> Champion.[16]

Rhaune offered the Free School the use of her house as the
venue for a twenty-four-hour advice centre and rather a nice
description crops up Robin Farquharson's book *Drop Out!*, in
which the radical thinker and academic recorded his experi-

ences living rough on the London streets for a week in December 1967:

> Rhaune Laslett runs a 'neighbourhood service' in w11. Release put me on to her; I explained I needed a bed for the night, and she asked me to come along to Tavistock Crescent. . . . I arrived at her address and was very warmly welcomed. Her office was obviously the scene of fantastic activity, a centre for social work, and particularly legal work of every kind. Analyses of work in progress hung on the walls . . . Rhaune gave me a hot drink and took me up to the bedroom of her son Mike, who had just returned from Sweden. The room's decorations were highly psychedelic . . . In the morning a chat with Mike (eighteen, I think) established that he was . . . certainly grooving. Rhaune had become somewhat alarmed by my graveyard cough, the result of a little sleeping out. She gave me a bottle of linctus, a sweater and two shillings for my journey. In the idiom she would probably have wished to use, she was a brick.[17]

I had been introduced to Mike, or Mouse as he is known to almost everyone, by a mutual friend, and he agreed to meet for a pint and to tell me more about his mother who passed away in 2002. Mouse proved to be a gentle soul – a softly spoken chap in his mid-sixties, with greying hair and a laid-back manner, born from a life spent on the road looking after rock'n'roll bands. These days he runs a gardening business and holds classes at The Tabernacle in Notting Hill, passing on gardening advice and tips. He was keen to emphasize that although his mother is often described as a 'community activist' and 'social worker', she had no master plan, or grand ideas; she simply liked to help people. 'Because she had knowledge people would come to her. There was no such thing as community leaders back then; people would come to her with their problems and she would do her best to help.' He vividly remembers his childhood and the days spent playing in streets that still bore the scars of the Blitz, telling me that despite the harsh environment there was a real sense of community.

> We weren't envious because we didn't know anything different. I mean, there wasn't even colour television, so there wasn't that thing of being able to see another world. There was a bit of local warfare going on in one form or another, but nothing too terrible. Kids went out to play at 7.30 in the morning and didn't come home till 7.30 or 8.00 in the evening. We would be playing on bombsites. There was no health and safety – you would be throwing bricks at each other. At least once a month I would be down at the local hospital. I was blinded as a kid for six months – legs, arms broken. That's just how it was, and if you survived you survived and a few died along the way.

The idea of holding some sort of carnival-style celebrations had been floated by the Free School during their discussions over possible fundraising activities. The minutes reveal that a number of possibilities were discussed, from a gala film night through to gigs at Bayswater Hall. At their public meeting on 8 March the idea of holding a local fair was mentioned in their opening address. The assembled crowd were told that they planned 'to run some local dances, carnivals in the summer, playgroups for children, street theatre and so on'. Unbeknownst to the Free School, Rhaune had long harboured a dream of holding an event on the streets that would bring the whole community together. In an interview given years later to *Touch* magazine, she recalled the genesis of the idea:

> It was 2 AM and I had just finished dealing with a landlord

and the tenant he was harassing. Suddenly I had this sort of vision that we should take to the streets in song and dance, to ventilate all the pent-up frustrations born out of the slum conditions that were rife at the time.[18]

Together, they set about organizing the Notting Hill Fayre which took place from Sunday 18 September through to Sunday 25. Mouse remembers his mother being very busy in the lead up to it. 'She went down to the cop shop and said, "This is what I'm gonna do." Everyone pulled together: there was a funeral director on Portobello who supplied a cart, and the Irish construction workers supplied a tipper truck that was decorated with bunting and made colourful. There was a costume hire shop where she got costumes. I was dressed as a Cavalier – my stepfather doesn't think the bill was ever paid!'

The *Kensington News* trumpeted the event in its Friday edition, stating that 'There will be floats, fancy-dress competitions and decorated cars, and everyone is cordially invited to join in on foot. In the evening a Festival of International Songs and Dances will take place in All Saints Hall, Powis Gardens.'

The Fayre began with a Pageant Procession on Sunday 18, starting at 34 Tavistock Crescent and proceeding through Notting Hill Gate and Ladbroke Grove. Steel band leader Russell Henderson lent his services to the event, leading a small steelpan band around the streets, having been asked by Rhaune's husband Jim, who knew him from The Coleherne pub in Earls Court, a popular watering hole with West Indians. Years later, Russell recalled the spontaneous procession route: 'People would ask, "How far are you going?" and we'd say, "Just back to Acklam Road", and they would come a little way with their shopping, then peel off and someone else would join in. There was no route, really – if you saw a bus coming, you just went another way.'[19]

In the evenings there were myriad events at All Saints Church Hall (the building has since been demolished), including music hall entertainment on Monday, a theatre group on Tuesday, folk on Wednesday and Thursday alongside poetry and jazz. The closing weekend saw Pink Floyd take to the stage for the first of a run of ten gigs taking place throughout the autumn months (see pages 169–179). The local press described the week as a roaring success that saw the community come together in a riot of sounds and fun. The *West London Observer* contained a detail account under the headline 'Jollity and Gaiety at Notting Hill Pageant'.

A Pageant organized by the London Free School, which filled the streets of Notting Hill with music and laughter on Sunday afternoon. Said Mrs Rhaune Laslett, the organizer: 'Without doubt we have succeeded in what we set out to do and that was to liven up the community spirit.' There are many different nationalities living in Notting Hill and during the pageant they all joined in with the singing and dancing in the streets. Four bands, including the London Irish Girl Pipers, a West Indian marching band, and an Afro-Cuban band, took part in the pageant. The route taken by the procession was through Ladbroke Road, Holland Park Avenue, Notting Hill Gate, Westbourne Grove, and Great Western Road, returning to Acklam Road. After the pageant, which was part of the London Free School's summer fair programme, an international song and dance night at All Saints Hall in Powis Gardens . . . was a 'complete sell out'. Mrs Laslett told the *West London Observer*: 'We didn't expect so many people at the pageant or the song and dance night.' Other events in the London Free School's week-long fair programme include a jazz and poetry evening tonight (Thursday) and a parade through Portobello Road on Saturday.

In 1970 Rhaune and her husband Jim handed the event over to the community, feeling that it was getting too big and commercial from the local event that they had started, and until recently she has been largely written out of Carnival history. Thankfully, her contribution was commemorated with the unveiling of a plaque on Tavistock Crescent in 2011 recognizing the crucial role she played. In later years she worried about the direction in which Carnival was going, telling Bill Tuckey in the *Touch/Time Out* 1998 Carnival guide. 'It doesn't seem to have the warmth that it used to have. I always feel a sense of guilt when there has been violence at Carnival, and I can't help but think that if it weren't for me this might not have happened. But then I can't take responsibility for people who disrupt things.' At the end of the interview, when asked if she will be attending that year's Carnival she says, rather sadly, 'I don't play a part now – I'm not invited anyway and I feel my contribution has been forgotten, but I've got no regrets about my involvement. Had it not been for my initiative and those that helped, Carnival would not have been, so we did turn a page of history.'

Westway Sun People Mural,
Emily Young

In 1972−3, Emily Young undertook a project imbided with the
spirit of the Free School. She chose to paint a series of murals
underneath the Westway. They have long since been covered
up and built over, and a gym, offices and a club now obscure
them from view, but they are still there, in the stretch between
Ladbroke Grove and Portobello, behind the bricks and cement.
When we met she told me about the project.

> During the Free School we would go dancing in the area
> that had been cleared, and we would get these huge old
> railway sleepers and make big bonfires and there would be
> a lot of free jazz and dancing. It was pretty wild, like the
> dark side of the moon. You didn't want to go there at night
> unless you were with a big gang of people. They were
> called happenings, and we would get cleared off by the
> police in the end. After the motorway went up I thought it
> was a bit of an eyesore, a bit of an imposition into an area
> that was actually a working community − you know, this
> grey concrete slamming across the market − and I thought
> we could decorate it. So I held a big party as a fundraiser
> and we made £3,000, which in those days was a huge
> amount of money, and with it
> we bought loads of paint, and I
> did a job-creation scheme so all
> these kids came and helped out.
> I did these huge figures so it
> appeared like they were holding
> up the road. Then I had these
> simple landscapes with suns −
> you know, balls of light − it was
> people, simple outlines.

Emily Young, 1966

Mas in the Ghetto:
Carnival 1973

Anyone leafing through *Time Out* in early June 1973 would have come across an advert placed near the back of the magazine aimed squarely at the residents of Notting Hill. It asked the question 'Do you want the carnival to continue?' underneath which it listed an open meeting, scheduled for the following Sunday at the Westway Theatre, asking local residents to come forward with their thoughts and ideas. In the six years since the 1966 event, when Rhaune Laslett and the Free School had taken the event onto the streets, things had been stagnating. It had failed to grow both in terms of the numbers attending and the scope of entertainment on offer, hovering at around the 3,000 mark. There was only one steel band involved and the parade was a short one. Interest appeared to be dwindling.

The *Time Out* ad had been placed by Anthony Perry, head of the North Kensington Amenity Trust, a newly created body responsible for developing 23 acres of land beneath the Westway for the benefit and use of the local community. Anthony was a firm believer in the ability of Carnival to bring the community together and – with the lynchpin of the preceding two Carnivals, Merle Major, pregnant and unable to take the reins – he was saddened to see no organizer coming forward that year. And when only five people turned up to the meeting the prognosis did not look good.

Fortunately one of the five people in attendance was Leslie Palmer, the man now credited with injecting new ideas into the

Leslie Palmer at the Book and Kitchen, 2013

way Carnival was presented and in the process laying down the blueprint for the modern day Carnival experience. Leslie was responsible for introducing sound systems, multiple steel bands, extending the procession route, using generators, seeking sponsorship and forming a committee of those involved. The results of these changes were immediately noticeable, as attendance levels shot up to 30,000–50,000 by the mid-1970s, and have continued to rise ever since.

Forty years later and I am standing in the basement of Book and Kitchen, a new independent bookshop situated half way along All Saints Road. Tonight it is hosting a rare screening of *Mas in the Ghetto*, a Super 8 film of the 1973 Carnival, part of a series of celebrations to mark its fortieth anniversary. I am greeted at the door by Tom Vague, head of the local history group and the man responsible for setting up tonight's event. As he busies himself plugging in the projector and fiddling with various USB cables, I find a spot at the back of the shop, slotting myself in among the children's literature.

Slowly, the old guard of Notting Hill appear, greeting one another warmly and helping themselves to juice or heading out to the garden patio to have a smoke. I recognize many of the faces, even if I don't know their names: these are the true guardians of the street, the people who have helped transform it into the multicultural and creatively inspiring place it is today. Also in attendance is Leslie Palmer himself, here to introduce the film and discuss the significance of that ground-breaking year in Carnival history.

Leslie is a spritely seventy-year-old, and it is easy to see why he was such a galvanizing force all those years ago. His enthusiasm is infectious as he chats to old friends, laughing and smiling. Gradually the audience settles down and he makes some introductory remarks, keen to make it clear what a pivotal year the 1973 Carnival was, describing the two years before as feeling like 'Carnival was dying a natural death – there were no costumes at all, no food at all, it was just the Trinidad guys reliving their youth and having a bit of a dance in the streets.' He describes it as a 'jump-up' rather than a carnival, a Trinidadian term for jumping up and dancing behind the band as the music was played. He was also worried by the fact that many West Indians were not taking part at all:

I saw all these other black people standing and looking at us, standing on the sidelines. That stuck in my mind. I thought, why aren't they in here jumping up with us? It was because they didn't feel part of it – you see, it was really a Trinidad thing. But over here we are all West Indians, so we must involve the other West Indians. That was the key!

Leslie had been an active player in the West Indian music scene ever since his arrival in London aged twenty-one in 1964. Settling in Kensal Rise, he would hang out in Ladbroke Grove, where he helped to form the Blue Notes Steel Orchestra. This was only a few years after the riots, and the police hassled Leslie and his friends all the time. But if anything this helped breed a sense of solidarity among the West Indians. As Leslie noted, 'Ladbroke Grove had a history of defending itself from the Mosleyites, so there was a sense of achievement and unity.' He took part in the indoor Caribbean carnival shows staged by Claudia Jones, as well as the street processions organized by Rhaune Laslett. But he could not understand why, with so much music being made by the West Indian community, there was only ever one steel band in the Carnival. And why they didn't include sound systems, which formed such a popular part of their social lives.

Because there was no place for us to go at the weekends, we used to go down into the basements and have parties which we called blues dances, run by the sound systems. So naturally if these sound systems supported us for fifty-two weeks of the year, and we are having a festive weekend, the sound systems should be there.

This was just the sort of idea that Anthony Perry had been hoping to tap into when he placed the advert in *Time Out*. When the pair met on that fateful Sunday at the Westway Theatre they hit it off immediately and Anthony invited Leslie to come along to his offices on Acklam Road the following day to discuss things further. Leslie recalls that day so clearly and passionately, he could be discussing a meeting that took place last week:

I sat down to speak to Anthony Perry and I said, 'I live in the neighbourhood and I think what you are calling a carnival isn't a carnival really. It should involve everyone, and it should have costumes and all that. There are so many music groups round here – sound systems and steel bands across the Harrow Road. We don't have to do just this one steel band every year; we can do a bigger thing.' And he liked the idea so that is how it all started.

Anthony provided Leslie up with an office and telephone at 3 Acklam Road. With a budget of just £700 and a volunteer staff made up of Robert Bigger Hamilton, Tony Soares, Geraldine Smith, along with two teenagers, Donald Francis and Leon Waithe, they set to work. With only seven weeks before the Bank Holiday weekend, there was no time to waste.

Leslie knew that if they were to stand any chance of success he must broaden their base of support and plug into the West

Indian communities across the capital. With that in mind he had some flyers made up: 'Calling all steel bands and mas bands. Carnival is going to happen in Notting Hill', with their address and telephone number in Acklam Road clearly printed at the bottom.

The next week was spent distributing these flyers. Their first port of call was the Coleherne pub in Earls Court a popular hang-out of West Indian men and where Russell Henderson and his band rehearsed. Russell had famously teamed up with Sterling Betancourt in 1952 to form one of the first steelpan bands in the country. Named the Russell Henderson Steel Band, they achieved instant success and were constantly in demand playing up and down the country, hired to play aristocratic functions and even entertaining royalty. They had been invited to participate in the 1959 indoor carnival event organized by Claudia Jones and had remained part of every Carnival since. The band were excited to hear of Leslie's plans and agreed to take part as usual, promising to spread the word as best they could.

Leslie and his team traversed the city, leaving flyers in likely pubs as far afield as Finsbury Park and Stoke Newington. Their hard work soon paid off, as Leslie began to field calls from bands eager to sign up and find out more about his plans. Keen to put down a framework from which future events could grow, Leslie organized an open meeting, at which each band or dance group were asked to nominate a leader to represent them at future meetings. From that, a committee was formed, meeting regularly in the run up to the Carnival weekend.

As the date drew closer Leslie was pleased to hear of Anthony's plans to film the occasion, having secured the services of a two-man crew. What emerged proved to be not only a unique historic document of the day but it also proved useful in the years that followed as a tool with which to woo potential sponsors. Leslie remembers showing the film regularly at the Westway Information Centre, and taking it on tours of local schools, borrowing a projector from the nearby Methodist Church on St Quentin Avenue.

Thankfully, technology has made the screening process somewhat easier to manage, and the film has been transferred onto the more portable DVD format. At Book and Kitchen the lights are dimmed and the film is under way. Flickering into life on the screen in front of us it bears the scars of its touring days, with some frames rather blurry and dark. But it is immediately apparent that we are witnessing the birth of the modern Carnival. Filmed using a single camera, we are led through the crowd mostly at street level, capturing viscerally the excitement of the day, and the colours are wonderfully rich and bright. We ride alongside a flatbed truck, a band crammed on top playing reggae, elbow to elbow, cigarettes dangling from their mouths, grooving along, smiling at the dancing crowds that gather in their wake.

One can clearly see the key elements of Carnival coming together: the costumes with their intricate construction are proudly worn; one man has a huge structure on his head which resembles a large chandelier, but he still manages to pull some dance moves. Most people seem oblivious to the camera, as there is so much to see and they are too intent on having a good time. We witness the age-old Carnival cliché of a policeman surrounded by a crowd of partygoers, having his helmet passed around and smiling on with a jovial grin.

The costumes stem from the tradition of mas bands – a shortened term for 'masquerade bands'. Their roots can be traced back to the days of slavery in Trinidad when, banned from taking part in the festivities, the slaves would hold their own celebrations in barrack yards, mimicking their masters behaviour while incorporating their own rituals and folklore. When slavery was abolished in 1838 they took their celebrations onto the street, using it as an opportunity to show their dignity, independence and pride.

After the credits roll and the lights go up, Leslie gets to his feet, readying himself to answer questions and hear the audience reaction to the film. With many of those in the room having been present at the Carnival, the images have brought back memories of just how poor the area used to be. A member of the audience comments on the decaying buildings visible behind the colourful figures. It is true the street did look different, less made up somehow. I am reminded of a description I read in Jonathan Raban's *Soft City*, in which he described what he saw in and around Portobello at precisely the time of the 1973 Carnival.

> Various hard-up community action groups have left their marks: a locked shack with FREE SHOP spray-gunned on it, and old shoes and sofas piled in heaps around it; a make-shift playground under the arches of the motorway with huge crayon faces drawn on the concrete pillars; slogans in whitewash, from SMASH THE PIGS to KEEP BRITAIN WHITE. The streets are crowded with evident isolates: a pair of nuns in starched habits, a Sikh in a grubby turban, a gang of West Indian youths, all teeth and jawbones . . . [20]

Though the area is still multi-ethnic, and has the very wealthy rubbing shoulders with the poorest in society, one would be hard pressed to square Raban's description with what we encounter today. Leslie is keen to emphasize that Carnival was not only a chance for the local community to come together and celebrate; it was also a chance for them to protest and air their grievances.

I called the film *Mas in the Ghetto* for a reason – St Ervan's Road and Wornington Road was a ghetto that had the most terrible housing conditions you have seen in your life – so I made the carnival go there! I said, 'Don't ask me to go Notting Hill Gate. I am not going to Notting Hill Gate and don't any of you go to Notting Hill Gate – keep the Carnival here in the ghetto!' And I used the phrase 'mas in the ghetto' to shame the council because Carnival is a voice of protest too, you know? It's not just about having a good time.

People nod in agreement. Many of those gathered feel that Carnival has lost touch with the local community. One woman points out that she doesn't know anyone on the committee. There is a murmur of agreement. Where is all the money that is made over the weekend going, another man asks. How have we let the Carnival be taken over like this, laments another. It is obvious that this is a complicated issue. Over the last forty years Carnival has become big business, and one element that has been watered down is the potential Carnival has as a vehicle of protest. To illustrate his point Leslie relates a story from 1973:

If you looked carefully at the film you might have seen a band called Prisoners on Remand. Because there were so many young Ladbroke Grove guys in Wormwood Scrubs, we invented a band and called it Prisoners on Remand. All the young guys made up T-shirts with the words 'Ladbroke Grove Jail Birds Prisoners on Remand' across them. So we were making a statement and sometimes you will see a band in Carnival and they are making a statement. And that is Carnival as a vehicle, a chance to tell the government how they are doing.

There is a chorus of approval as Leslie says this. Whatever the underlying issues that remain with the current set-up of the Carnival, the fact that the streets are taken over for two days in late August every year and bring so much happiness to so many is testament to the foundations that Leslie put down. As people ready themselves to leave he makes the final point that the achievement is not his but rather down to the community:

The most important thing I want to say to you is that this thing started because of the community. I could not have been successful at all if it wasn't for the community. I used to get the sound systems to play in front of people's houses, right out here on All Saints Road. There used to be a barber's shop and I would ask Joe the Barber: 'Could I plug in to your shop? Would you give us some power, Joe?' And Joe was delighted because maybe he can have a little drink with his friends and a dance. Jamaicans were delighted to hear their own music and that is what made the Carnival popular.

Heading up the stairs to leave I know I have plenty of questions to put to Pepe Francis, a member of the current Carnival Committee who I had arranged to speak with the following week. Pepe has long associations with Carnival, having attended since 1966 and is the Chairman of the British Association of Steel Bands and the Director of the Ebony Steelband Trust, one of the other major steel bands operating in the area.

He invited me to visit him at the Yaa Centre in Chippenham Mews, just off the Harrow Road. Getting rather lost finding the entrance I eventually find Pepe ensconced in an office upstairs, wearing a Manchester United cap twinned with a gold chain and ring. He ushers me into a seat opposite, yawning every few minutes, muttering something about having had a late night.

I ask him how the Carnival is administered, and he explains that there is a central committee made up of five people who represent the five different elements, comprising: steel bands, costumes, calypsonians, mobile sounds and static sounds. He represents the steel bands and has been on several committees over the years. He tells me he has seen thirteen come and go in the time he has been involved in the Carnival. I ask why he thinks that is. 'I think the reason for that is while the Carnival has developed the funding behind, it hasn't developed with it. On top of that we have had various committees who have had internal problems and people come and go with different ego trips. The committee I am on now has only been going two years.'

He explains that the council gives them a certain budget every year and that goes towards the infrastructure: 'The judging point, the Panorama Infrastructure and the stage on Powis Square – and out of that money we also have to pay for PRS and PPL and all of that stuff.' Pepe is referring to the performance rights organisations that collect royalties on behalf of artists when their songs are performed or played. The committee members are volunteers, he tells me, they are not on a wage; they employ someone only on a part-time basis around the event itself. They meet throughout the year but in the lead up to the event these meetings take place every Monday. I am surprised that the Carnival is run by volunteers – what about the reported £93 million that is made over the two days of the Carnival? 'That is coming to the traders, not the council. We have a problem but there is no way we can tap into it or get it. We keep trying. We would like to see local businesses contribute to it more, but they don't, and there is nobody to force them to and we don't have that power.'

I tell him that I have encountered local people who feel that Carnival is no longer representing the community, and they have lost their voice. He shrugs and says that is the nature of things, and they do try their best to represent the different elements that go into the Carnival. And what about the accusation that it is getting too big to be held in the streets of Notting Hill? 'No, it's not too big. I come from Trinidad and I know Carnival. I go to Carnival all over the world. I've been to New York and Berlin. Berlin Carnival is nearly on the same par with this now – it attracted a million and a half people; New York is the same; Miami is the same. Carnival is growing. It's part and parcel of what Notting Hill is about, and it can only get bigger. It's not going to disappear.' And what does he think we could improve on? 'I just think we have too many police. If you take Berlin: they have the same amount of people but only 400 police and we have 12,000 over two days. That, to me, is over-policed.'

Pepe has another meeting lined up so I leave him to his busy afternoon and head out into the mid-afternoon traffic on Harrow Road. I am intrigued by his assertion that the event is 'over-policed', and over the coming week I email several people at the Met asking if it would be possible to speak to someone from the Notting Hill station, or who has experience of policing the Carnival. I am eventually sent an email saying that an interview will be possible but I must pay £70 per hour plus VAT for their time. Having conducted countless interviews for this book, all given for free, I am reluctant to start paying for them now – it would be against the spirit of the whole project – so I decline. My thoughts turn to the upcoming Carnival and my adventures with the Mangrove Steelband.

Gaz's Rockin' Blues

Gaz Mayall is a flamboyant presence in the neighbourhood – a sharp dresser who is invariably turned out in a three-piece suit, spats and wide-brimmed Stetson hat with a feather neatly tucked into its side. He is impossible to miss, sculling down Ladbroke Grove on his Dutch bike, or walking arm in arm through the market with his statuesque girlfriend. He lives a short walk from Portobello, just over the Grand Union Canal on Harrow Road, in a flat above a Thai restaurant and next to a Moroccan rug shop. I popped round to see him one blustery October day to find out more about his life in the area and his involvement in the Carnival, where he hosts what is now the only live stage, dubbed Gaz's Rockin' Blues which has been a fixture of the event since 1989.

His stage is situated at 103 Talbot Road, outside the Globe and Gaz has built up a reputation for putting on a party with a real family vibe. Familiar faces appear year after year, getting down early to dance the day away. Over the course of the weekend, a series of bands play a mixture of reggae, soul and ska sounds. It has become my favourite Carnival destination, as you never know who you are going to catch playing. In 2009 Mick Jones took to the stage with the Rotten Hill Gang, strapped on a guitar and tore through the Clash classic 'Should I Stay or Should I Go'. The whole place erupted.

Answering the door, Gaz welcomes me into the warren-like building. He leads me upstairs to the sitting room before head-

Gaz at his flat on Harrow Road, 2013

ing off to fix us some tea, leaving me to take in my surroundings. His huge record collection sits in specially built shelves running the length of the room. There are instruments everywhere: a piano sits in one corner along with parts of a drum kit and an organ. On the coffee table I spot a pile of CDs by the Trojans, the ska band he has been fronting for the past twenty-five years, and as Gaz reappears bearing cups of tea he explains he has been busy packaging them up in preparation for their tour of Japan that starts later in the week. Now in his mid-fifties, there is something of the Keith Richards outlaw to Gaz and he talks in a West London inflected drawl, reminiscent of his punk contemporaries the Clash.

Gaz is the son of legendary blues guitarist John Mayall. He has lived in the neighbourhood since 1970 when his parents divorced and his father chose to move to America while his mother settled with Gaz and his siblings in Notting Hill. After enrolling at Holland Park Comprehensive he found it tough to fit in – an original character even then, who from the age of fifteen dressed exclusively in second-hand clothes bought from

Portobello Market. He spent very little time in the classroom, preferring to bunk off with his mates and hang out in the local Wimpy bar or go on 'nicking sprees' in the Biba shop. In the summer months they would go cool off in the round pond in Hyde Park or go round to one another's houses and listen to records. He tells me that he was able to maintain this routine for months before the school noticed, due to its vast size. He had worked out that as long as you were there for morning and lunchtime registration then no one would miss you.

Things eventually caught up with him, and despite several attempts to knuckle down he continued to find school intolerable. A plan was hatched that he should go and live in Wales, where his mother had recently acquired a holiday home, and lie low for a while, avoiding the authorities and missing his last year at school. While there he took to antique dealing, buying up furniture at local auctions and house clearances and selling them on from a huge barn he rented.

He had developed a knack for the trade on Portobello Road on Saturdays, where he had a stall at the front of a second hand clothes shop on Pembridge Villas. 'I'd buy stuff up on the poor end, the Golborne Road end, and sell it up outside Mr and Mrs Philips' second-hand clothes shop on a Saturday.' He had met them when he was playing truant from school. He always liked chatting to old people and learning from them, and when he needed some extra money they suggested he have a stall in front of their shop.

Though Gaz enjoyed his antique-dealing life in Wales he missed London and young people of his own age to hang out with. He would regularly come up for gigs and to see friends and it was during one of these trips that he first heard about Carnival. His friends raved about it, but it wasn't until 1976 that he was able to attend himself. He could not have chosen a more volatile year.

Truncheons out and tension mounting at the 1976 Carnival

Leaning back in his chair, he tells me that he enjoyed it at first, listening to the big reggae sound system that was set up at the top of Acklam Road. 'There was steam coming out and a cacophony of sound, and I was thinking this was the best thing I had ever been to.' As he stood on the corner of Cambridge Gardens and Portobello suddenly he was aware of a change in atmosphere.

All of a sudden I saw loads of people rushing towards me from the Ladbroke Grove direction. I remember standing back in the doorway of what is probably now Falafel King. I just stepped back and watched it all kicking off. Suddenly they stopped running that way and turned and started running in the opposite direction. They had been running away from the police, but then they must have realized they outnumbered the police and thought why are we running away. So they started chasing the police! It a real sense of 'We have the power!' I was slap bang in the middle of it and there was no way of going anywhere and as it grew wilder and wilder I thought the best thing to do was go to a friend's house, so I went round the corner to what is now Tavistock Square where a friend of mine lived. I was up on the first floor, sitting on the window ledge, legs dangling over with a cup of tea, watching it all kick off down below. There were cars everywhere back then and every time a car came round the corner hordes of youths would try and stop the car to torch it. And where Garcia's is now there was an electrical shop and everyone was looting it, but in a really helpful way, you know, passing stuff out of the window. 'Who wants this?' and 'Here's one of these,' and a little conveyer belt got going. That was quite something.

Accounts of how the riots were sparked vary, but it seems trouble was brewing from the outset. Police numbers had been dramatically increased from the previous, incident-free year, from 300 to some 3,000 uniformed officers. People recalled the 'sea of police' outnumbering Carnival goers, with coachloads more stationed at strategic points in the neighbourhood, primed and ready for action. The Sus laws, which gave the police the power to stop and search any individual, ramped up the tension as they were used indiscriminately to stop young black men. White fascist groups were at large in the crowd, and shortly after 5PM, when police tried to arrest an alleged pickpocket in the middle of the crowds, the trouble erupted. Bricks and bottles rained down on the police, as they sought to beat a hasty retreat, forced to use dustbin lids and road signs as makeshift shields against this onslaught of missiles. Pitched battles raged in streets around Ladbroke Grove and Portobello as windows were smashed and fires lit. Things calmed down around midnight and the count afterwards revealed some 35 police vehicles had been damaged, many of them torched, 300 officers injured, shops looted and 60 people arrested.

This extreme violence must be seen against the wider social context, with further riots to come in Brixton and Toxteth. Race relations in Britain were entering a troubled period. Whether the Notting Hill riots helped to push the Race Relations Act on to the statute book is a matter of debate, but what is certain is that the Carnival was about to enter a turbulent period as the police and the community locked horns and struggled to find a way of working together to ensure it became a peaceful and joyous occasion.

Though shaken by what he had seen, Gaz tells me had enjoyed Carnival before it had turned so ugly, and he just knew he had found his kind of party. He proudly informs me that he has never missed a Carnival since. By 1978 he had moved back up to London and was about to embark on his short-lived, though hugely successful, career as proprietor of a vintage clothes shop in nearby Kensington Market. This indoor market had long been a favourite destination for hippies, with many stalls selling clothes and household wares. By 1978 it was looking out of touch and out of time, but Gaz saw the potential. He had always had a strong sense of style and his timing could not have been more perfect. He started out sharing a small stall in a corner of the market and by January 1979 he had graduated to a prominent pitch with a window overlooking High Street Kensington.

He set about giving the place an overhaul, buying clothes rails, some bamboo furniture, and brought along a record player along with his own record collection. And he scoured Portobello for more stock, which he cleaned up and put out in the racks. 'In the first two days I took seventy pounds and the stock had laid me back about a fiver.' Kids started to hang out there and listen to records and, as a scene sprang up, other stalls in the market that had previously stood empty were taken on. When the Beaufort Market on the King's Road shut, all the kids from there gravitated to Kensington Market. 'By the summer of

1979 Portobello Road was empty and devoid of young people because they were down in Ken Market having a blast. There was a shop called Blue that had four T-shirts on sale, and the shop name was written up above in punk writing. All that they sold was speed in little blue tablets under the counter.'

With the Specials in the charts and Madness following hot on their heels, Gaz was on the crest of a wave. 'All the local skin-heads used to buy their clothes from me.' But as others caught on, and cheaper modern versions of these clothes came on the market, trade began to drop off and Gaz found it increasingly less fun. His attention changed to music, starting a club night in Soho called Gaz's Rockin' Blues in 1983, which is still running every Thursday night over thirty years later. Back in Portobello he was putting the Trojans together, with early band rehearsals taking place in the rat-infested basement of a shop called Risk, situated at 307 Portobello Road. In August that same year they set up outside and played during the Carnival. He explains that it was so much freer back then. 'We put a load of speakers out front and played records. We would play for an hour and then the sound system opposite us in front of the off licence would play for an hour and we would alternate throughout the day.' Smiling at the memory, he tells me that there was no curfew back then. 'It was an unwritten rule that even if they were trying to stop things in other places we would wait until a lot of the tourists had left, turn it off at sevenish and then wait until about nine o'clock and start it up again. By eleven we had our own local street party!'

He tells me of one memorable year in the late 1980s concerning Joe Strummer of the Clash. 'Joe lived at 37 and we set up a massive sound system right outside his house. It was great fun and the following year he wanted to do it again, but they wouldn't let him set up on the street, so instead we moved it to inside his house – we took the party there.' Again it was a great

Gaz outside the Globe, 103 Talbot Road, 1989

success and, despite the fact that Joe was keen to repeat the experience the following year, the police had other ideas, they had started blocking off Lancaster Road. 'No one could get in unless you could prove you lived there, so that screwed it right up when it was just starting to become a regular thing.'

His first year outside The Globe was in 1989, and it started at the instigation of his brother, who was managing it at the time. 'That first year it was tiny – literally just a few speakers and a record player outside the front door.' Gaz loved it. He felt instantly at home and over the coming years he found himself taking on the responsibility of registering the sound system at the newly inaugurated British Association of Sound Systems, better known as BAS. In 1990 he remembers that they held a competition to find the 'Best Dressed Sound System' with a cash prize of £1,000 offer – Gaz and his gang went all out to win it.

We made a massive effort to decorate ours with huge yellow rubbish shoots going all the way to the top of the house, two of them on either side, making them look like giant palm trees. In the middle we set up proper staging, designed as a ghetto blaster with the DJ inside it. We had wires suspended between two houses across the street, with records hanging off them and big letters spelling out SKA. It was on the TV and the news and everything. We really made an effort to decorate the whole street and make it three-dimensional.

For someone so consistently involved in the Carnival for over thirty years, it is wonderful to see that Gaz is still so enthused and excited about it. I ask if he thinks it has got too big and lost its sense of community. Shaking his head he says no, he doesn't buy into that at all. He still thinks it is 'a community party that belongs to the local people'. He tells me that he has been heart-

Gaz's Rockin' Blues pirate-themed stage at the Carnival in 2004

ened to see a recent return to its roots. 'It is making a bit of a swing back. I just found out at the debrief meeting that loads of people are using their own courtyards again to sell food, because it turns out there is a loophole – you are allowed to sell food from your own property, just not over the fence. And there were a lot more house parties this year, because they shut the sound systems off at 7PM.'

Gaz has a lunch engagement coming up so I leave him to get ready. Seeing me out to the front door, back down the narrow staircase, he says he can never imagine not being a part of the Carnival. He will carry on doing it as long as he can. He mentions an old local man who comes to his stage every year. 'He must be in his eighties or nineties, a really old stick, lived round here his whole life. He doesn't go away during the weekend, he really enjoys it and we look after him.' I can well imagine Gaz being just the same when he gets to that age, and you can be sure he will still be as immaculately turned out, gently tapping his stick to the ska beat.

The Mangrove Steelband

On the corner of Talbot Road, where it meets Portobello, Jerome O'Connell stands playing his steelpan all year round. With his sparkly red cap and weather-beaten features, he is a fixture of the street on market days, smiling at the tourists and nodding to the locals. His twinkling melodies instantly transport you back to the annual Carnival, even in mid-December, when he is surrounded by wreaths of Christmas holly. When I interviewed Damon Albarn he likened Jerome's presence to the ghost of Carnival past, and I rather like that description.

I had got to know Jerome over the years. He once played outside the Travel Bookshop for a book launch, hired by the author to add some Caribbean flavour to the literary gathering. I knew he would be the man to quiz about the steelpan bands who operate in the neighbourhood, and he suggested I talk to Matthew Phillip, general manager of The Tabernacle and leader of the Mangrove Steelband, one of the oldest and, according to Jerome, best steel bands in the neighbourhood.

I headed off to The Tabernacle, past Rough Trade Records and on through Powis Square, passing All Saints church. Asking for Matthew, I was ushered into the production office, where I was introduced to a tall man in his early forties, gentle in manner and softly spoken. After filling him in on my project he said he was happy to help, and invited me to come along and sit in on a band rehearsal, explaining that they took place twice a week on Mondays and Thursdays, in one of the rehearsal spaces tucked away at the back of the building. Thanking him, I promised to do just that.

In the meantime I did a little research on the steelpan. I was surprised to learn what a young instrument it was, having only been invented in Trinidad & Tobago in the early part of the twentieth century, though its roots can be traced back to the 1880 ban on percussion instruments introduced by the British colonial rulers. Drumming has deep historical resonance in the West Indies, and was used as a form of communication among enslaved West Indians. Following this ban they improvised at the annual Mardi Gras celebrations by banging on anything they could find, from biscuit tin lids and bottles to scrap iron. Tamboo Bamboo instruments grew out of this – these were tuneable sticks of bamboo wood, which were hit on the ground or with a stick to produce different pitches. When these too were banned in the early 1930s, the leap to steelpans came about almost by accident when a young man named Winston Simon started to bang on a drum that had become dented. He discovered that this created different pitches, or notes, and in the process transformed the drum from a rhythmic instrument into the melodic one we know today.

The steelpan first arrived on British shores in 1951, when the Trinidad All-Steel Percussion Orchestra, a band formed from various members of the steelpan community in Trinidad, was sent to perform at the Festival of Britain. This marked the first time that the instrument had been played abroad, and as the big gig approached the band displayed an inspired bit of showmanship that has been much retold over the years. The pans had grown rusty and dirty from sitting on out on the open deck during the long crossing, but rather than clean them up before the gig they chose to leave them just as they were, setting up their rusty instruments in front of the gathering crowd. Sounds of laughter and sniggering were clearly audible, but quickly silenced when they started playing, stunning the audience with the beautiful melodies they coaxed from the dirty old pans. Band member Sterling Betancourt recalled people looked around, confused as to where the music was coming from, trying to figure out what kind of black magic was at work.

After their short UK tour, Sterling was the only member of the band to stay on in Britain, and it wasn't long before he had formed a steelpan combo with fellow Trinidadian named Russell Henderson. Russell had come to Britain earlier in the year to study piano tuning at the Polytechnic of North London, and quickly picked up the instrument under Sterling's watchful eye. When the pair started to play gigs they found themselves in huge demand, an instant success playing at private parties and jazz clubs up and down the county, as well as recording sessions for the BBC. They were booked by Claudia Jones for the early indoor carnival parties and later on took part in the Rhaune Laslett Free School Fayre in 1966.

The steelpan is now an established part of British culture, having featured in the Jubilee celebrations in 2002 and more recently in the Olympic opening ceremony in 2012. It is without a doubt the sound of Notting Hill Carnival, and it is fitting then that the neighbourhood boasts the highest concentration of steel bands in the country, with four active bands in the neighbourhood – Mangrove, Ebony, Metronomes and Glissando.

I arrived at The Tabernacle soon after 8 PM to sit in on the Mangrove rehearsal. The terrace area at the front of the building was packed with people drinking and smoking, making the most of the first truly hot day of summer. Finding Matthew at the front desk he led me through the bar, past the small gallery space and down some steps to the rehearsal room. Finding a place to sit at the back, I surveyed the scene. It resembled the kind of rehearsal room I was used to from my band days – low ceilinged with a nondescript grey carpet – except that rather

The Mangrove steel band rehearse at The Tabernacle, July 2013

than a rock band set up with amps and a PA there were about fourteen steelpans arranged in rows across the room and a drum kit at the back. The band ranged in age from mid-teen through to forty plus. A smiley guy in his mid-twenties was addressing the group saying, 'I want to hear the rolls for that please,' before hitting the side of a pan with a drumstick to count them in, '1, 2, 3, 4 . . .' They sprang instantly to life, playing the same notes in unison. It was startling, I was surprised at how loud it was for an unamplified instrument and as the last note echoed out the young man seemed happy, saying, 'Okay lets hear it all together – 1, 2, 3, 4 . . .' and they were off. The music was incredibly uplifting – I wanted to jump out of my seat and dance around.

I barely noticed when a woman entered the room and sat down on the seat next to me. Smiling and gesturing hellos to the band members, she was obviously a well-liked member of the group. In between songs we got chatting. She told me her name was Rose and she had been a member of the band for many years. After a few more run-throughs the rehearsal came to an end and everyone headed out for a drink and to get some much needed fresh air. Rose was chatty and likeable, with a laugh to match her personality, full of life and happiness.

She explained that the band rehearsed throughout the year with a core membership of around twenty, but this grew radically over the summer months to accommodate seventy-five to eighty players as they prepared for Carnival and the annual Panorama competition. Panorama is held on the Saturday of Carnival weekend, pitting bands from across the country against one another.

Panorama is the highlight and it is also the eve of Carnival. So on the morning of the competition we meet early, have a prep meeting, get our instructions and head over there. For me, once that ten minutes is over and I have executed that piece of music as perfectly as I can, I breathe a sigh of relief and say, 'Right – now I can relax, let my hair down!'

Over the years, Mangrove has won several times, and this is what they would be focusing their rehearsals on – perfecting a piece of music arranged especially for the occasion by their musical director Andrew White. They would soon be transferring to the upstairs theatre and rehearsing four times a week with the full band in a couple of weeks' time.

I ask Rose how long she has been in the band and she lets out a long laugh before much concentration and counting of her fingers, working out that it must be about twenty-five years since she joined, saying, 'My family are very much into their music – it's a cultural thing.' Now in her early forties she was born and raised in the area and has been coming to Carnival since she was a small child, telling me it was almost inevitable that she would get behind a steelpan: she started learning the instrument from the age of twelve. At first she joined the Glissando band, based around Golborne Road. 'I had fun, I didn't take it that seriously. I was more interested in what was going with my friends and stuff. And then about eighteen months later I joined Mangrove.'

Over the years she has gone on tour with the band, including trips to Israel, Trinidad and Germany. She has also been the only female captain to date, helming the band between 1998 and 1999. She explained that the band captain was like that of a football team, leading the band during rehearsals and at competitions and gigs. When she joined, Matthew's father was still the manager and she watched as he brought on young players, giving them responsibility and a sense of purpose, and now she's seeing those young faces in leading roles. 'The band has given a huge amount of insight and opportunity for young people. It is about more than just playing, it is about developing positive relationships, discipline, respect . . . When you go to work you're not going to get along with everybody, but you have to learn how to work with people. It brings out a creative side to you.'

It is clear that the band is about more than just music; it fosters its own community and support network. 'A lot of the people in the band have followed their family into it, so are the second or third generation. But equally there are a lot of new people coming in from all over London – from South London and East London – who travel here to rehearse, so there is a high level of commitment and dedication.'

Leaving her to relax with her fellow band members I head off home, excited at the prospect of seeing the whole band perform.

A fortnight later, as I walk through the bar and head up the stairs, I can hear the sound before I open the double swing doors, but nothing prepares me for the next couple of hours. The first thing that strikes me is the sheer volume. If I had thought the small rehearsal room packed a punch, that was nothing compared to this. The combined sound of around seventy-five players, ranged across the venue floor playing in unison was awe-inspiring. I find a seat in the gallery and look around. There are a number of other people watching, entranced like me with smiles plastered on their faces. Some children are playing under the seats, immersed in their game.

I turn to find Matthew poking his head in from the back, checking out how the band is sounding, and I ask if we can have a chat. He explains that, like Rose, he has been coming to Carnival since he was a small child.

There is a photo of me taken in 1980 at one of my first Carnivals. It is of me standing outside The Tabernacle wearing a sailor costume. I remember before I played in the band my job used to be steering the float. In those days we didn't have a truck or a tractor pulling it. It was done by hand in a specially constructed float that my dad and a few of his friends had made. There was no set route – we would just get on the float whenever we felt like it and go around the block in any direction – it was much freer.

Matthew explains that it was his father who formed the Mangrove Steelband in 1980 with Frank Crichlow, the owner of the Mangrove restaurant on All Saints Road. 'Two or three years later they added a youth element and that has remained a tradition ever since because, after all, that is the next generation of the band as well as offering a positive diversion and focus for the younger ones.' When his father stepped down in 1992, Matthew and a few others kept things going and now he has taken on the management duties himself, though he is quick to credit his fantastic team as being equally important as him.

He is a great advocate of the pan's ability to bring people

together through the positive benefits of playing. The Mangrove hold open classes all year round (the teaching is done for free), and in recent years he tells me he has seen interest in the instrument on the rise, telling me:

It kind of died off for a bit, but in recent years more and more schools are cottoning on to the fact that it's a really easily accessible instrument. Up to fifteen people can learn to play it simultaneously with one tutor, and it is easy to get results and see improvement quickly. When people can see what they have achieved it kind of spurs them on to further learning. Even with group sessions on the pan you can tailor what you are showing people to the individual's ability – so if one or two people are doing better they can do something more complicated and it will still complement what people with lesser ability are playing.

The Tabernacle is the home of Carnival Village, which Matthew explains came into being about ten years ago when four Carnival arts organizations joined forces – the Mangrove Steelband, the Ebony Steelband Trust, the Association of British Calypsonians and the Yaa Arts and Community Centre. The aim was to 'broaden the horizons of Carnival' with The Tabernacle becoming the performance space as well as being home to the Mangrove.

I used to come here when it was a youth club, but the place was like a building site. You used to have to get up on a ladder to go up on the second floor and get into the main space. Nowadays you wouldn't be able to do that on health and safety grounds. There was literally a ladder tied up with some rope at the top, going to the next level, where there was concrete and graffiti everywhere. In 1985 there was a refurbishment that improved things, and then in 1997 the whole building was gutted and Lottery money was used to refurbish it.

It is now a multi-faceted space that acts as a community centre, hosting a wide range of classes, such as yoga and keep fit, alongside acting, singing and dancing. There is a small art gallery space that can be rented out, which often displays local history exhibitions. Matthew explains that it is not an easy building to manage.

It is very expensive, and the funding we receive from the council doesn't cover it, so we have to generate the money from hiring the space out and from the bar and kitchen. But then when you walk in here and see so many people all from different walks of life all enjoying themselves it makes it all worthwhile. There are a lot of different elements and communities that make up Notting Hill and you have to try and make sure they are all represented.

Matthew tells me he must get back to the rehearsals upstairs, and I thank him for his time. He reminds me of the details of the Panormana event, scheduled for two weeks' time and taking place in a small park area just off Kensal Road north of Portobello.

When the Saturday comes around the weather is far from perfect. Umbrellas and waterproofs have been pressed into service as I seek out a place towards the back of the crowd. The inclement weather has not affected their spirits; the atmosphere is excellent as we prepare to watch the six bands who are competing to win the annual prize. The Mangrove Steelband play fourth, arriving on stage to huge cheers. I find myself feeling unexpectedly nervous on their behalf, willing them to play well.

But I have nothing to worry about. They execute their song perfectly and look great decked out in matching red T-shirts. The applause when they finished is deafening and I can hardly wait for the last two bands to play before the results are announced. The talent on display is incredible, and as the last strains from the Croyden Steel Orchestra's rendition of 'Sapna (The Dream)' ring out, the judges confer among themselves to decide on the winners. It doesn't take them long. Ten or fifteen minutes later the head of the judging panel's voice comes over the PA: the Mangrove are awarded third place, with the Real Steal Band taking first and Metronomes Steel Orchestra second. There are whoops of joy as people congratulate one another and the judge on stage thanks everyone for coming and for their ongoing support and love of the pan. It is clear that this event is not about the winning positions. There are no cash prizes on offer, and the bands even paid to enter. It is about celebrating the music and the sense of community that brings everyone together, musicians and supporters alike. I can see that the band is busy celebrating with their friends and family. With the skies still grey and drizzly I head home. I need a good night's sleep because tomorrow will be the start of Carnival, and two days of drinking and dancing.

Fox Friends:
The Maverick Masquerade Band

Over the years I have watched the Carnival procession from various vantage points along its route, dancing to the music and marvelling at the costumes on display, as helicopters hum and swoop overhead. The smell of burning charcoal permeates the air, as chicken and sweetcorn are cooked and cans of Red Stripe are drunk and discarded at an alarmingly fast rate. I normally find myself squashed between sweaty, drunken revellers, jostled by the crowds at the front or caught in jams of people at the back, as the police try to regulate the flow of the crowd. By late afternoon if I'm not drunk enough my feet begin to hurt and I am ready to keel over.

It is at this moment that I think back to my most comfortable Carnival experience. It took place about ten years ago when I lived in a flat on Ladbroke Grove, right on the procession route. All I had needed to do to secure my ringside seat was push up the huge sash window in the bedroom and lower myself gently down onto the wide window sill. Sitting there above the ebb and flow of the crowd was bliss. I could fetch a cold beer straight from the fridge and nip to the loo whenever I needed to. Perfect.

To be honest, this was about the only time I was happy to be living in that flat. In all other respects it was awful: there was no central heating, the floor was covered by sticky laminate of indeterminate age and colour, and the 'kitchen' was nothing more than a sunken corner of the room with a hot plate and a

rusty sink. I was glad to leave it after one year. But on that Bank
Holiday weekend in late August, none of that mattered – it was
transformed into the perfect flat.

It was during that Carnival, sitting there on my little promon-
tory above the crowds, that I fully grasped just how much work
went into each float, or 'band' as they are called. I saw women
decked out in colourful outfits with matching headdresses
twirling in the sun. The costumes are all handmade, each one
individually tailored. Bands of drummers flanked by women in
bikinis would move in time to the music with the whole scene
choreographed to create maximum effect. When it worked it
was truly something to behold, and you could see the ripple of
excitement move across the crowd.

Masquerade bands, or mas bands as they are known, are an
intrinsic part of the Carnival experience. They are made up of
small groups who gather together and decide upon a theme,
designing and making costumes and devising a dance routine to
go with it. Many hundreds if not thousands of hours go into the
design and preparation work, with mas camps springing up in
the months before Carnival, and the finished results are as much
a celebration of teamwork as self-expression.

That day on Ladbroke Grove, one float stood out from the
rest. Towards mid-afternoon a band came into view made up
almost entirely of children, from the very young to teenagers,
wearing a uniform of matching bright yellow T-shirts. They
were all smiling and holding up umbrellas that had been embel-
lished with various bits of fabric and eye-catching glitter, which
they then proceeded to hold aloft and twirl in time to the music.
The effect was dazzling. It was a far simpler than the other
floats I had seen that day, but that was what made it stand out.
Thinking about my carnival experiences for this book, I knew I
had to seek out that band and try to discover who those children
dancing so happily down Ladbroke Grove that day were.

I discovered that the band in question was the Fox Carnival Band, the brainchild of a local woman named Fiona Hawthorne and based out of Fox Primary School, from which they took their name. Fox had been taking part in the Carnival since 1995, and was now one of the biggest attractions in the procession, with up to 600 people dancing behind the float, ranging in age from babies to grandparents.

I found their website and sent Fiona a message asking if she would be willing to talk me through the history of the band. She responded a few days later saying she was happy to meet up and talk to me about her Carnival experiences. A date was fixed and we arranged to meet.

It was then that a strange coincidence occurred. Cycling home northwards along Portobello Road one evening, I encountered some colourful paintings attached to the long stretch of wall between Oxford Gardens and Chesterton Road. They formed part of a council-led initiative to bring Portobello and Golborne Markets closer together, for this stretch of the street has always been a bit of a no-man's-land on non-market days, leaving the uninitiated to think this must be the end of Portobello with nothing more to see, when of course, Golborne Road lies just beyond, full of cafés and interesting vintage and antique shops. Slowing down and dismounting my bike I took a closer look at the paintings. They were large, perhaps ten or fifteen feet in length and width. Executed using a mixture of photography and painting they depicted a whole range of Carnival scenes, from the floats to the sound systems, all the way through to the bin men dealing with the detritus left in the Carnival's wake. Reaching the informative board at the end I was astonished to discover these paintings were part of a project called 'Aspects of Carnival' by Fiona Hawthorne, the woman behind the Fox Carnival Band. I hadn't realized that she was an artist and she had been too modest to mention this project when we emailed.

Fiona Hawthorne's *Aspects of Carnival* artwork
adorns Portobello Road, 2013

What a wonderful way to celebrate the spirit of the Carnival, I thought, and I looked forward to hearing all about how these paintings came about.

Fiona is all smiles when we meet. A glamorous woman in her early forties, she arrives exactly on time and instantly puts me at ease. When I mention her paintings on Portobello she beams with pleasure, asking me what I made of them. I tell her that I think she has done a wonderful job in capturing the vibrancy and diversity of the weekend. She tells me she has been thrilled by the response, receiving several emails a day from people telling her how much they have enjoyed looking at the paintings and of the memories they evoke. 'Old guys who were involved in Carnival have come up to me and said, "Thank you for representing something of our story." Or people who have lived here for generations have said to me, "We have lived through all this change and it is great to see how you have captured that in your paintings."'

Fiona has certainly seen the area change since she first moved here in summer 1984 after graduating from Chelsea College of Art. Moving in a couple of weeks before Carnival, she was unprepared for what to expect and was blown away by her experience, so much so that she has never missed a Carnival since. She has four children with her husband, the actor Colin Salmon, whom she met while he was busking on Portobello and who is as passionate and involved in carnival as she is.

The idea for the Fox band began to germinate in 1997 when her eldest child, Sasha, entered Fox Primary School. Fiona was astonished to discover they had no direct links or involvement with the Carnival, despite the fact that it was taking place on their doorstep. 'They had no connection to the Carnival, they didn't have a float and it wasn't included in the curriculum in any way. And I just thought, wow, that is such a shame because it is such a resource, it is such a learning tool.'

Rather than accepting this state of affairs Fiona took action. She decided to form a masquerade band of her own and, with the help of some fellow parents and supportive teachers, they set about designing traditional-style costumes in preparation for the upcoming Carnival. The work was fiddly and time-consuming, with the adults forced to take the lead if they were to be ready in time. As the weeks went by she realized that the children were being sidelined from the creative process. It didn't feel right. Nevertheless, when the Carnival weekend arrived the small group paraded proudly down Ladbroke Grove.

Fiona explains that in the weeks that followed she 'realized that the way a lot of it is done is very adult led – you know, those big shimmering costumes, each one the same as the next one, whole sections of glittering bikinis and sequins. It requires a production line and I didn't want children to be doing a production line. How could you argue that that involved the children?

The Fox Carnival Band shaking their umbrellas at Carnival 2005

So we decided to challenge it and to make it into something that was about children's work.'

Fiona was still unsure as to how exactly this would work, until an idea came to her one afternoon when she was helping out at Fox school, showing a group of children how to use some digital painting software. With minimal instruction she asked them to create some pictures inspired by the Carnival and within minutes they came up with wonderful colourful paintings of masks and outfits they had seen. It was then that she had her lightbulb moment – why not take this art that the children had created and somehow use it for their costumes? Perhaps the paintings could be printed off and laminated and displayed by the children? Of course the idea needed fleshing out, but in essence she felt she was on to something.

Pitching this idea to the official Carnival committee she was greeted by a sea of blank faces. She remembers how they dismissed it, saying, 'No, that is not Carnival.' Despite these

The Fox Carnival Band proudly display their artwork at Carnival 2010

protests she stuck to her idea, convinced that the children would feel far more involvement if their own work was being used. Slowly, she tells me, she won them over, and the following year, in 1998, the children wore a uniform of matching T-shirts and held aloft their artwork of carnival masks, which had been laminated and mounted on sticks. Shaking them in time to the music they made their way along the route.

She tells me that the reaction varied from the supportive, to the bemused and even the downright hostile. But they kept going, year on year, steadily growing in popularity, so that by 2012 they were the biggest group taking part in Carnival. Throughout this time they have stuck to their design principles, using cheap and easy-to-find objects that are then transformed by the group. They have included a windsock magically trans-formed into a fish, monsters created from plastic bags and children's umbrellas decorated and attached to long poles. She explains how: 'They usually hold their work on sticks and move it time with the music, there is no showing of bodies in bikinis and all that. We all wear the same colour T-shirt. We are very strict about the look – a strong sense of uniformity is important, giving people in the audience a really good show.'

Their 2012 theme took its inspiration from the riots of that summer, using brushes and brooms brought from home or bought from the pound shop, adapted by the group and waved in solidarity with the clean-up operation.

She is adamant that Carnival must be an inclusive experience, telling me it is as much about the audience as the band. 'It isn't about us guys having a party that you can witness. It is about giving the audience a drama and that drama is created through the art, through the uniformity and through the numbers.' And she is keen to stress that Fox is an affordable way to get involved: they differ from other floats who order their elaborate costumes at a higher price online. She explains, 'What we are trying to do is give kids a safe and affordable route into being involved in the Carnival, because buying those traditional costumes isn't cheap, it is unaffordable for a lot of people. If you've got three or four children you'd be spending the same as going to Portugal for a week.' Money aside, she explains how the children that take part 'see how numbers can come together and have this crazy, incredible artistic impact that moves people. If children are part of creating that drama it changes their perception about possibilities for the future.'

Fox took a year off in 2012 and I can see why. It has been quite a journey for Fiona and her family. Putting a band on the parade route is a year-round task. Not only does she co-ordinate the creative side of things, she also has to attend meetings and deal with all the attendant bureaucracy. But Fiona takes it in her stride; her passion for the neighbourhood and for an inclusive community is awe-inspiring. This brings me back to the paintings on Portobello – she has promised to give me a guided tour, and with our coffees drunk we leave the café to take a closer look at her work.

I ask her how she got the commission. 'I saw it advertised, but at the same time about six people sent it to me and said, "You've got to do this, you've got to get this job!"' Her CV could not have been more suited to the job, not only was she a local resident but she had been coming to Carnival for twenty-five years. She won the commission and set to work. Shaking her head in disbelief she recalls the speed at which she worked. The council wanted new work to cover as much of the 100-metre wall space as possible. 'I started on 14 February and finished on 14 April, so I did it all in eight weeks, which was insane!' In a sense, though, Fiona had been working on this project for almost thirty years, ever since her first Carnival experience in 1984.

Incorporating photographs and using digital technology, the paintings are full of local landmarks and characters. 'There were a few people I decided had to go in. There is a Carnival character called Sister Monica, who is an incredibly positive force. Then there is an old guy who is a pan player who I included. In one of them I have put loads of photographs of all the Fox people because, aside from anything else, they have become such good friends over the years.' With rainclouds gathering, I say goodbye to Fiona who is heading off to her studio in Shepherd's Bush.

A week later I speak to her eldest daughter Sasha, who is now in her early twenties and has been part of the Fox Band since she was seven years old. She proves to be just as eloquent and passionate about the Carnival as her mother: 'It's the only time where people of all creeds stand side by side and dance together. The area houses such opposites – all different races – and the gap between rich and poor is bigger than anywhere else in London.' When I ask her if there was a particular moment over the last fifteen years that sticks in her mind, she answers without missing a beat: 'Seeing a young Dutch millionaire heiress holding the hand of a young black boy, helping to customize his T-shirt – both residents of the area who I doubt would have ever met outside of Fox. They didn't seem to even be aware of their differences in this moment. Now they are Fox friends.'

PART THREE

IN LOVE WITH
ROCK'N'ROLL

A rock'n'roll inspired mural near Portobello Road

The Caribbean community that settled around Portobello in the early 1950s brought with them not only a new palette of sounds, but also a nonconformist, DIY spirit that has been a trademark of the music scene here ever since. This spirit is apparent in the early sound system selectors, such as Count Suckle and Baron Baker, who DJ'd at the illegal shebeens that were in abundance in the area in the 1950s and '60s. It is also in the work of visionary record producer Joe Meek who set up his first home studio at his flat on Arundel Gardens during the skiffle boom of 1957. Since then, music of all genres, from rock'n'roll to punk via reggae, prog and psych has poured out of these streets, as bands have formed and gigged here, studios have sprung up, and pioneering shops and record labels have been founded.

In 1964 Beatlemania appeared on All Saints Road when the Fab Four stopped by to film a sequence for *A Hard Day's Night* featuring Ringo running away from a pair of screaming girls before taking refuge in a second hand shop. Two years later, in the autumn of 1966, Pink Floyd, the toast of the emerging London underground scene, played a series of gigs at All Saints Church Hall that saw them transformed from an R&B covers bands to into a fully fledged psychedelic experience, ushering in a wave of psychedelic rock that would take London by storm the following year.

By the late 1960s with acid replacing dope as the drug of choice, the neighbourhood became not only the headquarters of the counterculture, home to underground publications like *Oz* and *Frendz*, but also its musical centre, arguably becoming London's answer to Haight-Ashbury in San Fransciso. Bands flocked to this run-down and seedy corner of the city, attracted by cheap rents or the possibility of squatting, and the hippie scene blossomed. Eric Clapton formed Cream while living here; Van Morrison lived on Ladbroke Grove and immortalized it in the song 'Slim Slow Slider' from his *Astral Weeks* album; and design duo Hapshash and the Coloured Coat designed and produced their iconic psychedelic posters from the sitting room of 52 Princedale Road.

In 1968, in the attic room of 57 Blenheim Crescent, Marc Bolan strummed an acoustic guitar composing 'Ride a White Swan' and bonding with original Tyrannosaurus Rex bongo player Steve 'Peregrine' Took. The Edgar Broughton Band moved down from Warwick after signing a deal with EMI, and Leicester's soul-prog finest Family lived at 187 Oxford Gardens. But it was former mod outfit the Action, who morphed into Mighty Baby and relocated to the Grove, who best encapsulated this new feeling of inclusive optimism and experimentation, releasing two incredible albums before getting into Sufism and splitting in the early 1970s. Sextet Quintessence formed in Notting Hill and shared their love of Eastern religion through their music, which was based around mantras and ragas, including the song 'Notting Hill Gate' on their *In Blissful Company* LP.

The more out-there wing of the hippie freak scene was exemplified by the Pink Fairies and the Deviants, whose leader Mick Farren was the self-styled king of the freaks and a long-time resident of the neighbourhood, but it was Hawkwind who were elected as the house band, embracing a people's band philosophy that chimed with the times, playing regularly for free under the Westway.

In the late 1970s, as flares gave way to the drainpipes and

leather jackets of punk, the neighbourhood had its own conquering heroes in the form of the Clash, the ultimate local gods. Rough Trade pioneered a new type of record shop, first on Kensington Park Road before moving to their current location on Talbot Road, becoming the hub for the DIY fanzine scene. Equally important to the punk revolution was Ted Carroll's shop Rock On at 93 Golborne Road, which boasted an unrivalled selection of R&B, northern soul, rockabilly and US punk and garage. Numerous record labels operated from the area: Virgin moved into Vernon Yard in early 1974, expanding their office space on the proceeds of Mike Oldfield's *Tubular Bells*; Island Records operated from offices on Basing Street; and Miles Copeland's HQ label was based on Blenheim Crescent, releasing classic albums by the likes of REM, the Fall and the Police.

In the wake of Joe Meek's home set-up, numerous more professional studios sprung up, including Lansdowne Studios and Basing Street (now Sarm West). These have been joined in more recent years by Damon Albarn's studio, XL's basement studio, and celebrated musical innovator Brian Eno, who rather fittingly operates from a quiet mews house, where his studio set up includes a Helios desk that he bought from the original Island Studios in 1975.

The 1980s saw local band Aswad shoot up the charts, finding a receptive audience with their brand of pop reggae, and Mick Jones' post-Clash outfit Big Audio Dynamite posed for photographs in front of Trellick Tower the 31-storey block of flats designed by revered modernist architect Erno Goldfinger in 1966. In November 1984 the cream of the British pop establishment visited Basing Street Studios to record the Band Aid classic 'Do They Know It's Christmas?'.

The 1990s saw Pulp's Jarvis Cocker make Ladbroke Grove his home, name-checking the street on 'I Spy', a track on their acclaimed *Different Class* album. Blur's Damon Albarn moved into a flat on Kensington Park Road in 1990 and has never left, with the area continuing to inspire him both musically and lyrically almost twenty-five years later. In the mid 1990s girl band All Saints named themselves after the notoriously troubled street known locally as the Front Line, going on to huge world-wide success; while at the same time cult West London power trio My Drug Hell recorded their lost classic 'This Is My Drug Hell 2' on vintage gear in a basement on St Charles Square. The most recent label to set up shop here is Heavenly Recordings who moved their operations from Soho to Portobello Road in 2009. The following chapters contain interviews with some of those movers and shakers who have helped put the neighbour-hood on the musical map over the last half century, and who continue to make it a relevant and exciting area to live in.

Pink Floyd Go into
Interstellar Overdrive

Peter Jenner, a twenty-five-year-old assistant lecturer in social administration at the London School of Economics, sat in his small Central London office on Sunday 12 June 1966, contemplating the large pile of exam papers lying on the desk in front of him. He had been in the job for two years, since graduating from Cambridge with a degree in Economics and moving to London. But he had to admit he was growing bored of his duties and the daily drudge of lectures and tutorials, not to mention all this marking. His life outside the university was proving far more interesting. As a founding member of the London Free School, he moved in middle-class, liberal intellectual circles, smoking dope, talking radical politics, listening to Beat poetry and indulging his love of jazz.

He had been introduced to this London scene through Hoppy, the leading light in the London Free School who was so instrumental in organising the first Notting Hill Free School Fayre (see 'Pageant, Fireworks, Music, Plays and Poetry: The London Free School and the 1966 Carnival' in Part Two: Lord, Don't Stop the Carnival) More specifically he had met Hoppy through scoring dope at his Westbourne Terrace flat when he had first moved to the city. The pair had soon become firm friends and earlier that year, along with fellow travellers Felix de Mendelsohn and Ron Atkins, had founded an avant-garde record label which they christened DNA records, inspired by the avant-garde American label ESP. They had even secured a deal through

Elektra Records, brokered by Joe Boyd, another Free School member and friend. Earlier that month he had accompanied their first signing, free jazz outfit AMM, into the Sound Techniques studio to record their debut album.

By mid-afternoon that Sunday, Peter had worked his way through about half the exam papers, using a red pen to scribble his comments in the margins. But his mind wasn't really on the task in hand. He kept gazing out of the window towards Soho. There was a gig happening that afternoon a few streets away at the Marquee Club, with a band he had been hearing good things about due to play. As the clock on the wall inched around to 4PM he put his pen down, stretched out his arms and made a decision. Enough was enough. Jumping up from his chair he retrieved his jacket from the hook on the door, slung it over his shoulders and was out the door. The rest of the marking would have to wait until Monday.

It did not take him long to walk from his Holborn office to the Marquee Club, which was located halfway along Wardour Street at number 90. Since relocating from its former Oxford Street address two years previously, it had become *the* place catch the latest bands. Everyone from the Who, the Spencer Davis Group, David Bowie and the Moody Blues had shuffled onto its small stage. But that afternoon's event was not the usual Marquee Club affair. Since January of that year, avant-garde filmmaker Steve Stollman had been promoting a series of 'happenings' dubbed 'Spontaneous Underground', or simply 'the Trip'. Fliers had been distributed around the hip neighbourhoods and sent out using the mailing list of the ever-helpful Hoppy. They were invitation-only, alcohol-free affairs with the fliers promising 'dancing, painting, sculpture, homosexuals and jazz musicians'.[21]

Featuring acts signed to ESP records, the label run by Steve's brother Bernard, they were among the first truly psychedelic events in London. Founder of the Indica gallery and bookshop Barry Miles wrote in the underground newspaper *East Village Other*:

> Nothing is advertised, no one is billed, no tickets, about five phone calls are made. When they are there, they do things, meet people, happen. Unorganised events have included Donovan, in red Cleopatra make-up, singing to one sitar and five conga drummers, AMM in white coats with electronic tapes, films projected onto dancers.[22]

The band booked to play that night was billed as the Pink Floyd Sound. They had already played over half a dozen times for Stollman at these Sunday happenings and found the audience receptive to their set of American R&B covers given a psychedelic makeover, with one or two original numbers by the band's lead guitarist and singer Syd Barrett, an art student enrolled at Camberwell Art School. The rest of the band were made up of three architectural students from the London Polytechnic on Regent Street, in the form of drummer Nick Mason, bassist Roger Waters and Rick Wright on Farfisa organ.

Peter arrived shortly before the band took to the stage, descending into the club's mirrored interior with its raised stage at the back set against a painted stripy backdrop done out to resemble the inside of a big top circus tent. Finding a spot at the back he stood and waited as the band strapped on guitars and tuned up. The set that followed was unlike anything he had seen or heard before. Standard R&B covers like 'Louie Louie' would veer unexpectedly off into echo-laced discordant jams, as a makeshift lightshow projected colours onto the walls and the band themselves, all of them immersed in the sound. 'Roadrunner' was covered in wailing feedback and screeching noise. Peter found it impossible to discern whether the sound

The late, legendary leader of Pink Floyd, Syd Barrett

was emanating from the heavily reverbed guitars or the Farfisa organ, both of which were being fed through a Binson Echorec unit, giving the sound a washed-out shimmering quality that allowed the music to float around with the lights. The whole thing was also very, very loud.

The Pink Floyd Sound had been together in this line up for little over a year, playing sporadically wherever and whenever they could. They were a middle-class, intelligent group who took their studies as seriously as their music, although privately certain members were beginning to doubt the likelihood of their ever making it in the music business. Roger and Syd had grown up together in Cambridge, bonding in their teenage years over a shared love of the Stones and early blues records. Roger, three years older than Syd, had moved up to London first and met Nick and Rick on his architectural course. After several abortive line-ups and name changes, Syd had joined on guitar and vocals when he had moved to London in autumn 1964.

Peter approached them after the gig as they set about packing up their equipment. Bowled over by what he had just witnessed, he offered to sign them to his DNA label. They treated his enthusiasm with polite detachment. This gig was to be their last before the end of term when they broke up for the long summer vacation. Over recent months it had proved a hard slog combining their studies with the band and they were looking forward to a well-earned break. With this in mind they told Peter he would have to wait until the autumn when they would be back in London for the start of the new term.

Fast-forward almost fifty years and I am sitting opposite Peter discussing his early days with the band, perched on a sofa in the comfortable sitting room of his house on Bravington Road, just off Harrow Road. Over the course of the afternoon he explains to me how he and his business partner Andrew King came to manage Pink Floyd and oversee their early rise under the genius of their sensitive lead singer and songwriter Syd Barrett. I am here to discuss a specific series of gigs that Peter booked for the band at All Saints Church Hall, just off Powis Square, in the autumn of 1966. During that ten-gig residency their set was transformed with the R&B covers dropped as a wealth of new Syd Barrett-penned songs were incorporated into the set, songs which would make up the backbone of their self-titled debut album released a year later. Playing in tandem with the light shows, they emerged from those gigs as the fully fledged psychedelic pioneers soundtracking the burgeoning underground scene.

But we are getting ahead of ourselves. Peter is explaining to me how, in early September 1966, he did just as they had suggested and looked them up after their summer vacation. From Steve Stollman he obtained a piece of paper with an address in Highgate. There was a determined spring in his step as he set off to find them. Over the summer he had talked things through with his childhood friend Andrew King, who was now as keen as him to work with this band. The pair had been best friends since childhood, having grown up together, (their fathers were both vicars), and they would often spend school holidays together. Andrew had a steady job at BAE, but was growing increasingly bored by corporate office life, so the idea of releasing records and working with Pink Floyd sounded like an interesting escape.

When Peter arrived at the house in Stanhope Gardens he rang the doorbell and waited. He was feeling nervous. Rather like a travelling salesman he practised his pitch as bassist Roger Waters opened the front door. Surprised to see this strange chap from the gig on his doorstep he ushered him inside. A brief conversation ensued in which Peter once again asked if the band would be interested in signing to DNA records. He was met with a reply he had not anticipated. Roger told him they didn't need a label – what they needed was a manager. Laughing at the memory today, Peter says, 'So I said, "Well OK, we'll be your managers then." I didn't know what a manager was. I didn't know what a label was. We didn't know fucking anything!'

Going back to the flat he shared with Andrew on Elbrooke Road, he told him the good news. Rather fortuitously Andrew had just come into some money. 'An aunt had left him some money so he put that into the pot and said, "Let's go for this!"' They decided that their first step should be to invest in some new equipment because wasn't that what managers did? They purchased a top-of-the-range Selmer PA system, a fender bass for Roger, and WEM amplifiers. With the Free School Fayre scheduled for the end of the month and the All Saints Church Hall booked for a series of events it offered the perfect opportunity for the Pink Floyd to play. 30 September was duly set to be their first gig at the venue and their first with Peter and Andrew at the helm.

The band were not initially thrilled that the first bookings from their new managers were a series of church hall gigs, but went along with it. As Nick Mason recalled in his memoirs:

Playing church halls wasn't what we had expected our new managers to be aiming for. But in fact it turned out to be one of the best venues we could have found, since W11 rapidly established itself as the hub of the alternative movement. The whole district of Notting Hill was becoming the most interesting area in London, mixing cheap rents, multicultural residents, activities like the London Free School and a thriving trade in illegal drugs.

The hall has since been knocked down, replaced by an old people's home, but it was by all accounts a pretty basic venue.

Large enough to accommodate about 250 to 300 people, it had polished wooden floors and a high ceiling, and a small raised platform at one end acted as a makeshift stage. With the venue more used to hosting coffee mornings than psychedelic happenings, tea urns stood at the edge of the room on long trestle tables. Peter tells me that they never anticipated the success of these gigs. 'We thought that we would get forty or fifty people.' As it happened, they were soon turning people away. 'By the second week it was absolutely packed. You couldn't get in.'

The sound itself was pretty poor. 'You couldn't hear much. The PAs weren't great back then so you couldn't really hear the vocals.' It was the light show that proved to be the crucial element not only in making these shows unique, but also in shaping the sound of the band. In charge of the lights at the first couple of shows were Joel and Tony Brown, two visitors from Timothy Leary's League for Spiritual Discovery in New York and early pioneers of the light show. They just happened to be in town and brought a projector and some coloured slides along, putting on a light show as the band played. 'That was really how the whole idea of lights started, bringing a multimedia element to the gig, which was really important for the initial idea for the Floyd.'

The lights quickly became such an important element that when Leary's cohorts disappeared after the second gig, presumably back to the US, Peter and Andrew were forced to concoct their own makeshift lighting rig. With no experience and no contacts in the theatre world, the pair went down to the local builders' merchants and bought some standard spotlights, which they mounted onto a length of wood. Armed with some tubes of paint, slides and a projector they set to work. Andrew described the system as 'this absurd system put together with domestic lights, which I operated by flicking the on/off switch very fast.'[23]

It seemed to do the trick, though, and the light show allowed the band room to experiment as the audience looked at the colours rather than just staring at the band. They began to play more original compositions, though covers still formed a part of their set. A review of the first All Saints gig in *Melody Maker* magazine urged the band to explore their psychedelic side further, saying, '... if they can incorporate their electronic prowess with some melodic and lyrical songs – getting away from dated R&B things – they could well score in the near future.'[24]

Peter and Andrew had been urging them to do just this. 'So that was the point when Syd started digging out songs that he had written at his Earlham Street flat that autumn, quickly incorporating them into the set.' A set list from mid-October finds them playing several songs that would go on to appear on their debut LP including 'The Gnome', 'Interstellar Overdrive', 'Take Up Thy Stethoscope and Walk' and 'Astronomy Domine'. The new songs went down well, and the lights and the sound combined to tremendous effect. Drummer Nick Mason noted with pleasure the audience reaction. 'They responded so well and so uncritically to the improvised sections in our set that we began to concentrate on extending those rather than simply running through a sequence of cover versions.'[25]

A regular attendee of these gigs was Emily Young, the fifteen-year-old schoolgirl who lived in the neighbourhood and would sneak out of her home at night to hang out at the Free School (see 'Pageant, Fireworks, Music, Plays and Poetry: The London Free School and the 1966 Carnival' in Part Two: Lord, Don't Stop the Carnival). When we met she described these early Floyd shows to me:

It had this great energy. Everybody danced and you could get really lost in it. It got very multimedia and creative. They were definitely pushing that. You might drink a little wine, smoke a little dope, see your friends. It was people coming together and that was the thing about Portobello: it was people coming from all over the world because there was some sort of smell in the air. They could taste it and smell it and they wanted to be part of it. There was something happening. I quite liked the music but I was more interested in the people talking about stuff. I thought Syd was magical. I think at the time running all through London there was this feeling of things changing and new possibilities opening up, and Syd had a spark that was magnetic. He was incredibly alive, and dripping with that sense of being arty and creative. He was very attractive to be near, a Pan-like character, a creature of the forest. He looked otherworldly and had this wildness, this quality of not being urban. He had a sense of English wildness.

Her link to Pink Floyd goes further than just attending these gigs. In spring 1967 Pink Floyd released their second single, an upbeat psychedelic pop nugget called 'See Emily Play'. It was said to be inspired by Emily and her looning around at these All Saints shows. When I asked her about this she told me she feels that she was a muse rather than inspiration:

I think he already had that story inside him. It was about himself, not about me. I was just the image – it was actually about something that he needed to address: his over-taking of drugs. He knew the poet in him was in terrible danger and was going to die because he wasn't protecting it. I think this song was about him trying to have a conversation with himself about the creative instinct and how you can plunge down to the depths and the difficulty is staying alive and safe and still being able to function in the real world. It was an unconscious conversation between himself and his poetic intuition. This was like a huge alarm bell going off, and it did happen. What he was afraid of did happen.

Syd's trajectory from psychedelic seer, writing some of the most innovative and influential songs of the era, to burnt-out acid casualty leading to his departure from the band in early 1968 has been well documented. But at that moment in autumn 1966 he was at the peak of his powers and Pink Floyd were fast becoming the toast of the London underground. It is worth noting just how quick their rise had been and although we may think that the idea of the 'buzz band' is a modern, Internet phenomenon, Pink Floyd illustrate that the notion goes back fifty years. Peter is still surprised at the way it unfolded.

It took off very fast. By Christmas we had got features in the *Melody Maker*. In three months we had got to the point of centre-page spreads saying, 'This is the big thing for next year,' including a big article in *Queen* magazine. It was a middle-class intelligentsia thing. There were links with people like Barry Miles from Indica, who was connected to the Beatles. The launch of *International Times*, the first Roundhouse gigs, the start of UFO . . . all these things were happening that autumn.

Although Pink Floyd had to wait until 1973 to find mainstream success with the release of their multi-million selling *Dark Side of the Moon* album, the importance of these early shows cannot be over-estimated. These ten shows in an old church hall off Portobello Road signalled the start of their transformation from an R&B covers band to the stadium-filling group of the 1970s, connecting with millions of people across the world.

Hapshash and the Coloured Coat

The exotically named duo Hapshash and the Coloured Coat
were in fact Michael English and Nigel Waymouth, who
created some of the most original psychedelic art of the era,
designing posters for bands like Pink Floyd, The Crazy World
of Arthur Brown, Soft Machine and The Incredible String
Band. They drew on artists like Max Ernst, René Magritte
and Alphonse Mucha, with a heavy dose of Art Nouveau, to
pioneer a visual style that was uniquely their own, using
colours to maximum visual effect and achieving a clarity and
depth of ambition that is astonishing. Looking at their work
today it is all the more astounding to think that they created
these works using screen-printing techniques in their makeshift studio at 52 Princedale Road, now in the heart of
gentrified Notting Hill. Nigel explained to me that he was
familiar with Portobello Market, having visited many times
with his girlfriend Sheila Cohen on buying trips, when they
were setting up their fashion boutique, Granny Takes a Trip.
He shifted into poster design in late 1966, when he was introduced to Michael English by a mutual friend, record producer
Joe Boyd, who was looking for someone to help Michael
design their posters for gigs at his UFO Club, as well as the
recently formed *International Times* magazine. Joe felt there
was something 'missing' and suggested the pair get together.
With that in mind, in January 1967, Nigel caught the bus from
Chelsea and headed over to Michael's flat on Princedale Road.
'We instantly liked one another and started doing some
sketches pretty much straight away. Michael was a brilliant
technician, very precise and very tight, and what he needed
was a burst of ideas that were wilder than what he was doing.
And what I needed was someone who could show me how to
properly put it down.' Commissions quickly flew in. 'Joe or
Hoppy would look in and say, "Pink Floyd need a poster this
week for the UFO Club. Can you do it?" or Track Records

Nigel Waymouth and his psychedelic posters, 52 Princedale Road, 1967

would swing by and say, "Jimi Hendrix needs a poster".' With such beautiful posters appearing on walls and in venues across London, it wasn't long before people were ripping them off the wall as quickly as they were going up. They tried to capital-ize on this by producing extra editions to sell on, but it didn't quite work out as planned. 'It was a Mickey Mouse business, as Miles said to me the other day. It was crazy – it cost us 7 and 6 [the equivalent 37½p today] to produce these posters and we were selling them for 7 and 3 [the equivalent 36p today]. The spirit of capitalism was certainly not abroad!' These days, Nigel is a sought-after portrait painter, and rather fittingly he has ended up living on Princedale Road after more than a decade in America. 'It remains a special place for me. All of the posters were done there. The Hapshash experience was all very much based in Notting Hill and Holland Park.' But he notes sadly that the area has changed beyond recognition from the one that he pitched up in half a century ago. 'It was a very down-at-heel neighbourhood back then. Nowadays in Portland Road and Princedale you can't find a worker's cottage for less than £5 million, and the little terraced houses now have Bentleys and Porches parked outside.

Cover of Hawkwind's 1974 album, *Hall of the Mountain Grill*, named
after the popular greasy spoon café at 275 Portobello Road

Hawkwind:
The House Band

In summer 1969, Clearwater Productions, a band management company based in Westmoreland Mews, decided to break into the lucrative gig promotions market by staging a number of shows at nearby All Saints Church Hall where Pink Floyd had played their legendary shows in the autumn of 1966 (see previous chapter: Pink Floyd Go into Interstellar Overdrive). The gigs mainly showcased bands from their roster, including psychedelic folk rockers Trees and prog-leaning outfits High Tide and Skin Alley. Attendances were good, attracting up to 250 people, with David Bowie even turning out to play one night.

On 29 August the hall was booked for a night to be headlined by High Tide. Late that afternoon preparations began for the show: equipment was unloaded and carried into the hall, amplifiers were plugged into the ancient-looking wall sockets and the PA was gingerly tested out. At around 5PM, a dark green Morris van pulled up and parked outside, and a conversation ensued between the van's occupants before the driver got out.

Dressed in a dirty old pair of flared jeans with long greasy hair and a straggly beard tied at the centre, he walked into the hall. Sidling up to one of the guys unknotting mic cable, he informed him that he was in a band and enquired about the possibility of their playing later on. He was duly introduced to the promoter, Douglas Smith of Clearwater, and after a few minutes it was agreed that they could play a short set at the end of the night.

Only one question remained: what was the band's name? The long-haired man scratched his head and replied, 'Group X.'

Like most bands playing their first ever gig, Group X soon changed their name, becoming Hawkwind Zoo, before slimming it down to simply Hawkwind. That first gig would prove to be an auspicious occasion for them, for in the audience that night was John Peel, the influential radio DJ. At the time Peel was living around the corner in a tiny studio flat on Stanley Square, and had come along to check out High Tide, only catching Hawkwind's set by accident as he was heading to the exit. Intrigued, he stuck around and listened. He was blown away. Before leaving he advised a member of the Clearwater team: 'That Group X – get them.'

It is easy to see why Peel had been so impressed, the gig must have been quite something to behold. The band did not run through a rehearsed set list of songs. Rather, they played an improvised jam lasting around fifteen minutes based on the riff from the Byrds' 'Eight Miles High'. They were led by guitarist and singer Dave Brock, a veteran of the blues scene, who along with fellow guitarist Mick Slattery set about creating a wall of Hendrix-style feedback, holding their guitars up close to the amps. Drummer Terry Ollis beat the living hell out of his kit, while bassist John Harrison kept things rooted with his steady bass runs. Former roadie and electronics genius Michael 'Dik Mik' Davies sat off to the side, fiddling intently with an old audio generator that he had twinned with an echo unit to create weird electronic whooshes. Nik Turner stood in the centre, behind Brock, playing saxophone lines that weaved in and out of the mix. The audience stood entranced as the liquid light show and strobe effects added to the audio-visual assault. It would not be an understatement to say that they were quite unlike anyone else gigging at the time, years ahead of the pack, offering a multimedia experience before the term even existed.

Heeding Peel's advice, Clearwater signed the band up and set in motion a career that is still going strong to this day. But it is the early years that I am most concerned with here, specifically the period between 1970 and 1975, when the band released their five most commercially successful and critically acclaimed albums. I arranged to talk to Nik Turner, saxophonist with the band until his departure in 1976. Nik is often credited as the heart and soul of Hawkwind, having co-written many of their most enduring songs and been instrumental in bringing their collaborations together. Throughout this period the band became synonymous with Ladbroke Grove, and they linked up with some of the key figures of the underground, from writers and poets through to artists and dancers. They would regularly play free gigs in various local venues from Bayswater to Wormwood Scrubs. One could say they were the area's house band.

Nik Turner is one of the most colourful members of the countercultural vanguard still making music today. Touring under the Space Ritual banner he laces his sets with old Hawkwind numbers. He exudes the free spirit of the era, happy to give me his time, looking every inch the ageing rocker in a frayed western shirt and a pair of black jeans. He is deeply proud of what Hawkwind achieved and stood for all those years ago, and smiles when I remind him of their first gig at All Saints Church Hall, specifically Peel's reaction. 'He was very impressed because we were like the Sex Pistols of that era. We were very expressionist.'

Born in 1940, Nik's journey to the ranks of Hawkwind had been a circuitous one. Spending his teenage years near Margate, he was a clever child, winning a place at the local grammar school, where he was a popular pupil. He was encouraged to be creative and musical by his mother, herself an enthusiastic boogie-woogie piano player, and he took up clarinet lessons at seventeen. At twenty-two he joined the merchant navy as an engineer, sailing to Australia and back before settling in London where he secured a job with London Transport.

It was 1963 and the British R&B boom was in full swing. Nik spent his nights going to clubs like the 100 and the Marquee, or checking out the Yardbirds and the Stones at the Station Hotel in Richmond. But the boredom of his day job was too much to bear. He quit in 1964 and moved back to Margate, where he found work on the beach selling sun hats, postcards and other paraphernalia to the holidaymakers who flocked to the coast throughout the summer season.

But it was a trip to Berlin in the winter of 1968 that proved to be a turning point, opening his mind to a new way of thinking. 'I went over to Germany and worked with all these free jazz musicians, and they convinced me that you didn't need to be technical to express yourself. So from that moment really I wanted to play free jazz in a rock band.'

Inspired by what he had seen in Germany, Nik resolved to move back to London just as soon as he had enough money. By spring 1969 he felt the time was right. He had acquired an old green Morris van and in early May he tossed what few possessions he owned in the back, including a saxophone, and headed for the capital once more.

With nowhere to live but plenty of friends in and around Notting Hill, it was the obvious destination. He was to spend the next two years sleeping on friends' floors and sofas where he would limit his visits to one night, never wishing to outstay his welcome. He made what money he could doing deliveries with his trusty van. One regular job involved moving the bulky silk screens around for the owner of the Dogg Shop on Blenheim Crescent, one of the first 'head shops' in the country, specialising in selling smoking paraphernalia along with countercultural magazines and books.

When old Margate contact Dik Mik mentioned that some

mates of his were getting a band together and needed a roadie with a van, he jumped at the chance. Soon both Nik and Dik Mik were helping Dave Brock, Mick Slattery, Terry Ollis and John Harrison move their equipment into a small theatre at the back of the Royal College of Art. They had secured the space rent-free for a period of intensive rehearsals that summer. Hanging out with the band it wasn't long before they encouraged Nik to bring along his saxophone and he started honking along during rehearsals. Dik Mik got involved too, setting up an old audio generator and echo unit he had picked up. He began to make weird noises as the music flowed around him. The roadies had joined the band.

Following their infamous gig at All Saints Church Hall and the subsequent deal with Clearwater Productions, the band embarked on a schedule of playing gigs both local and national. A record deal was inked with Liberty Records, with sessions at Trident Studios in Soho resulting in their debut LP, released in 1970. But they continued to spend most of their time in the area, using the offices of underground magazine *Frendz* at 307 Portobello Road as their unofficial HQ.

Frendz had started life in December 1969 as an off-shoot of *Rolling Stone*. Originally titled *Friends of Rolling Stone*, it re-launched in 1970 as *Friends*, and from May 1971 until its closure in August 1972 it became *Frendz*. Although it is perhaps not as well known as other underground papers from around the same time, such as *International Times* or *Oz* magazine, it was just as important. Nick Kent got his first writing gig there when he turned up on their doorstep in January 1972 offering his services as a music journalist. Legendary rock photographer Pennie Smith also got her start there before, like Kent, moving on to the *NME*. It was while hanging out at the offices one day that Nik was introduced to Barney Bubbles, graphic artist and art director for the magazine.

Nik tells me he liked Barney immediately and speaks fondly of his old friend. 'The two of us hit it off really well and he said, "Where are you living?" and I said, "Nowhere," and he said immediately, "Well you can sleep on my floor," so I moved onto his floor, or more accurately I slept in a cupboard.'

Barney Bubbles, christened Colin Fulcher, was a key mover in the late 1960s and 1970s underground, becoming well known for the light shows – which inspired his adopted surname. He created bubbles by mixing oils and water on the slides during his shows at venues like the Roundhouse and Middle Earth. It was Barney, in fact, who had taken on the lease at 307 Portobello Road in 1969, along with entrepreneurs Edward Molton and Stephen Warwick, planning to use the premises to launch his graphic art studio Teenburger Designs. While things went moderately well, designing covers for the first Quintessence LP and for some artists on the Vertigo label, his partners jumped ship in 1970. *Frendz* magazine stepped into the breach and took on the lease, with Barney retaining an office and becoming their art director.

While staying with Barney, Nik invited him to design the cover for *In Search of Space*, Hawkwind's second album. With its iconic cover art and concept, it encapsulated the Hawkwind philosophy of collaboration drawn from the creative melting pot that was Portobello Road at the time. The album's concept was a journey into space, and Nik enlisted the help of his old Margate friend Robert Calvert to write the lyrics. Robert had been writing for *Oz* and *International Times* and proved the perfect candidate to translate Hawkwind's space rock sound into words.

The LP was housed in a fold-out sleeve complete with log-book outlining their journey into space. Discussing it today Nik becomes animated, excitedly describing how they devised the live presentation to tie in with the record. 'Barney devised

Hawkwind played numerous free gigs under
the Westway in the early 1970s

the stage presentation for it based on the Music of the Spheres,
with the band's astrological signs and the corresponding colours
involved with the light show. And Robert, Barney and I put
the whole thing together.'

It may sound self-indulgent today, but Hawkwind were all
about the spectacle, mixing rock'n'roll with the avant-garde
and creating an inclusive gig for all to enjoy. Nik was crucial in
bringing it all together:

> I think we attracted creative people because we were seen
> as a creative medium. People could be off-the-wall and
> revolutionary with the things they tried. It wasn't just
> people going through the motions – we created a platform
> to do really experimental stuff. I think that was part of the
> attraction and the creation of the success – because all these
> people contributed to it and helped to create that success

for the band. I mean, we ended up having a huge amount of grassroots support.

That grassroots support was down to the fact that they were truly a band of the people and for the people, sharing their time and their drugs with the fans decades before bands like The Libertines were credited with having broken down audience/performer barriers with the help of the Internet. Nik remembers one occasion when they were heading to the Isle of Wight Festival in 1970 as typical of Hawkwind's interactions with their followers:

We picked up all the dropouts in Portobello Road and put them in our van and drove down to the Festival with them. Those people were our grassroots support. We had the support because we were so open and sociable and helpful towards people that didn't have very much and needed some help.

By 1970 rock was entering its imperial phase, as the accountants and managers realized just how much money could be made from touring and record sales. Yet Hawkwind chose to play for free as much as they could, happy to tie their colours to the mast of any worthy cause:

We kept practising what we preached really, doing free concerts and doing benefits, playing in unusual places. We played in Wormwood Scrubs prison, Chelmsford prison, gigs for CND and protest gigs at places like Aldermaston. We made ourselves available as a band for these kinds of benefit gig. Basically, we would do any gig because it was a good way to get exposure and it was a good way to help people and turn people on to a lot of good times.

Turning people on to good times could have been the band's manifesto at this point. Nik tells me he still gets approached today by people relating a life-changing experience they had at one of these early Hawkwind gigs. And as we are chatting, as if on cue, a woman stops at the table and excitedly tells Nik that she was at a gig he did in Camden twenty years ago and it changed her life. As the woman walks away smiling, he remembers:

> One of our roadies – a guy called John the Bog – used to work as a rent collector, or enforcer, for Rachman. But then he took loads of LSD and completely changed his ways and became our roadie. He was a local lad, and he and another guy used to have an LSD factory. They would come along to Hawkwind gigs and give away loads of LSD. Our gigs were a bit like drug dealers' conventions really. Hawkwind became synonymous with drugs quite quickly. At our gigs, people took LSD whether they wanted to or not.

A strong cup of coffee and greasy fry up usually saw the band right after one of their gigs, and the place to go was 275 Portobello Road, the home of the Mountain Grill Café. The band would usually be found sitting at one of the tables, Dave Brock would be hunched over a pile of change in front of him, counting up his earnings from a morning spent busking on Portobello. Dave had come up through busking and continued to do this right through Hawkwind's early years. The band immortalized the café on their fourth album *The Hall of the Mountain Grill*, released in 1974.

Nik tells me how he would buy apples, oranges and bananas in large boxes from the fruit and veg traders on the market and give them away at gigs. 'I just thought it was a nice thing to do and it didn't cost very much. I used to pay out of my own

pocket.' While handing out fruit at the end of a particularly raucous gig at Bayswater Hall, Nik remembers a strange collision of
eras, when he was introduced to Larry Parnes, the famous pop
star impresario of the late 1950s, who had a stable of singers
whom he would take on and rename, such as Vince Eager and
Marty Wilde. Nik chuckles recalling the incident:

> He turned up at the gig wanting to manage Hawkwind! He
> was a friend of the photographer that did a lot of work for
> us, called Phil Franks. He invited Larry along to the gig and
> introduced me to him afterwards. Larry said to me, 'I would
> very much like to manage your band.' I just thought it was a
> bit of a joke really and said, 'Not today thanks!' Looking
> back, I probably should have taken him up on it – he would
> have turned us into superstars overnight!

But being superstars was never something Hawkwind aspired
to. At more than a forty-year remove one can appreciate what a
unique band they were, and they could only have come out of
the Ladbroke Grove scene of that time. They were the perfect
example of how this new generation were tearing up the rule-
book. But it could not last for ever. By 1975 the atmosphere in
the neighbourhood was changing as the hippie idealism of a few
years before was punctured by the growing popularity of hard
drugs.

> When people were taking LSD that was great and really
> creative, but the drugs changed and ultimately did for
> the scene. People began to get deluded on cocaine, and it
> became popular to take amphetamine sulphate, though I
> didn't. The Hells Angels were being really rude and outra-
> geous. I lived with a whole load of Hells Angels in a house
> on Ladbroke Grove, and they needed some wood for the

fire so they cut the bannisters down. When I left I think they were in the process of cutting the stairs down so you would have to climb up to the next floor.

But perhaps one group of people did not lament this passing too much: gig promoters. Hawkwind were so renowned for playing free gigs, and so well loved by the community, that on the rare occasion that they were playing a ticketed event, Nik could not risk leaving the house on the day of the show for fear of the huge amount of guest list requests that would come his way. With a glint in his eye he tells me:

I remember one time we had a gig at the Rainbow Theatre, part of a big all-nighter. I had arranged with a friend who worked as a chef at Biba to cook a lot of food, which we then gave away at the gig. But by the time we arrived at the venue I had accumulated a guest list of around 350 people. And the promoter said, 'Well, I'm not letting all these people in', and I said, 'I've told them that they are on the guest list so unless you let them in I'm not going to go on stage.' So he let them in.

The Death of Hendrix

The so-called '27 Club' of rock stars who have died at that young age is a roll call of legendary names, featuring among them Jim Morrison, Janis Joplin, Amy Winehouse, Brian Jones and, of course, the messiah of modern blues, Jimi Hendrix, who choked on his own vomit in room 507 of the Samarkand Hotel at 22 Lansdowne Crescent some time in the early hours of 18 September 1970. His final hours remain shrouded in mystery and counterclaim, but what is beyond doubt is the fact that he was pronounced dead on arrival at St Mary Abbot's Hospital in Kensington at 12.45 PM. He had been discovered by on/off girlfriend Monika Dannemann earlier that morning, who found him unresponsive after he had ingested a large quantity of sleeping pills. At first it was thought that he committed suicide, an idea given credence when old friend Eric Burdon, who was one of the first on the scene, discovered a scribbled note titled 'The Story of Life', but this has since been attributed to be the lyrics to the last song he composed, inspired his turbulent affair with Monika. Though he was in a fragile state at the time, both physically frail and mentally exhausted, it is not thought that he took his own life, but rather that a tragic accident occurred when he mixed red wine (which he was not used to) and strong sleeping pills. The day before he had sat in the garden of the hotel, drinking tea and posing for photographs that Monika snapped off on her camera. The pair then went up to Kensington Market where he bought a leather jacket and some shoes, and ran into ex-girlfriend Kathy Etchingham, whom he invited to come round to visit him at the Cumberland Hotel where he had a suite, an invitation she would always regret not following up. Lansdowne Crescent has become a site of pilgrimage for fans of the guitar god, looking for the spot where it all ended so tragically for Jimi over forty years ago. Interestingly, it is not the only address associated with Hendrix in the neighbour-

22 Lansdowne Crescent: still a place of pilgrimage

hood. In early 1967 he stayed at 167 Westbourne Grove, a property that at the time was painted a lurid shade of purple, reportedly inspiring his second single 'Purple Haze', released shortly afterwards.

1976: Rough Trade and
the Birth of Punk

There is no blue plaque screwed onto the wall above 202 Kensington Park Road, no hordes of tourists posing for photographs or excited fans whooping with joy. This is definitely not an address etched in the annals of rock'n'roll mythology, nor is it a site of pilgrimage like the Père Lachaise cemetery in Paris or the Abbey Road zebra crossing in North London – yet it is arguably as iconic as these. For it was here in February 1976 that a record shop called Rough Trade opened its doors, and in the space of just twelve months became a key outpost in the punk and DIY movement.

Rough Trade was the brainchild of the then twenty-four-year-old Geoff Travis, who, over the intervening three and a half decades has gone on to become one of the most important and influential figures on the independent music scene. In 1982 the shop was bought out by its staff and moved around the corner to new premises at 130 Talbot Road, where it remains to this day. Geoff left to concentrate on the label of the same name, signing an incredible array of seminal bands, from the Smiths to the Libertines and the Strokes. The label is rooted in the neighbourhood, operating from offices halfway along Golborne Road.

I was keen to find out how and why he came to choose the area for his initial foray into the music world. Sitting in his neatly laid out cubby hole of an office, he talked me through the genesis of the shop, in his gentle North London murmur punctuated by rolling bursts of laughter.

Geoff is a Londoner, born in 1952 and raised in Finchley. His love of music began at an early age, and as an eleven-year-old he could often be found in his local electrical shop, flicking through the box of 7-inch singles on the counter, picking up Kinks and Beatles hits. His secondary school in Angel was located conveniently close to the West End, allowing for lunchtime excursions to record shops like Musicland and One Stop – long-gone institutions whose names are whispered in reverential tones by those who frequented them. Returning home laden with the latest American imports and obscure singles Geoff would spend hours in his bedroom listening to his finds and dissecting the sleeve notes.

When he graduated from Cambridge University in 1974, Geoff – like many of the baby-boomer generation – was more certain of what he didn't want to do than what he did. He toyed with the idea of teaching and academia, but he always came back to his first love: music, specifically rock'n'roll.

As a huge fan of Beat poetry he headed off in search of its spiritual source, hitchhiking his way across America and Canada in a post-university haze. He spent time in Toronto and Chicago before wending his way down to San Francisco, where he immediately sought out the hallowed ground of City Lights bookstore where he was staggered to find poet and proprietor of the shop Lawrence Ferlinghetti perched behind the counter. Geoff spent hours scanning the shelves in the basement, picking out volumes of poetry, which he would read sitting on one of the chairs dotted around the room. There was a seemingly never-ending flow of coffee available from the counter, and no push to force one to make a purchase and leave the shop. In fact, quite the reverse: people seemed to show up just to hang out, chat and see who was around. 'That was a revelation – there weren't many shops like that. I was used to the Wimpy system here where the lights are bright and they want to get you in and out in ten minutes.'

With his visa running out, Geoff knew he had to make a

decision about what he would do when he returned to London. It was while hanging out with his friend Ken Davidson, a fellow Londoner who had joined him in San Francisco, that the idea for a record shop was born. During his travels Geoff had accumulated a huge stack of around 200 LPs and while he was making arrangements to have them shipped back home Ken suggested he start a record shop, using these records as the basis of the stock. Mulling it over, and with Ken a willing volunteer to help run things, Geoff decided to do just that.

On the long flight home he thought of what he had experienced at the City Lights bookstore and resolved that he would incorporate its laid-back philosophy into his own venture. He wanted to create an environment where people could hang out and chat as well as shop for records. It is a philosophy Geoff has used to guide him through his working life: 'You know: make your life your play, that whole Situationist thesis. You don't want to go to work, you want to go to play. And when the two things meld together your life is a lot more fun.'

Back on home turf, Geoff and Ken set about putting their plan into action. Geoff secured a loan from his father, an insurance loss adjustor, who offered cautious yet encouraging advice to his son. As the hunt for suitable premises began, Geoff heard on the grapevine that one of his favourite record shops in Cambridge was closing down. Red House Records had been a regular haunt during his student days and so he quickly borrowed a van and bought up much of their stock, as well as their record bins and shelving units.

They soon found a shop to rent, located on Duddenhill Road in Kensal Green. It needed a bit of sprucing up, but it seemed ideal to Geoff and Ken, who had by this time been joined by Geoff's best friend from Cambridge, John Kemp, and his girl-friend, Jo Slee. Together the four of them set about stripping away layers of wallpaper and began repainting the walls. The shelves and bins from Red House Records were unloaded, and appointments were made with the sales reps from the major record companies.

One of the first to show up was the Polydor rep. Geoff remembers that day clearly: 'He said, "What are you doing here?" and we said, "What do you mean?" and he said, "There's no passing trade," and we looked at one another and replied, "What's passing trade?" and he said, "It's people!" And we thought, you know what he's right, it is a pretty nowhere street, really.'

They immediately downed tools and hopped into their clapped out old Transit van, hitting the streets in the hunt for more suitable premises, somewhere less hidden away. Heading towards Ladbroke Grove they felt on safer ground. Geoff was familiar with the neighbourhood, as at the time he was squatting with Vivien Goldman at 145a Ladbroke Grove. Vivien was one of the first journalists to write about reggae in the UK music press and a regular contributor to *NME* and *Sounds*.

Geoff was aware that their budget would not stretch to renting a shop on Portobello Road, so they sculled around the side streets nearby. 'We just drove around and were attracted by a big cartwheel that was hanging from outside number 202. We thought it looked interesting.' On further investigation, it transpired that the print works that presently occupied the shop was moving and the place was up for rent. A few phone calls later and, after a little negotiation, the place was theirs. And it had that elusive 'passing trade'.

The shop was laid out with the records lining both walls. A large round table and chairs stood in the centre, encouraging customers to sit around and hang out. Potted plants were dotted around, giving the place the feeling of a countercultural common room. New and second-hand vinyl peeked out from the record bins, ranging from hip singer-songwriters like Jackson Browne and Kevin Coyne to more popular bands like Steely

Dan and 10CC. There was a large reggae section and a good stock of rock'n'roll and garage garnered from Geoff's American adventures.

Geoff explained to me that there was no marketing plan to help bring people through the doors – it happened naturally. 'We didn't really worry that anyone would come, in our naïve semi-arrogant way we just thought we would make a great shop and people will come.'

In retrospect, the timing of its opening could not have been more serendipitous, chiming as it did exactly with the birth of punk. The Sex Pistols appeared in the national music press for the first time on the same day that the shop began trading in February 1976 and in March the band played their legendary gig at the 100 Club, lighting the touchpaper on a movement that was much more than merely musical. Punk was year zero for a culture that had grown complacent and a record industry that had become bloated and self-satisfied.

The extravagant prog rock and self-indulgent singer-songwriter fare heard on the radio bore little relation to the economic realities of life in Britain. As Harold Wilson handed over responsibilities of the state to Jim Callaghan, unemployment had reached an all-time high of 1 million. IRA bomb threats hung like a cloud over the city, with rubbish going uncollected and strikes leading to the three-day week. Neil Taylor, in *Document and Eyewitness* – his exhaustive history of Rough Trade the shop and label – goes as far as to propose that had it not been for the emergence of punk, 'the shop would not have survived'.[26]

Credibility was cemented by visits from Patti Smith, Talking Heads and memorably the Ramones, who did a signing session in July 1976. Early staffer Steve Montgomery remembered that 'Kids mobbed the place. Shane McGowan was there and Mark Perry ... At one point it was noticed that Joey Ramone had gone missing so I went to try and find him. The bemused fruit and veg

Geoff in the stock room at Rough Trade's first home at
202 Kensington Park Road, 1979

lads in Portobello Road soon pointed me in the right direction.'[27]

Geoff's shop was fast making a name for itself as the place to find obscure records and bootlegs by the likes of Iggy Pop, Talking Heads and Pere Ubu, which were not stocked anywhere else. Ari Up, leader of the Slits, recalls the scene when she would visit in late 1978: 'I just remember it being very chaotic. A pile of records like a mountain, a mountainside. Piles and piles of records and shelves and everything thrown down on the ground and piles of papers and piles of scattered girls running around. That's what I remember walking into that shop – total chaos.'[28]

They began to operate a mail order system, supplying other shops around the country. This led in time to the formation of the Cartel – the first independent distribution company –

distribution being something the big record labels had traditionally had a monopoly on.

It wasn't just music that Rough Trade was selling. They soon became one of the key suppliers and distributors of fanzines, *the* literature of the punk movement. They became the first shop in London to stock *Punk* magazine, which they bought directly from its publisher John Holmstrom in New York. They went on to stock almost every fanzine produced in Britain between 1976 and 1983. Fanzines were as important as the music to the punk movement. Geoff described them as 'a call to arms. They gave people the ammunition to do their own thing.'[29] Of course, the 1960s countercultural movement had produced its own array of literary outpourings, such as *Oz*, *Frendz* and the *International Times*, but by the mid-1970s these publications had run out of steam, lacking any kind of cohesion or anything new to say.

It is difficult to understand the importance of fanzines in our post-Internet world, where information and opinions can be batted around the globe at the click of a button. They provided a way of communicating with one's peers from within the scene, as it happened and, most importantly, spreading the idea that anyone can do this, so go and do it yourself. The most famous example of this was in January 1977 in the fanzine *Sideburns*, which showed an illustration of three chord shapes accompanied by the words: 'This is a chord, this is another, this is a third. Now form a band.' It was later reproduced in the Stranglers fanzine *Strangled*, and has become the ultimate example of the DIY creed.

Geoff was heartened to see these stapled pamphlets of intent offered to the shop.

The shop in a way was supposed to be a Socialist experiment, where we would try to encourage everybody. So if someone came in with a fanzine we would buy it from them and stock it. We would also help them with it, and lend them the use of the printer to help them print it up. Mark Perry used to come in and put *Sniffin' Glue* together. We knew everybody in that punk community.

Geoff ran the shop along Marxist lines, with everyone paid the same wage no matter what their job was. His flatmate Vivien firmly believed he was trying to 'make a utopia there in the ghetto of Ladbroke Grove. The idealism was very real, it wasn't a put-on, it wasn't pretentious or a façade. Geoff was giving it a go. He wanted to shatter the paradigm. You could say it was an experiment because nobody knew how it would turn out.'[30]

Talking to Geoff it becomes clear that these early days at the shop were incredibly important in laying the groundwork for a career that has never taken the easy route. The blueprint he laid down in 1976 is still in evidence today, with the shop operating successful branches on Brick Lane in East London and more recently in New York. But looking out onto Golborne Road, Geoff says, 'This area is Rough Trade's home. It feels like a good place for us.'

The Clash

The Clash are without a doubt the ultimate Ladbroke Grove band. Their journey from the Westway to the world captivated a generation. The came together under the initiative of manager Bernie Rhodes, who introduced singer Joe Strummer to guitarist Mick Jones and bassist Paul Simonon in the spring of 1976 and secured them a deal with CBS Records shortly afterwards. Their ties to the neighbourhood are many – from Joe Strummer's pre-Clash gigs with the 101ers at The Elgin pub on Ladbroke Grove, to their debut single 'White Riot' in March 1977, which was inspired by the Carnival riots of the year before.

One of their most extraordinary moments came on Christmas Day 1979, a few weeks after the release of their third album *London Calling*, when they played two free gigs at Acklam Hall. Joe Strummer biographer Chris Salewicz was present at the gigs and described them to me as 'fantastic! The posters only went up the night before on Christmas Eve in the area, at places like the fish and chip shop on Ladbroke Grove. It was snowing, and I remember Pete Jenner who was managing them at the time was there in the dressing room beforehand, handing out presents. He gave Joe some reproduction painting.'

In the audience that night was local boy Ed Vulliamy, the hugely respected foreign correspondent and writer. Twenty-five years old at the time, he was home for the holidays and heard about the gigs in the pub the night before. Squaring it with his parents to miss Christmas lunch, he and his brother went along.

> I wasn't a punk and I wasn't a fan of punk. I was still listening to Dylan, but when I saw them I was converted. I had seen the Sex Pistols, who I thought were interesting but didn't particularly like, but when the Clash played they

Back cover of the Clash's debut album,
featuring the 1976 Carnival riots

were just superb. There weren't many people there – it's a
small hall and it was more like a private concert. It was
brilliant, but it wasn't really punk, it was rock'n'roll! And
I didn't realize what a great guitar player Mick Jones was
until I saw them. I remember we came back and we had
Christmas presents and tea and cake beside the tree.

Youth (left) and Alex (far right) relaxing in their
squatting days on Ladbroke Grove

Killing Joke:
The Adventures of Youth

On a balmy late August evening in 1978, in the basement flat of 85 Ladbroke Grove, eighteen-year-old Martin Glover, or 'Youth' to his mates, dipped his paintbrush into an industrial sized pot of white paint before daubing it liberally onto the wall in front of him. His old school pal Alex Paterson crouched next to the turntable in the middle of the otherwise empty room, cueing up the only record they owned: a 12-inch copy of 'Rapper's Delight' by the Sugarhill Gang. As the familiar drum intro kicked in, they stood back, retrieved their rollies from the ashtray, lit up and admired their handiwork. They had been hard at it for eight hours straight, as this one-song soundtrack charted the room's journey from grubby brown to brilliant white.

85 Ladbroke Grove was the first of several flats, all situated within a stone's throw from Portobello, that Youth would squat over the coming years. He would live at each address for around six months before the owner gathered the relevant paperwork to have him moved on. He had come to the area to be close to Killing Joke, the band he had recently joined, which would prove to be one of the most interesting groups to emerge in the post-punk era. Despite being over fifty now, he still retains his youthful nickname, and since those early days has become a highly successful record producer, working with everyone from the Verve to Paul McCartney. He is an enigmatic figure known for his unusual studio techniques and charismatic manner.

Though he now lives in Wandsworth, close to where he grew

up, Youth tells me he still visits Portobello. 'Every two weeks I have to go up. It's more centred around Golborne Road now – that's the authentic bit of the market that is left. People say it's all gone, but it hasn't, you know? It's still got this mix of poor and rich. It's still full of writers and musicians.'

He explained that he joined Killing Joke through that tried and tested route of answering an ad that caught his eye in the *NME* in 1977. The ad read: 'Total exploitation. Total Anonymity. The Killing Joke.' A few phone calls later and he was meeting up with Jaz Coleman, the singer in the band and the guy responsible for the ad. After a brief audition Youth was in. A band manifesto was duly written up, stating their somewhat lofty ambition to 'Define the exquisite beauty of the atomic age in terms of style, sound and form.' They were up and running, with Youth taking care of bass duties. When Jaz moved into a squat on Ladbroke Grove, he invited Youth and his old school mate Alex to join, tipping them off that the basement was empty. They moved in almost immediately.

As luck would have it, Alex drops in to see Youth as we sit and talk in his kitchen. He is happy to pitch in with his memories of the time, proving to have an uncanny recall for dates and addresses. He roadied for the band in the early days, before forming dance duo the Orb, who are still making music today.

Back in 1977 the area around Ladbroke Grove was overrun with squats, where many of the crumbling old Rachmanite buildings and mansion blocks lay tantalizingly unoccupied. Squatting afforded Youth and Alex the time to play music and be creative without having to worry about making the rent by clocking into a job they hated. Looking back on this period in his life, Youth says, 'It was an amazing experiment. My generation was so lucky that we could basically sign on and get about fifteen quid a week, which wasn't much, but it would feed you – and you could squat. It was like having a grant to go and be an artist and for a good six, seven years – it really helped.'

The two of them would spend their days in Mike's Café, nursing cups of coffee or watching films at the fleapit of a cinema, the Electric on Portobello. With a wistful look in his eye, Youth recalls the experience of watching a film at the cinema. 'You'd slide down with your cushions, get a bong going, drop a hit of acid and watch *Apocalypse Now* nine times and still come out scratching your head. Hahaha . . . !'

They describe the local pubs as rough and ready, and they were more inclined to spend time hanging out at various friends' flats or going to house parties. However, this changed in the summer of 1980 when they were turned onto a money-making scam by an enterprising friend of theirs named Wally. Alex leans forward in his chair and explains it to me in hushed tones.

This friend Wally, who was a bit of a Shepherd's Bush villain, came into the squat one day and we mentioned we were a bit strapped for cash. He said not to worry, and showed us how to hit the different pubs on Portobello Road and do the fruit machines. I can't go into too much detail . . . hahaha! We'd get £25 a night and spend half of it on weed and the other half we'd spend down at the 24-hour shop up on Golborne Road.

Notting Hill had been the heart of countercultural London in the late 1960s and early 1970s, but by the time Youth and Alex arrived in 1979 the party was well and truly over. Punk had hammered the final nail into the coffin with its year-zero manifesto, making the days of Hawkwind and *Frendz* magazine seem dreadfully old-fashioned and self-indulgent. Despite this shattering of the cultural axis, the area was still home to many old 'heads' and hippies who refused to give up on their lifestyle, proudly wearing their hair long and their jeans flared. For Youth and Alex, two teenage punks into speed and beer, these older characters offered them an initiation into the psychedelic counterculture, opening their ears to unfamiliar sounds and expanding their minds into new ways of thinking.

Smoking endless roll-ups that he produces from a small square tin, Youth recalls some of the people he encountered when they moved into Ladbroke Grove, and who were to have a significant impact on his life.

We were very quickly catapulted into this Portobello Road, Ladbroke Grove psychedelic alumni. Brian Barritt became a close friend – he had written a book with Timothy Leary, followed by a seminal psychedelic book called *Whisper* that really set me going: I was whispering to everybody for a bit. And John Michell the writer, who recently passed away, was there, along with Raj Rama from Quintessence and Lemmy and Hawkwind, along with various Pink Fairies and Jolly from Better Badges had a shop there

Two figures in particular helped to shape Youth's worldview and in the process save his mental health. The first was a neighbour who lived on the top floor of his second squat on Royal Crescent, known to all as the Wizard. Youth smiles as he describes him to me: 'He never wore shoes, had a seven pointed star tattooed on his face, wore a cloak and had a dog called Helden along with about fourteen stray cats living up there with him.' It wasn't long before Youth had enlisted the Wizard's help at Killing Joke gigs, where he would blow fire and dance. 'He was the fire master. He would ritually draw a pentagram on the dance floor and do his ceremonies. Then during the show would just blow fire. There was no health and safety in those days!'

Brian Barritt, the psychedelic evangelist, and friend and

Big Paul, Geordie, Youth and Jaz: Killing Joke in 1980

cohort of Timothy Leary, became the other key friendship. Barritt had been turned on to LSD by Alexander Trocchi in the early 1960s, and had become a Cosmic Courier, part of a small group who distributed LSD around the world, believing it to be their spiritual duty to turn the world on. After spending time in India and Afghanistan, Barritt ended up living on Ladbroke Grove, which is where he met Youth. At the time Youth was happily experimenting with hallucinogenic drugs when he took one trip too far, after sampling some potent Californian Sunshine Acid. Luckily for him, Brian was there to offer counsel and advice to the young man. Youth recalls:

I had this infamous acid meltdown when I was about twenty-one, and it featured Portobello Road quite heavily. I was completely in Syd Barrett land – I was heading for the river, convinced that bombs were dropping and the sky was turning green. Of course, I got arrested and slammed in this mental hospital, and I kept on going, 'I'm not mad. You're all mad.' and of course that is when they know you are really mad. Wizard and Brian would come up every day. I was only in there a couple of weeks before I straightened up enough to get out, and Wizard brought me this little crystal and said, 'Meditate on that and it will bring you your truth.' And so I meditated on it the night before I was due up before a board of doctors who were due to section me. The spirit guardians came through the crystal and said to me, 'Just tell the guys you have had some LSD, you are tired and you want to go home and see your mum and they will let you go. And whatever you do, don't say, "I'm not mad. You're all mad."' So I did that and they let me go! Wizard and Brian were real kind-hearted guys and took the time out to help me and said, 'Look, you're not mad, you're just going through this shamanic initiation, and we're here if you need some advice.'

Throughout this period, Killing Joke were recording and touring relentlessly. They would rehearse at the Free People's Hall, headquarters of the infamous Frestonia (see 'Heathcote Williams and the Ruff, Tuff, Cream Puff Squatting Agency' in Part Four: Bricks and Mortar), also popular with other local luminaries like the Clash and Motörhead.

It was the most amazing rehearsal studio because we shared one big room with Motörhead, just us and Motörhead! It became one of our ambitions to be louder than Motörhead, because when we walked in they would still be playing and we would go, 'Fuck they are *so* much louder than us! We gotta get bigger amps or something!' The Clash had a room upstairs and we had this long-running feud with them because I had gone up to their room and put a dollar sign through the S of the huge Clash poster they had on the wall. They always thought it was Jaz. In the end he made it up with them in some bar in the middle of nowhere in America. He said, 'Why have you always been so off with us? What have we ever done to you?' and they said, 'Well, you put that dollar sign through our S on our poster,' and he said, 'That wasn't me that was Youth!' and they both laughed and became really good mates.

They recorded their self-titled debut album at Basing Street Studios, released in August 1980 on the EG label. It was while recording at Basing Street that Youth got to know a notorious West Indian resident of the area: Aloysius 'Lucky' Gordon, who was working as a chef at the studio. Lucky had risen to prominence in 1962, due to his part in the Profumo Affair when his relationship with Christine Keeler and subsequent violent actions proved to be the catalyst that blew the affair into the public consciousness, almost bringing down the government. Youth has fond memories of Lucky. 'I remember a couple of Christmas Days when I had no family to go to, or they were already doing stuff, and I would have a few friends round the squat. Lucky would say, "Come round the studio," and do a big Christmas dinner for us. A lovely, warm-hearted guy, and he still had all the press clippings from the Christine Keeler case!'

By late 1981, Youth was finding some of his squatting experiences a little more hair-raising than he would have liked. He remembers a brief period of living on All Saints Road in a squat next to the infamous Mangrove restaurant, run by West Indian community activist and civil rights campaigner Frank Crichlow. At the time the Mangrove was under almost constant police surveillance, not an ideal location for Jaz's then girlfriend to carry out her small-time pot-dealing business. There was a distinct feeling that things were getting a little too heavy.

She had done a deal with some of the gangsters – sort of pre-Yardie gangsters – in the Mangrove whereby they could stash some of their drugs and weapons in our roof. So I came in one day and she'd be going, 'This is Jack, or John,' and he's just pulling out a gun from the roof or something! It did get quite heavy. At the time I got stopped four or five times a day, because the police policy was that if you were white and in that area – on the front line in All Saints Road – you were only there to buy drugs, so you were fair game to be stopped. In the end they said, 'Look, come down to the station and we will give you a card with your address on it saying you live here so you can show it to the officer when you get stopped and they shouldn't hassle you.' That worked, but then the dealers would say, 'Right, you're taking this over here for us: you've got the magic card!' Hahaha! I think it was just after that that I thought it was about time to move out.

The doorbell rings and Youth heads off to answer it. A group of musicians carrying guitars and amplifiers appear in the hall-way before heading up the stairs to Youth's in-house demo studio. I take this as my cue to leave, thanking Youth for his time and generosity before leaving him to his music making.

A week or so later I am walking down Ladbroke Grove towards Notting Hill Gate when I realise I am about to go past the first house that Youth and Alex squatted almost thirty-five years ago. Stopping outside number 85 I walk to the front steps and peer in through the basement window. I can't see much, the only things visible being a pram and some children's toys scattered on the floor. Turning back, I am struck by how immaculate and well tended the small garden is, and at that moment a smartly dressed woman opens the front door and descends the two steps to the street. I jump back and try to look innocuous, pretending to scan the names on the door buzzers. As I continue my walk up Ladbroke Grove I think about how much things have changed. Being able to live rent free during that formative period in their lives had been incredibly important to Youth and Alex, giving them time to make music and be creative. With property now at such a premium in this pocket of London, it is difficult to see that happening around here again. But then that is the nature of the city: ever changing and shifting beneath our feet.

Damon inside Honest Jon's Records, 278 Portobello Road

Under the Westway:
Damon Albarn

As a teenager growing up in rural Herefordshire in the mid-1990s at the height of Britpop, I would read with envy about the club nights and gigs going on in London. I learnt that Camden was the scene's Mecca, centred round pubs with names like the Good Mixer and the Dublin Castle. It all sounded terribly glamorous to my adolescent ears. But as an avid Blur fan, I heard references in Damon Albarn's lyrics to another area of London: Portobello Road, the Westway and Trellick Tower. Looking back, I suppose this was my introduction to the neighbourhood, and when I ended up living here in the early 2000s I not only discovered the places he had referenced but also often saw the man himself sculling around the streets on his bike or strolling through the market.

Over the last ten years he has proven a prolific artistic force, forming the hugely successful virtual band Gorillaz, and turning his hand to film composition, opera, several African music projects and his super group the Good the Bad and the Queen featuring former Clash bassist Paul Simonon. But it is the area that anchors him, helping to feed his creativity, and he remains as passionate about it as when he first moved here in 1990. 'I'll never live anywhere else in London, or else I won't live in London,' he tells me when we meet. It is a bright June morning at his recording studio, which is housed in a former car paint garage near Ladbroke Grove. 'On the record I have just finished I've got references to All Saints Road, Westbourne Grove and

Brunel Estate in one song. It is about the post-Carnival world where I have all these African animist gods roaming around the neighbourhood.'

He first visited Portobello Road as a schoolboy, venturing over to see his aunt, who had an office in Notting Hill. 'She worked for the cartoonist Mel Calman. She was his accountant and I would visit her. As a kid it seemed like a very long way away from my home in Leytonstone.' The Albarn family had moved to Essex shortly after he was born in 1968, with his father Keith going on to become head of the North Essex College of Art. It was a bohemian background, where acting and music making were encouraged, and after dropping out of drama school aged eighteen, Damon formed Blur – or Seymour, as they were originally known – with friends from Goldsmiths College of Art. Playing early gigs (which he describes as 'chaotic') throughout 1989, he paid the rent by working behind the bar at the notorious Portobello Hotel at 22 Stanley Gardens. Since opening in 1971, it had become famous for attracting a rock'n'roll clientele, including Van Morrison, Mick Jagger and Tina Turner. Damon explained his duties there:

> I was living in Greenwich, so I had to cycle there, work all night, and then cycle back. My shift was 8 PM to 8 AM. I did that for about a year. It was interesting because there were lots of very famous people staying up all night and I was barman and I had to give room service and all that. So it was a great education for me. That was right at the start of Blur. Graham [Coxon] and Alex [James] were still at Goldsmiths so we were just doing our first gigs. First on the bill at an indie all-dayer at the George Robey pub in Finsbury Park which meant we were on at eleven in the morning and just got pissed for the rest of the day, taking advantage of the beer coupons.

When I ask if he has any juicy stories from this period he laughs, saying, 'Yeah, there's plenty of anecdotes but I'm not giving them to you because they're for my book!' He goes on to explain that he moved into the area shortly after, in 1990, by which time Blur had signed a record deal. 'I moved here first after meeting a very bright, beautiful girl called Justine Frischmann. My first real time spent here was when I moved in just off Kensington Church Street and then, because she came from quite a well-to-do family, she bought a house on Kensington Park Road near Elgin Crescent. So I was there for the whole of the 1990s. Then we split up and I bought a flat over Tom's Café before buying a much bigger place just up Westbourne Grove.'

In that time he has seen the neighbourhood change immeasurably. 'When I first moved onto Westbourne Grove there were pubs and a 24-hour garage, but virtually every other shop was an interesting antique or knick-knack shop. Now it is very soulless in that sense.' But he is adamant that the creative, bohemian population is still at large.

We are all still here; we are just not as extrovert as our neighbours, so to speak. I genuinely don't think that the people who live here and call it their home socialize with those who are more transient, who live here because they have got a great job and fancy living in West London. In time they'll be gone – they are not here for ever. Westbourne Grove itself has a history of transients. When it was first built, it was a boutique shopping mall for wealthy Londoners. The same thing happened then as now. Rents became extortionate and people left. It all goes in cycles.

He has worked from a number of studios in the area, the first of which was in the more cramped environment of the Buspace complex on Canlon Street. 'I did the first two Gorillaz albums in that little studio, and then had enough money to find somewhere else. I nearly bought the old church on Golborne Road that Stella McCartney moved into, but at the time I had enough money to buy it but not to do it up, so I passed on that.'

When the old garage came on the market in 2006, he snapped it up and is obviously immensely proud of it, giving me the guided tour. The studio itself is full of keyboards and guitars, with exotic-looking African instruments propped up against the walls next to samplers and tangles of cables. Upstairs there is a large roof terrace backing on to the railway and Westway flyover. As a train trundles past he excitedly tells me of his plan to have a giant mural painted on the exterior wall depicting all the musicians who have recorded here – a roll call of names featuring, among others: Terry Hall, Martina Topley-Bird, De La Soul, Snoop Dogg, Bobby Womack and even former Oasis nemesis Noel Gallagher.

In the last fifteen years, Damon has shown the ability to absorb new styles of music and incorporate them into his own unique voice. He explains how local record shop Honest Jon's (located at 278 Portobello Road) has been crucial in this process. 'I really got my taste together at Honest Jon's and have been really influenced by them – first as a punter. I remember first going in there and being absolutely terrified and so ignorant – they just seemed so learned. But I got to know them and bought a lot of records. And that really was my passport, musically, for going to Africa and to Mali in particular.' He has made a number of trips to Mali, most recently to record the album *Maison des Jeunes* in one week as part of Africa Express, a cross-cultural collaboration that brings together Western and African musicians. 'That has had a massive impact on me. After ten years of being in a band and the orthodoxy of that I found myself sitting in the back of minute little clubs in the backstreets of Bamako, just playing my melodica for hours on end. It was just a fantastic education.'

His friendship with Honest Jon's has led to the formation of a record label established in partnership with the shop, something Damon is clearly passionate about. 'It has done brilliant work and really helped to document the black music especially of this part of London. We have put out a lot of records directly relating to West London.'

But despite this ever-expanding musical palette and trips to Africa and China, he always returns to West London. It is here that he feels rooted and in touch with a certain creative energy that feeds into his work. His blue eyes sparkle as he enthuses about the sunsets on his home stretch of Westbourne Grove. 'I am sure the Westbourne Grove is very ancient and that 2,000 years ago there was some sort of spiritual focus on top of that hill, because you get the most extraordinary sunsets up there. You feel as if you are directly underneath it, the colours and light are just incredible.'

Recording Studios

The neighbourhood's rich heritage of recording studios was inaugurated in July 1957 by legendary record producer Joe Meek, with his first makeshift home set-up at 20 Arundel Gardens. He filled the small one-bedroom flat with a raft of equipment including tape recorders, a Binson Echorec unit, speakers, amplifiers and microphones, along with a honky tonk piano purchased in the market, and used to great effect five years later on the worldwide hit 'Telstar', recorded at his more famous home studio located above a furniture shop on the Holloway Road. But he didn't last long at Arundel Gardens. When a release party, for his skiffle-produced tune 'Sizzling Hot' by Jimmy Miller and the Barbecues, got a little out of hand, with a reported 150 people attending, it was the final straw, neighbours complained and he was asked to leave.[31] But this was not the end of his recording legacy in the area. Between 1957 and 1959 he was installed at Lansdowne Studios where a tube console desk was built especially for him by EMI, finished in purple with gold edge trim. Here, he recorded hits for Lonnie Donegan, Chris Barber and Humphrey Lyttelton, becoming known for his unusual recording techniques and stunning results. The studio eventually closed its doors in 2006, after recording albums and singles by the likes of Queen, Rod Stewart and MC5.

The most famous studio in the neighbourhood is undoubtedly the former Island Records studio, which opened in January 1970 on Basing Street, on the site of a former church. The list of the hugely influential albums recorded here is too long to print in full, but it includes Led Zeppelin, Jethro Tull, Mott the Hoople, the Eagles, Black Sabbath and Bob Marley and the Wailers. In 1975, it changed its name to Basing Street Studios and by the early 1980s had been rechristened Sarm West, under its current ownership of Trevor Horn and ZTT Records. Although Sarm is still in use today, it is undergoing

Pioneering record producer Joe Meek who had his first
home studio at 20 Arundel Gardens

a massive redevelopment that will see the studio rehoused
in the basement with the upper floors turned into luxury
apartments.

The Rise of XL Recordings

Dotted around throughout the neighbourhood are a number of mews. These date back to a time before the motorcar, when horses would be stabled there. They have long since been converted into houses or carved up into flats and offices, acting as pockets of tranquil calm removed from the general hubbub of the street. On the walls of numbers 1 and 1a Codrington Mews there is a large mural, depicting the city of London being swept away by a tidal wave, with landmarks like the Gherkin and St Paul's toppled and lashed by the fierce waters chopping at their foundations. It is the work of London-based artist Stanley Donwood, entitled *A London Scene*, and was commissioned by Richard Russell, founder of XL Recordings to adorn the front of their London office. It could be read as symbolic, with the wave representing XL, an unstoppable force going from strength to strength as the rest of the music industry flounders in the post-Napster digital age. It is the latest in a long line of record companies – including Virgin, Island Records and Rough Trade – to be based near Portobello Road, finding success with bands as diverse as the Prodigy, the White Stripes, Radiohead, Dizzee Rascal, recently hitting supernova levels of success with Adele, whose second album *21* has sold 26 million copies worldwide and counting.

Arriving at the offices early on a weekday afternoon, I wait on a battered old leather sofa in the reception area. Every inch of the walls has been plastered with old gig posters and flyers advertising record releases and launch parties. Stylish-looking young label employees filter in and out of the front door. It has a relaxed atmosphere, feeling more like a university common room than the headquarters of a multi-million selling record label.

Label founder Richard Russell soon arrives and we head down to the in-house studio. In his early forties, he is an intelligent and intense individual, imbibed with a sense of confidence and drive that is infectious. He is a well-known face in the neighbourhood, having lived here since the late 1980s. 'I was drawn to the multiculturalism of it because Edgware, where I grew up, wasn't very multicultural at the time, and I think I felt a bit stifled by that. The vibrancy of this area just felt very appealing to me. And with the music and the Carnival it felt right, it was exciting and it felt like an inclusive place. I immediately felt part of it around here.'

A lover of music from a young age, Richard explains that the Beatles were his first real obsession, he tells me how he learnt to play all their songs on the guitar, watched all their films and devoured documentaries and biographies on the band. He cites them as crucial in shaping his creative outlook. 'I think it helped to develop this certain seed of ambition, that is based around a creative idea that you could see with them. They didn't think there were any limitations to anything at all, and if you think like that then there aren't any limitations. I think I was really lucky to have that going in.' As a teenager, he fell for hip-hop in a big way and he would regularly spend hours holed up in his bedroom perfecting his mixing skills. His mother recently remarked that he was luckier than most because 'on one side there was a main road and on the other side there was a deaf neighbour'.

Soon Richard had broken out of his bedroom and was DJing at parties and in clubs, securing a regular Friday night slot at The Tabernacle in 1987. Eschewing university, he spent a year in

New York working at legendary record shop Vinyl Mania before returning to the UK, where he rented a flat on Cornwall Crescent with a friend. 'The first night we moved in we had a party and two bottles of poppers got spilt on the floor. The smell never went for the whole time we were there!'

Rave was in the ascendant, and he explains that Portobello was home to several key labels, such as Kickin', who had their offices and studio in the basement of 280 Westbourne Park Road (the address that would later become famous as the Blue Door), and Vinyl Solution, at 231 Portobello Road. He enjoyed hanging out in the neighbourhood, doing a 'huge amount of record buying round here at Honest Jon's, Dub Vendor and Rough Trade', and cutting his first rave-inspired demos at The Tabernacle's in-house studio.

In fact it was as an artist rather than a label impresario that Richard first tasted success, as one half of Kicks Like a Mule, a duo who had a top-ten hit single in 1992 with 'The Bouncer'. But XL was about to take off, they had just signed Essex's finest rave outfit, the Prodigy, who released their acclaimed debut album *Experience* in September 1992. They made the top ten with singles like 'Firestarter' and 'Breathe', followed by their 1997 album, *Fat of the Land*, which went triple platinum. It was this new level of success that prompted their move into Codrington Mews. He remembers that the vendors were

> thrilled to get rid of it! It was in quite a state, having been derelict for ages. It was very cheap and they were just really happy that someone wanted it. It had been being used for some sort of industrial purposes – it was virtually a factory. But it has an interesting history, from what I have pieced together. Miles Copeland was here for a while, and apparently three or four of the members of Monty Python used to work here at some point.

Since then, Richard and his team have been busy building a creative environment akin to Warhol's Factory. 'As soon as we moved in it just felt right. It has been great for us. We have been able to do all the different things we want to do here.' Murals adorn several interior walls, with spaces constantly updated and added to. The whole place has the feel of a cottage industry – they do everything here, from screen-printing merchandise to programming the website. It buzzes with creative energy. XL taps into the great tradition of self-sufficient creativity that the area is famous for, from Joe Meek and *Frendz* magazine through to Rough Trade Records and Virgin. 'Being here has been a massive part of that, because over the past fifteen years we have had our own space and I think it has developed out of that. I think most people don't know that we are here and that has been quite helpful. Although it is a busy area, you wouldn't trip over us.'

The studio that we are sitting in is housed in the former garage. 'At first it was more of a writing and rehearsal room and then at a certain point I thought, "You know what? It's only a demo studio because we are calling it a demo studio. Let's turn it into a proper studio." The first record that we made in here was the XX. I worked on the Gil Scott-Heron record here. And the Horrors have used it.'

In the wake of their successes, rather than expanding and upping their release schedule they have stuck to releasing between six and ten records a year, giving each record the attention it deserves. 'The label has gone backward in that regard: it has become smaller and more creative as we have gone on. Unlike most labels, who start off that way and get bigger.'

Richard is keen to point out that although the label came out of the rave scene, he had always envisaged turning it into a bigger operation, drawing inspiration from labels like Island Records where he had worked as a teenager. He felt they had 'really good taste running through everything they did. It felt like a fantasy really, and that is what I had in mind to do with my own label.' Similarly, he namechecks Def Jam and the first wave of American rap labels, describing them as 'pure magic', and adds Virgin Records and A&M Records to his list, explaining, 'You look at the inner sleeve of one of those labels and it will show this extraordinary array of LPs that the label have released, and I wanted to achieve that. I think while the label was in the process of doing that, you don't really notice it, until one day you look at the albums we have released and you see a Radiohead album next to a Prodigy album next to an Adele album next to a Gil Scott-Heron album, and you think, OK! The twenty-year-old me would be buzzing about that!'

He is as enthusiastic about new music as he ever was, and regularly pops into Rough Trade on Talbot Road to get his hit of new sounds. In fact, it was on one such foray to the shop in 2001 that he was turned on to the bluesy stomp of a boy/girl duo from Detroit called the White Stripes. He picked up their two LPs released on American label Sympathy for the Record Industry, and was hooked. 'By the time they played their first show in London there was a huge amount of excitement around them, even though they were just doing what they had been doing for quite some time. I remember the gig well at the 100 Club – it was a hot, sweaty summer's night and it was very amazing. But back in the States they were still just thought of as this blues group, so it was that classic thing of being misfits. The same thing had happened to Hendrix – they were misfits in America so they had to come here to get noticed before people would then take notice of them back in America. Now England is very good at recognizing the originality in something.' Richard promptly dispatched one of his A&R people to Michigan to investigate further, and the rest, as they say, is history. The band went on to sell over 3 million albums

Stanley Donwood's mural *A London Scene*
on Codrington Mews, XL Recordings HQ

worldwide, playing to hundreds of thousands of people and
becoming festival favourites.

Richard describes Portobello as 'the soul and the spine' of the
neighbourhood.

So much of creative importance has happened in this area.
The fact is that, whatever happens, there is still that bohemian feel to it. You can't kill that off – it is ingrained in the
fabric of the place. For one thing, there are different types
of housing round here, so however expensive the billion-
aires' houses get there is also housing for normal people and
it is all mixed up. It's not perfect, obviously: with the rise in
property prices there have been unfortunate side effects,

but nonetheless you walk around here and you see what is going on and it is a cosmopolitan area. You can feel that.

I ask him if, despite what he says about the heritage of the neighbourhood, he has been tempted to move operations east-wards. Surely it would make more sense for him to be operating out of Hackney or Shoreditch, among the young creative brands and labels. But he is emphatic in his reply:

The fact that what we were doing when we moved in was not particularly unusual for round here, and now – fifteen years later – it is unusual, underlines the importance of it. Among all these people who go off to work in banks in the City, this is a building with a mural outside and people inside, busy making things in a creatively uncompromising environment. That doesn't make me think we should move away. It makes me think we should make a stand. I feel very much part of this area, as do Eno and Damon. There is a reason why people of that creative calibre haven't moved out of this area. It is because this place is still great at feed-ing creativity.

Leaving the offices, I step out onto the mews, and the mid-afternoon sun picks out patterns on the Stanley Donwood mural. Richard is right: it is important that creative spaces exist here, in spite of the soaring property prices and gentrification of the neighbourhood. In an age of creative conformity, it is inspiring to see a label like XL flourishing, keeping alive the countercultural currents that still flow through the neighbour-hood like one of the city's lost rivers.

PART FOUR

BRICKS AND MORTAR

The opulent face of Portobello, 2014

Notting Hill is home to some of the most varied architecture in the city, from ornate Victorian family homes and beautifully proportioned Georgian and Edwardian villas through to stunning Modernist structures. Until the early nineteenth century the area retained a rural character, which only began to change when property developers like James Weller Ladbroke formulated plans that they hoped would create a fashionable suburb, attracting wealthy families who might otherwise have chosen to live in Mayfair or Belgravia. The building work got underway in the 1840s, but the hoped-for demographic shift did not materialize, with many of the large houses designed for single-family occupancy immediately split up into self-contained flats. Soon the area was well known for its air of seedy dilapidated grandeur, where a building's classical façades bore little relation to what lay inside. Art critic, author and cartoonist Osbert Lancaster, memorably described such dwellings in his book *All Done from Memory* (1963): 'Vast stucco palaces that had long ago been converted into self-contained flats, where an ever-increasing stream of refugees from every part of the then civilized world had found improvised homes, like the dark age troglodytes who sheltered in the galleries and boxes of the Coliseum.'[32]

By the 1950s, notorious slum landlord Peter Rachman had moved into the neighbourhood, building a property empire that included over a hundred mansion blocks that he managed from his offices at 91–3 Westbourne Grove. He became known as one of the few landlords willing to rent to black tenants, something he quickly realized could make him even richer as he charged hugely inflated sums to immigrants desperate for somewhere to live. When news of the Profumo Affair broke, shortly after his death in November 1962, his notoriety was assured when it was revealed that he had not only been involved with both Christine Keeler and Mandy Rice-Davies, but he also owned the mews house in Marylebone where the pair had lived.

From the ashes of Rachman's empire, the late 1960s and early 1970s witnessed a huge surge in the activities of community action groups campaigning for tenants' rights and protection, in an area which became a key outpost for the squatting community. Heathcote Williams established the Ruff, Tuff, Cream Puff squatters agency, and John 'Hoppy' Hopkins founded the BIT information service, both of which offered key support to the underground community.

The most significant change since the 1960s and 1970s has been the shift in property use from multiple-occupancy blocks to single-family use, ironically the demographic that the developers had in mind 150 years ago. Decade after decade of gentrification has seen the area become one of the most sought-after and expensive destinations in the city, with hedge fund managers and bankers moving in *en masse* in the wake of Richard Curtis's 1999 romcom. A *Newsnight* feature in November 2013 described Kensington and Chelsea, the borough that contains Notting Hill, as 'the Monaco of London', declaring it to be 'home to some of the richest people in the world'. It is true that house prices are astoundingly high, with the average price of a semi-detached property clocking in at a cool £5 million, increasing by 120 per cent since 2005, far more than anywhere else in the country. These statistics, however, hide the fact that the area includes a significant portion of the social housing, with

People's News, October 1971

organisations like the Notting Hill Housing Trust and the Octavia Housing Group helping to maintain a degree of social mix, at least for the time being. But the following chapters are not only concerned with buildings and property but also the lives of those dwelling within those walls, as we cross the threshold of some key addresses in this incredibly vibrant and creative neighbourhood.

Dunworth Mews, 2014

A Legal Matter:
Goodwin & Knipe

On any given weekday between 1967 and 1981, at 9.30AM on the dot, a small blue car would pull up in Portobello Road and park neatly opposite number 204. A small grey-haired, middle-aged woman would get out dressed in a sensible suit and clutching a battered brown leather case. Walking across the street she would take a set of keys from her bag and open a door set just inside Dunworth Mews, climbing the fifteen steps to the first floor. Standing on the landing she would be faced by two doors: one led to the flat upstairs, while the other led to Goodwin & Knipe Solicitors, the firm that she had bought in 1966. Unlocking the door to her office, she would make her way to the desk in the second, smaller room overlooking the street. Soundtracked by the murmur of the fruit and veg traders and the clatter of metal that signified a delivery at the Welsh dairy directly below, she would get to work.

The woman sitting down to work each morning was quite extraordinary. Her name was Eleonore Mann, known to everyone as Lore, a German-born Jewish refugee who, after qualifying as a Doctor of Law, had been forced to flee Nazi Germany in 1933 along with her husband. After retraining as a solicitor in the 1950s, she had set up on Portobello Road with the express intention of helping the poorest and those most in need gain access to legal advice and representation. She was unique in that she only took on legal aid work, and as a staunch feminist most of her cases saw her representing women. She was a genuine trailblazer, operating before the North Kensington Law Centre came into being, before Release, the drugs advice line was set up and before the advent of Women's Refuges. A fiercely intelligent and determined woman who shunned the limelight, she would have been uncomfortable with the idea of anyone writing about her life.

I had become aware of her almost by accident while interviewing a fruit and veg trader. At the end of our chat I had asked him about any characters he remembered most in the street and he immediately mentioned her, though not by name, referring instead to 'that lawyer up above the dairy'. I jotted 'solicitor Portobello Road' in my notepad, adding it to my list of leads to follow up and track down. Months later I was talking to my agent when she mentioned that one of her clients had grown up not far from Portobello Road and that her mother had worked as a radical lawyer there. Scouring my notepads I made the connection and that is what led me to take tea with Eleonore's eldest daughter, Jessica Mann.

Meeting Jessica in a café a short walk from Portobello I was astonished at the story that unfolded when we sat down to talk. Jessica Mann, who is a successful writer and journalist now living in Cornwall, explained how her mother and father had met at Berlin University in 1929, where they were both studying for their Doctorates in Law. Indeed, Eleonore would become one of the first women to qualify as a Doctor of Law in Germany.

In 1933, her father Francis accepted a job offer from a firm of lawyers in Munich, and on 28 February took the night train from Berlin to Munich to start work. That date coincided exactly with the Reichstag fire, an event seen as pivotal in the establishment of Nazi Germany, allowing Hitler to extend and consolidate his power. Eleonore could foresee the danger that they now faced as Jews, and persuaded Francis, now her fiancé, to return to Berlin. Together they began to make plans for their emigration to England, with Francis securing work in London and going ahead in April 1933. Francis returned in October and both he and Lore sat their post-doctoral exams for professional qualification on 11 October. The following day they were married and, with their bags packed and tickets booked, left that afternoon, arriving in London four days later on 16 October.

Eleonore was horrified when her papers were returned to her, forbidding her from undertaking any paid work in England, as high levels of unemployment now meant that only one member of a refugee family could be legally employed. Still, they were relieved to have arrived safely and it wasn't long before they were starting a family. David was born in 1935, joined by sister Jessica in 1937. It gives one an insight into just how driven and intelligent Eleonore was that while raising two young children she undertook an external degree in mathematics from the University of London.

When war was declared in September 1939 they were living in a small rented cottage in Surrey. Jessica recounts a favourite family story of how a knock at their front door revealed the local village policeman standing on the threshold and looking rather sheepish. It turned out he had been dispatched with orders to arrest Francis and have him sent to an internment camp on the Isle of Man. 'The policeman said, "You know I have been sent to arrest you but I know you're not a spy and so I am going to go back and tell them that I won't do it." I always thought that is one of the nicest stories I have ever heard, because it says so much about the British character.'

During the war Jessica and her brother were evacuated to Canada for three years, while Eleonore helped the war effort by working at the Osram lightbulb factory. The children returned from Canada in 1943 and the family soon grew by one: their sister Nicola, born in 1944. By this time, the couple had bought a house on Addison Avenue, securing it for under £1,000 at a time when few people wanted property in the war-damaged city. After the war, Francis began to carve out a formidable reputation as a solicitor, first at a small firm and then at Herbert Smith, where he excelled in international law as well as becoming one of the most influential legal writers of his generation. In 1949, with Nicola enrolled at school, Eleonore went back to law school, retraining to practise in this country.

It was while working at a firm in Shepherd's Bush that she became convinced of the need for social law, particularly in and around Notting Hill, where conditions for the average family were very hard. With Francis earning enough money for both of them, she could devote herself wholeheartedly to the job of helping the community, particularly women, who she felt lacked a voice. With this in mind she duly set about scouring the area for suitable premises from which to set up on her own.

When her estate agent rang in September 1966 informing her that they had a vacant office on Portobello that had until recently been home to a solicitors firm called Goodwin & Knipe it proved to be the perfect location. It seemed Mr Goodwin and Mr Knipe had set up shop in this run-down neighbourhood in the hope of making money by representing criminal cases, but when clients failed to materialize they decided to move on. Eleonore was fond of telling people how she found numerous scraps of paper tucked inside her desk when she first arrived with things like 'Back in ten minutes', 'Back in thirty mins' or 'Out for lunch' scrawled on them.

Jessica suggested I get in touch with her mother's articled clerk, a woman called Barbara Thomson, who had worked closely with her mother throughout the years at 204 Portobello Road. Barbara now lived and worked in Norfolk but was only too happy to meet up with me and talk about her experiences. She was just seventeen when she joined Eleonore, weeks after completing her A-level exams. Having grown up in leafy, middle-class Richmond she was shocked at the poverty that existed in Notting Hill. With crumbling houses where families slept three or four to a room, and children running about on the streets with no shoes, it was like turning the clock back a hundred years, she says.

The offices were pretty basic, essentially two small rooms split up by a thin room divider, with brown utilitarian linoleum flooring throughout. Eleonore would drive home for lunch every day (she was a vegetarian in the years before this was an accepted social norm) at 1 PM and be back at her desk by soon after 2 PM. The main threads of their work were matrimonial, housing and immigration issues.

Right from the start they were busy. People would often turn up unannounced on the doorstep desperately seeking advice about bullying, violent husbands and unreasonable landlords. Soon the Citizens Advice Bureau on Ladbroke Grove was sending clients their way and word got out that if you were in trouble or needed legal advice then you should head to 204.

Local landlords were in for a shock, as tenants suddenly had access to legal advice and began to learn that they had rights too. Barbara remembers one trick that landlords had been used to using to get rid of tenants:

A very common trick that we encountered was that when a landlord wanted vacant possession, they would simply not collect the rent. So the tenants, often on social security and very hard up, would just spend the money on their living costs. The landlord would wait until a chunky amount of arrears had accumulated, say six months or more, or until there was no chance that it could be repaid, and then sue for possession. That was how they emptied the houses. Tenants would come to us for advice and say, 'Look, he won't take it – I can't get him to accept the rent.' Often we would say,

'Well, pay the rent to us, instead.' It would go into our client account and we would then write to the landlord and say, 'You are refusing to accept the rent – we don't know why. Your tenant will pay the rent to us each week and we have it in our client account ready to pay to you whenever you want.'

Domestic violence was a largely ignored, unspoken social problem in 1967. Women's refuges did not appear until 1971 and there was very little help available for women who found themselves in abusive relationships. Eleonore sought to address this by representing women in divorce cases, keen to make them realize there was an alternative to staying with an abuser. This could occasionally prove dangerous when an angry husband took it upon himself to seek out these solicitor troublemakers down on Portobello. Barbara remembers one occasion vividly:

I was eight and a half months pregnant and the husband of one of our clients came to the office to tell me that he was not a violent person and had never hit or touched his wife. As our meeting went on he got more and more agitated and started throwing things around the office. In the end he started shoving me around because, as he said, I really needed to understand that he was really a very quiet person who wouldn't hurt a fly. By then a shoe shop had opened up underneath replacing the express dairy, and this man had obviously been making such a racket in the office that the owner of the shoe shop appeared with their window cleaner and a market trader who saw the man off the premises and checked I was all right.

In 1981, aged seventy-four, Eleonore was diagnosed with terminal cancer. She faced this with her usual strength and tenacity. Unwilling to be a burden to anyone, she booked in to a nearby hotel and took an overdose of sleeping pills, slipping away quietly and without fuss. Barbara remembers visiting the office shortly after her death. One of the market traders pulled her aside, saying, 'She had the respect of the market, you know?' Smiling at the memory, Barbara thinks Lore would have been happy with this.

North Kensington Law Centre, 74 Golborne Road

When it opened in July 1970, North Kensington Law Centre was the first of its kind in the country. Its offices were at 74 Golborne Road, on the site of a former butcher's shop, and it remains there to this day. The intervening decades have seen it joined by fifty-five other law centres across England, Wales and Northern Ireland, staffed by solicitors and barristers who specialize in areas of civil law – such as housing, employment, welfare benefits, immigration and discrimination – and with a commitment to providing access to justice to those who struggle to afford it. They are born of a collective desire to offer 'justice for all' from a new breed of lawyers who felt uneasy at the way the law discriminated against the poorest in society. Indeed, as one of the founders of the North Kensington Law Centre, Lord Gifford, commented, 'In my early years at the bar there was truly one law for the rich and one for the poor.' He was among a radical group of lawyers for whom 'justice rather than money or status was the motivation',[33] as he himself put it. These new law centres were located on high streets and in busy shopping districts in order to promote the idea of openness and accessibility to the law; they were embedded in the community they served. Speaking in 2010 at their fortieth anniversary Lord Gifford said:

> What we started at North Kensington Law Centre has become part of a revolution in the way law is practised. North Kensington Law Centre is still reaching the parts that others cannot reach because of its commitment to its community. ... Access to justice must be supported by properly resourced advice services to enable the most vulnerable to enforce their rights. Access to justice is bereft of meaning without the tools to achieve it.[34]

The tradition of free access to legal advice still remains, Golborne Road

Funding for law centres has always been problematic. They rely on a combination of local authority grants and legal aid, and with recent cuts to the legal aid budget there is a fear that their future could be at risk. Lord Gifford commented in an article published by the *Guardian* in June 2013 that despite their leaps forward over the last forty years it is now at grave risk. 'Now it is all in danger of being smashed.'

In Search of a
Furnished Room

Walking through the market on a bitterly cold winter's day with snow underfoot and the temperature measuring −5 degrees, I felt admiration for the stallholders, if a little bit smug as I headed to the warmth of the bookshop. They all seemed to have their own coping strategies. Some danced around blowing on their hands, while others drank endless cups of coffee decanted from flasks, trying to keep themselves cheered up as transistor radios blared out football results and music. They were all wrapped in multiple layers, like living mummies, with only their eyes and the tips of their fingers visible.

One regular stallholder with whom I had become friends had her pitch outside the health food shop directly underneath the Westway flyover. Her name was Laura and her stall was like a piece of modern art, almost entirely wrapped in tarpaulins designed to keep out the merest hint of a draft. She stood behind it in all weathers, with greying hair and kind eyes, selling socks, stockings and tights.

One day, we ran into one another on Blenheim Crescent as I came out of the bookshop. After a brief chat she asked rather hesitantly whether we would be interested in stocking her first novel from 1961, titled *The Furnished Room*, which was about to be republished. I was taken aback, I had no idea she was a novelist. Looking up the book later on, I was even more astonished to discover that it had been adapted into a film, retitled *West 11*, starring Diana Dors and directed by Michael Winner.

Laura Del-Rivo now in her sixth decade on the market

It transpired she had written three novels since moving into the area in the mid-1950s, and had taken to working on the market to supplement her writing income. She explained to me that she has dealt in 'books for a while, second-hand jeans, tweed jackets, furniture when I worked for some house-clearance people, army surplus. But I won't move from tights now. They're not my favourite thing. I get bored with things, and basically I am bored with tights, but I am too old to move on to something else now.'

Laura Del-Rivo was born in 1934, growing up in Sheen and moving to London in 1952 aged just eighteen with the aim of becoming a writer. She has lived at the same address on Blenheim Crescent since 1963, starting out on the ground floor and moving up to the top flat underneath the eaves where she currently lives. The space is filled with books and paintings, the floorboards are stripped and there are numerous potted plants creating a mini rainforest in the kitchen. She sits opposite me on the corner of her bed. Her voice is quiet and soft, but as she forgets about the red blinking light from my Dictaphone she speaks a little more loudly and seems to enjoy recounting her old way of life.

Her first job in London was at Foyles bookshop on Charing Cross Road, which she describes as 'a dreadful place to work. They hired and fired on a revolving basis so no one ever stayed there long enough to learn anything.' But the one advantage was that it introduced her to Soho and its coffee bars, where she whiled away her non-working hours, sitting in the corner smoking endless cigarettes and people watching. 'It was right next to the St Martin's School of Art, so we used to see these exotically dressed art students going past. A lot of the time it was quite boring, but having invested so much time sitting in the café you were determined to wait until something interesting happened. And if you sit in a café everyone meets everyone eventually.'

Her investment paid off as she gradually began to mingle with the vibrant literary scene of 1950s Soho. She met exiled Hungarian writer John Rety, who was the first to publish some of her short stories in his seminal underground paper, *Intimate Review*, alongside other notable contributors such as Doris Lessing and Bill Hopkins. But it was her introduction, in the spring of 1956, to a rather serious-looking young man dressed in an ill-fitting tweed suit, that would prove especially auspicious. The young man in question was Colin Wilson, who was on the cusp of publishing his sensational debut *The Outsider*, the book that would define his career. Laura recalled her first reaction. 'I felt instantly that he was something special. I mean, you can tell if someone is very good at something: if he is a runner you can see him running fast. It's the same thing with writing: you can see if they are good and very intelligent, and I always knew he was much more intelligent, better read and better at writing than me.'

Wilson provided Laura with her entry to Notting Hill,

inviting her round to his room at 24 Chepstow Villas, one of the long narrow streets that link Portobello with Westbourne Grove. 'It was a beautiful house, but very empty. It had been an expensive house so all the rooms had these noble proportions, but it had simply gone to wrack and ruin. I mean, there was still only one bathroom for the whole house, because all these homes were built as one family houses, but a lot of them were multiple-occupied right from the start.'

The house was divided up into eight rooms, with a revolving cast of writers, actors, painters and artists living there at any given time. Laura remembers how Wilson was fond of informing visitors that a few years previously Dylan Thomas had lived in the basement, and Beat writer Alexander Trocchi had taken an upstairs room along with the Scottish painters Colquhoun and MacBryde, who would have violent screaming matches on the landing. By the time Laura was visiting, the list of residents was no less impressive, including writers Bill Hopkins and Cressida Lindsay along with painters John Eyles and Roland Jarvis and actor Dudley Sutton.

The huge success of *The Outsider* bolstered Wilson's ego still further, leading him to declare, without a hint of irony, that he considered himself a genius. The press lapped it and when his next book appeared in 1957, titled *Religion and the Rebel*, they could barely disguise their glee when it received a critical mauling. His star had well and truly fallen. 'He went from being the golden boy to the devil in the space of one year,' Laura says, shaking her head, adding, 'People like to eat their gods.'

Finding it increasingly difficult to work in London, and keen to escape the glare of publicity, he decamped to Cornwall and handed his room over to Laura. Though sad to see her friend leave London under such inauspicious circumstances, she was happy to have found a room of her own. Moving in on a particularly cold night in mid-February, she laid out her few possessions,

Front cover of the 1963 paperback edition of *The Furnished Room*

making the room as cosy as possible. She can still remember how she arranged her books on the shelves left by Wilson, and set her typewriter up on the rickety table in the corner. Her boyfriend spent that first night with her, though they planned to wake early so he could slip out undetected by the landlady who lived on the first floor. 'But very early in the morning there was a knock at the door and it was the landlady. Panic! And she sort of drifted in and simply asked, "Have you possibly got some coffee I could borrow?" Bliss – it was a totally bohemian house. Everything was easy.'

Laura was temping at an office in the West End by day and would return to the creative atmosphere of 24 Chepstow Villas by night, sitting up late and working on her first novel. 'It was a very happy time really because I was writing and the house was full of people writing and painting and talking.' As she made steady progress, the story unfolded on the sheets of thin white paper that littered her room. Occasionally she showed what she had done to Bill Hopkins or John Rety, but more often than not she kept her neatly typed manuscript to herself.

By the summer she had got a job working as a bookseller at Peter Russell's bookshop on D'Arblay Street in Soho. One day, flipping though the trade press, she spotted a notice placed by Hutchinson publishers looking for new writers to publish. She noted down the address on a scrap of paper and tucked it in her shirt pocket. Back in her room that evening, she took a fresh sheet of paper and wound it into her battered Remington typewriter. She composed a covering letter, signed it 'L. Del-Rivo', attached it to her manuscript and posted it off to Hutchinson the following day.

A couple of weeks later she received a letter addressed to Mr Del-Rivo. It stated that Hutchinson were eager to meet, having read and enjoyed *The Furnished Room*. Laura had known that she stood a greater chance of acceptance, or at least a fair reading, if she neglected to mention her gender and it had worked. The book was published and she tells me that 'Peter Russell's bookshop gave me a launch party. He was more of a publicist than me, and he was promoting his bookshop in passing and selling my book. The photographer Ida Kar lived above.'

In fact, Ida Kar, the renowned Russian-born photographer, shot Laura in the bookshop and she tells me she thought nothing more of it until the pictures were included at a 2011 retrospective of the photographer's work at the National Portrait Gallery. They capture Laura as she changed from the shy young girl from the suburbs into the bohemian young woman standing in the bookshop dressed in a loose-fitting painters smock, her hair cut into a bob with cigarette in one hand. She thinks back on those days in Chepstow Villas with great affection. 'It was my golden age, I think. I can imagine people thinking their time at art school or university was theirs, but when I look back, that was mine, at Chepstow Villas. To be part of a group who all like each other and have a sense of "us against them".'

10 Rillington Place

The most infamous address in the neighbourhood is certainly 10 Rillington Place, where John Reginald Christie lived between August 1943 and March 1953, murdering eight women and burying them beneath the floorboards and in the small back garden. His actions were only uncovered after he had moved out of the property in March 1953, three years after Timothy Evans, his former upstairs neighbour, had been wrongly accused and found guilty of murdering his wife and baby daughter. This was actually the work of Christie, for which he was hanged.

Christie had passed himself off as an upstanding member of the community, employed as a special constable during the war, and known for his supposed in-depth medical knowledge. He preyed on prostitutes, picking them up in local cafés and pubs and luring them home, where he gassed and strangled them. Shortly after he had vacated the property on 24 March his upstairs neighbour Beresford Brown discovered the bodies of his last three victims stuffed behind the wall of a small alcove in the kitchen. A nationwide manhunt began, and Christie was picked up by police officers on the embankment near Putney Bridge on 31 March, having spent the previous few days drifting in and out of cafés across the city. At the trial in June he confessed to the murders, entering a plea of insanity that was rejected by the jury, who found him guilty on all counts. He was hanged at Pentonville Prison a month later. As a grisly finale, the 1971 film adaption of Ludovic Kennedy's bestselling book *10 Rillington Place*, which charted the miscarriage of justice over the unsound conviction of Timothy Evans, was filmed on location in Rillington Place, or Ruston Close as it was known by that time. The street had been renamed in 1954, but it was the very same slum that Christie had lived in seventeen years before. The film is eerily powerful, and features superb performances from Richard Attenborough, John Hurt

Children playing outside 10 Rillington Place in October 1966

and Judy Geeson. As soon as filming wrapped up in October 1970, a team of demolition workers moved into the street and slowly tore down the houses with pickaxes and shovels, making way for a new development and getting rid of a particularly gruesome address in the process. The exact site where 10 Rillington Place used to stand is now occupied by 22–29 St Andrew's Square.

Poster for *Performance* (1970)

Performance and
Powis Square

25 Powis Square was an address I knew long before I lived in the neighbourhood as the bohemian home of Turner, the reclusive rock star played by Mick Jagger, in Donald Cammell and Nicolas Roeg's legendary film *Performance*. The film merged London's ultra-violent gangster underworld with druggy rock 'n'roll. Chas, an East End hard man played by James Fox, falls foul of his boss and goes on the run, hiding out in Turner's basement. It is an incredibly complex and strange film that survived almost being shelved by Warner Bros. to become a cult hit now widely regarded as a classic.

In the decades that followed the two directors' paths diverged completely, with the charismatic yet troubled Cammell moving to Hollywood, where he struggled to make further films before shooting himself in 1996. Roeg, on the other hand, went on to make over a dozen hugely successful and critically adored films from *Don't Look Now* to *Walkabout*. I met with Sandy Lieberson, the producer of *Performance*, to discuss some of the myths surrounding its production in the summer of 1968.

Performance was his first outing as a producer after he moved to the UK from Hollywood in 1965 as an agent, working for CMA and looking after their client Peter Sellers. He met Donald Cammell during the production of the 1967 film *Duffy*, for which Cammell supplied the script. The pair got along well and Sandy agreed to represent him as a writer. He explains that one of the first ideas he came up with was an early draft of

Performance, at this stage titled _The Liars_. 'There wasn't a hell of a lot of difference: it charted the conflict of this rock'n'roll singer who had dropped out and the London underworld – those two worlds intersecting. I mean, it developed and changed in the ways scripts do, but it was essentially what he came up with.'

Sandy explains that Cammell had hoped that Marlon Brando would play the part of Chas, but when he proved to be unavailable James Fox was suggested, an unlikely candidate for the role, given that he had been making a name for himself playing upper-class Englishmen in films like _The Servant_ and _Those Magnificent Men in Their Flying Machines_. But he famously threw himself into the role, immersing himself in the gangster underworld to such an extent that he experienced a nervous breakdown in its aftermath and disappeared from acting for ten years.

I ask how Mick Jagger was chosen for the role of Turner and Sandy explains that he met him rather by accident.

I'd seen a spread in _Vogue_ magazine on Marianne Faithfull, and of course she had 'As Tears Go By' in the charts. I thought she could be an interesting character for films so I arranged to meet her. At the time she was living with Mick in a mansion block on Marylebone Road, and as we were chatting I noticed someone lurking in the kitchen and it turned out to be Mick. Apparently she had only agreed to the meeting because Mick was interested in representation and moving into acting. So he came out and we chatted. We subsequently met again and talked, and he wanted to know what else he could do outside of the Stones in the way of acting.

Sandy went on to represent the Stones and Mick for their film work, overseeing _The Rolling Stones Rock and Roll Circus_ as well as the Jean-Luc Godard movie *One Plus One* (better known as *Sympathy for the Devil*).

It wasn't long before Mick was passed a copy of the *Liars* script. He already knew Donald Cammell socially through the Chelsea set, and promptly agreed to play the part. Sandy explains that Donald suggested they approach Nicolas Roeg with a view to co-direct. 'I thought Nic was a brilliant cinematographer. He was already well established and wanted to move into directing. I thought that this would be a good combination. I can't even recall the last person to co-direct in England at that point. So it was a difficult sell for Warner Bros. to buy the concept of co-directing, but they eventually did because they had no choice – it was either agree or don't make the film. So they agreed.'

The sequence marking Chas's arrival in Powis Square comes about fifteen minutes into the film, locating us firmly in the neighbourhood. We follow Chas as he gets out from a taxi on the corner of the square and walks up to number 25 (though in the film we are told it is number 81). We are in the heart of this crumbling post-Rachmanite corner of Notting Hill, the houses are in varying states of disrepair. We see a couple of black people walking along the opposite pavement, a long-haired bohemian girl almost collides with Chas and a child dances across the pavement. The camera switches angle to reveal rubbish and rotting pieces of furniture strewn across the square as Chas reaches number 25 and mounts the steps. Was the setting important to them I wonder? 'Portobello and Notting Hill Gate were the focus of the film, absolutely. That is where it was set. I think we tried to represent what Notting Hill was and what it looked like. I think it was accurate – you know, it didn't distort it. It looked like that at the time. It was very representative of the period and that area. There were kids running around in the streets with no shoes. That little girl in the film was somebody we picked up from Notting Hill Gate – she was just cast from locals.'

While the film is set in Powis Square, the interiors were shot in a large house in Knightsbridge. 'It was only the logistics that prevented us from making the entire film in Powis Square, because of the way the rooms were constituted. They were too small and there was no ability to move around, whereas in Knightsbridge it was a deserted and bigger house.' The eleven-week shoot is so imbued with myth and rumour that it is difficult to sift the truth from the reality, with stories of drug taking and mind games in almost every account. When I bring this up Sandy comments, 'It was amazing we held it all together. It was a volatile set, but in a positive way.' He goes on to clarify:

I think there was a substantial amount of drug taking, and a lot of paranoia, but not on the set. I mean, people weren't walking around smoking a joint, or snorting coke or inject-ing heroin, or whatever they were doing. There may have been some of that going on in the dressing room, but it wasn't flagrantly done on set. But there was a degree of neurosis, because people like Jagger and Donald are sur-rounded by groups of people who always like to inject their own opinions about things. And of course there was tension between Mick and Keith over the fact that Anita was in the film, and there were rumours about Anita and Mick and all that. But who knows?

Sandy is referring to the fact that Mick spent a large portion of the film cavorting with Keith Richards' girlfriend Anita Pallenberg, leading to stories that had a furious Richards refus-ing to set foot on the set, waiting outside to pick her up at the end of each day's filming.

When Warner Bros. saw the results of what they had been

bankrolling they 'freaked out', taking exception to the levels of violence and sex, and the fact that Mick Jagger, the bankable pop star, didn't appear until halfway through. Shaking his head at the memory, Sandy recalls a preview screening held in LA: 'It was a complete and utter disaster. They had to stop the movie halfway through because the audience were so incensed with it. All the Warner Bros. executives were there, including the representative from the ratings board, who was a psychologist and said, "This is an X -rated film." At that time, well still today, none of the major distributors released X-rated movies. But when you look at it from today's standards, it is rather modest in terms of the sex and violence.'

The film sat in the Warner Bros. vaults, where it could easily have remained were it not for the enthusiasm of one man. 'Finally new management came into Warner Bros., and there was one person in particular named Fred Weintraub, who was the producer of the movie *Woodstock* and owned a club in New York. He was a music person. He pushed things and said, "Hey, you know this should be revived."' Warner Bros. were persuaded to consider a recut, so long as it was completed in LA where they could keep an eye on how it progressed. With Nicolas Roeg due to start work on his next movie *Walkabout* in Australia, the task fell to Cammell.

The studio finally released the film in August 1970 and rather fittingly the UK première was a benefit for Release, which is a local drugs charity founded by Caroline Coon and Rufus Harris to help those caught in possession of drugs seek legal advice and representation. 'When Caroline approached me about the possibility of doing the première for Release, we all thought it was a good idea because we believed in them and what they were doing. We had called on her for help because one of the actresses, Michele Breton, was arrested for smoking dope during the making of the movie, and Release lawyers helped.'

The movie shown this time was very different after its LA recut.

You could say that it became a different film, certainly in terms of the editing style and use of images. The images were all created by Nic and Donald but how they were used changed quite dramatically, and that was one of the things that made it very distinctive: the fact that the narrative wasn't told in a conventional way. It was told in a frag- mented way in order to get Mick Jagger in the movie early on. And I think ultimately that made it more distinctive, more ground-breaking and more unusual. So in a way the negative aspect of having to recut the film and make the compromises actually enhanced it considerably and changed the style of the film.

Performance is now a staple on film school syllabuses, studied for the ground-breaking use of cuts and imagery that Sandy talks of. But for students of Notting Hill it offers a look at the neighbour- hood before the money and the bankers, when it was still the bohemian centre of London.

Powis Square

While cameras rolled outside number 25 in 1968, Powis Square was also the focal point for local community action. The People's Associations urged the council to buy the square and turn it into a playground after several children were run over playing in the street. Local historian Tom Vague recalls: 'To the hippies, opening the garden squares of the former Rachman slum area became a symbolic mission to convert "unturned on people" and start (as Neil Oram put it) "a tidal wave which is about to wash away the square world". In 1968, Notting Hill became the radical hippy Interzone A, plotted out in the map issue of *International Times*. 'As students took to the barricades in Paris, the Powis Square gates were stormed by hippies disguised as pantomime animals.' The locals soon got their wish when the council bought the square for £6,000 and turned it into a playground. Tom Vague informed me, 'The opening party banner proclaimed: "At last the square belongs to the people. The council have learned a simple lesson from the local people and children. The council is the servant of the community."' Powis Square became an important element of the People's Carnival events in the early 1970s, and during the 1971 event it was the venue for a gig that saw future Motörhead main man Lemmy debuting, with the band on bass with the Pink Fairies and Julie Driscoll sharing the bill.

Further Limits:
Duncan Fallowell

On a damp and cold mid-November day I walk from Notting Hill Gate along Bayswater Road, looking out for Ossington Street where I am due to meet local writer Duncan Fallowell. Duncan's latest book *How to Disappear* is subtitled *A Memoir for Misfits* – an apt description of his own career, that has seen him author several acclaimed novels, along with travel books and biography, all the while writing articles for a range of publications from the *Spectator* to the *International Times* and interviewing everyone from Mick Jagger to Diana Mitford. I had first met Duncan years ago at the Travel Bookshop, and we had struck up a conversation which had somehow turned to music. I was astonished to discover that he was good friends with the legendary krautrock group Can, and in the 1970s had even been asked to join them as lead singer, an offer he declined after what he described as a 'dark night of the soul'.

I was intrigued to find out more about him and his life in the neighbourhood he has called home since moving here in 1970. Rather than conduct a sit down interview, I had arranged to tour the area with him acting as my guide, taking in the places he has lived, along with some local literary landmarks. When he mentioned that some of the addresses on his itinerary did not pertain strictly to Notting Hill I told him not to worry. I felt this was in keeping with his writing and outlook on life, which has never confined itself to a prescribed area, geographical or otherwise.

Arriving at the top of Ossington Street I find Duncan waiting for me. He is not difficult to spot with his head of well-coiffured hair, brandishing an umbrella against the persistent drizzle. Pointing to The Champion pub opposite, he explains that this was his introduction to the area, part of his 'breaking out', when a friend took him there in the late 1960s, it was the first gay pub he had ever been in. 'I remember when tourists would come in and start to giggle or leave when they realized there were rather too many moustaches and leathers!'

Coming down from Oxford in 1970 having read History, he scored a job at the *Spectator*. 'I just wrote to them and said you've got nobody writing for you under the age of forty.' He was soon installed as their first rock critic and paid the princely sum of £20 a week. He immediately set about scouting out somewhere to live, keen to escape the confines of his family home in the Thames Valley. After briefly considering Chelsea he opted for Notting Hill, feeling it chimed with his hippie lifestyle, combined with the fact that 'it was cheaper here, and also quieter. There is a lot less traffic – one of the reasons why I think the area has retained its charms. It is not really on the way to anywhere; it is a destination in and of itself, so you don't get this terrible surge of traffic. And since I was into taking acid the last thing I wanted was to be run over by a bus!'

He explains that he found a bedsit at 27 Ossington Street after scanning through the 'To Let' section of the *Evening Standard*. We walk northwards down the street to find the house in question and Duncan explains that the tall, well-proportioned houses were originally built to accommodate the servants of nearby Kensington Palace. Tall plane trees are planted the length of the street, and we take cover underneath one opposite number 27. The flat was a self-contained attic bedsit, with kitchenette and bathroom. The rent was £12 a week, leaving him £8 to live on. He tells me he got along well with the family there, an upper middle class sort who had a house in Norfolk and whose own children had left home. The only tension arose when the shared telephone in the house, situated on the upstairs landing, rang out constantly for Duncan. The chant of 'It's for you, Duncan!' eventually led to the decision that were the phone to ring it would be assumed that it was for him and he would descend the stairs to answer it himself.

It was no wonder Duncan was so popular – working as a music journalist in London in 1970 could not have been more glamorous. Duncan had timed his arrival perfectly, getting the gig just as the party was getting into full swing. Continuing on down the street he explains, 'Corporate entertaining was tax deductible, and the music industry was lavishly entertaining itself. My little *Spectator* column was as welcome as anyone.' He describes the era as 'awash with money and terribly self-indulgent'. He would go to gigs in the evenings and record company launches at lunchtime, where champagne flowed and free records were abundant. He was able to supplement his income by freelancing for underground press titles like *International Times*, *Ink* and *Frendz*, and by flogging his promo records to a second-hand shop in Soho.

We reach the end of Ossington Street and hit Moscow Road, passing a large mansion block where Edith Sitwell lived from 1914 until 1932. Duncan dryly notes, 'A lot of people we would be familiar with, like T. S. Eliot, Siegfried Sassoon, Virginia Woolf, Robert Graves, E. M. Forster and Graham Greene made pilgrimages here, and would be given dried-out cake from some dreadful bakery on Queensway and a cup of tea washed down with lots of rather violent conversation from our most distinguished imagist poetess.' Duncan tells me that he later became friends with Edith's brother Sacheverell, whom he counts as one of his literary touchstones.

He was very important to me. I had four big influences and I met them all and became quite good friends with three of

Duncan – beautiful youth – great wallpaper, at Ossington Street, 1971

them: Andy Warhol, William Burroughs, Sacheverell Sitwell and John Betjeman. They represent my English side and my Greenwich Village, tripped-out side. It has produced this peculiar chemistry in my own work. People don't know whether I am right-wing fascist or a completely deranged leftie. The truth is I am neither, I am just me.

Our next stop takes in one of these touchstones. We walk eastwards to 7 Prince's Square, where William Burroughs stayed at the Devonshire Hotel in 1964. Duncan explains that Burroughs was spending more and more time in England in the early 1960s. 'He moved around in this area a lot after he had been in Tangier. He increasingly came to London because he had two English boyfriends and his doctor was here. So he developed an intense relationship with London. In the early 1960s he was also further east at 5 Lancaster Terrace and 51 Gloucester Terrace – but I think these were rooming houses rather than hotels.'

We walk on, with Duncan keen to show me Leinster Square, just south of Westbourne Grove. 'It is one of the most extraor-

dinary streets in London, where the tradition of having the
houses facing onto a private square – as opposed to a publicly
visible square – has produced this very odd effect where you get
two rows of back doors.' He is absolutely correct. Approaching
from Hereford Road we find a street of beautiful white houses
that appear back to front, most of them seedy-looking, crumbling hotels. The street is empty as we walk along and peer in
through the rotting sash windows, many of which lie open to
reveal shoes sitting out in the damp air. Rusty old bikes are piled
up in the basements or locked on to the original railings. When
we reach the eastern end of the street Duncan turns to me and
says, 'It's started already,' pointing to the boarded up house on
the corner. We peer in through the open front door as builders
come and go, to see the guts of the building being pulled out.
Looking back at the street Duncan sighs: 'This is the last echo of
West London grot. A complete anomaly in the brave new world
of Notting Hill.'

Crossing down onto Westbourne Grove we walk eastwards
until we find Newton Road, searching for the house that Duncan moved into in 1972. He explains it 'cost a bit less because it
wasn't a flat it was simply a room with a cooker. And a shared
bathroom.' The street still looks grotty today and Duncan can't
remember for a moment whether he lived at number 7 or 9,
made more confusing by the fact that they have identical red
front doors. He is certain, though, that he took the room on the
top floor because 'I liked to sunbathe on the roof.'

It was an eclectic household, which included a retired chip
shop owner who 'existed entirely on a diet of fish and chips',
with the consequence that whole of the ground floor smelt of
fried food. On the first floor were 'a lovely old couple from
Wimbledon, who had been bombed out in the war' who were
'immensely proud to have the first floor drawing room into
which they had crammed all their belongings from their previous life in a Wimbledon mansion.' Finally, there was Joel, a rent

boy turned shoplifter – or 'hoister', as he liked to call it – on the second floor.

Duncan remembers one of Joel's regular visitors was a chap called Freddi, who would often pop round to smoke a joint and would knock on Duncan's door asking if he had anything to drink. He told Duncan he was responsible for Bowie's Ziggy Stardust look, a claim Duncan didn't take completely seriously at the time until years later, when he saw the name Freddi Burretti in an exhibition catalogue, credited with creating Bowie's iconic look, and he realized that he was the same young man who he used to hang out with. 'To me, this is part of the romance of bedsit London at the time. I remember I was very low one day. Freddi was visiting and he came across the landing to my room. Sensing my mood, he said, "Duncan there is only one rule in life," and I said, "What's that, Fred?" And he said, "Well, it's only one word, actually," and the word was "strut". He got everywhere on that one word.'

Our next stop is now well and truly out of my geographical domain, falling into Bayswater rather than Notting Hill, but we walk on and Duncan keeps me entertained with stories of his adventures all those years ago. 'I mixed everything. I was never addicted to one thing. I was freewheeling.' He had got into acid while at Oxford and during the Michaelmas term of his final year in 1969 he discovered the band Can, who had just released their debut album *Monster Movie*. The cover caught Duncan's eye as he browsed – it depicted a robotic, futuristic figure reminiscent of Jacob Epstein's *The Rock Drill*, standing above the clouds, a range of purple mountains at his feet.

Taking the LP into one of the listening booths he dropped the needle onto side 1 and was instantly transfixed. 'I thought, "Oh, this is mine!" and then when I tripped to it on acid and it became even more mine. What I loved about it was that I had been looking for something that combined the two wings: highly intellectual classical music mixed with very visceral rock

Velvet flares, roll-ups and basketweave sofas – Duncan rapping with
friends, Brook Mews North, 1974

music. I have always loved dancing, I can dance for ever once I
hit the groove and suddenly there it was in one band. I just knew
that they knew about music.'

He went to Germany to interview them shortly afterwards
and they became firm friends. 'Aha, here we are,' exclaims
Duncan, as we approach a rather grand looking block of houses.
Walking to the end of the row we stop in front of what was the
Averard Hotel. Rather fittingly, it is boarded up, seemingly in a
state of development purgatory, with no sign of workmen. This
was the hotel that Duncan would book Can into in the latter
part of the 1970s, a formerly grand hotel gone to seed. 'It had
the original staircase, with great marble statues and rather worn
carpets and wardrobe doors that didn't quite close. Faded
brocade sofas. It just screamed the 1920s. It looks like it has
been gutted now. Even in the 1970s it was an anomaly.'

We turn a corner and drop down a slight incline to Brook
Mews North and admire what was once a pub with a few rooms

above, where Duncan lived with two female friends. He explains
that Can hung out with them, 'bean bagging', smoking joints
and listening to LPs. It wasn't unusual for Brian Eno to pop
round; it was very much an open house. 'This was the hedonistic
climax of the whole of the 1960s and 1970s revolution. We
took taxis, never public transport, to the Albert Hall, and the
Rainbow to see Queen, Captain Beefheart, the Grateful Dead,
Jefferson Airplane, Led Zeppelin, Pink Floyd, Rod Stewart and
the Faces.' But the lifestyle was beginning to take its toll. 'Too
many drinks, too many drugs, too many parties, too many night
clubs, too many rock concerts, too many fashion shows. Too
much of everything. That's when I moved to Hay-on-Wye and
wrote my first book for Tom Maschler at Cape, which was a
biography of April Ashley, a sex change friend of mine.'

We start to head back to Duncan's flat. The rain has cleared by
now so we can finally fold our umbrellas away. Duncan rumi-
nates on how the area has changed, identifying two key factors
that he feels have had a huge impact:

This was very much a rooming and council area. The two
big changes in the last forty-five years are the rich people
arriving, turning the houses back into single occupancy, and
the Muslims arriving in council and housing trust flats, and
they don't drink alcohol. This has dampened down the local
nightlife. There used to be all-night films shows, all-night
clubs like The Globe and The Talbot, and a couple of all-
night supermarkets. So although the pubs closed at 11 PM,
there was a lot of life afterwards which was started in the
1950s by the West Indian clubs and has been killed off now.
But it's still a gorgeous place to live. I can't think of another
inner city area in the world that is so leafy and green and
charmingly gentle on the soul. It is under threat but it still
has that.

Pavement Poetry

The eagle-eyed visitor will have noticed something rather special about the neighbourhood's coal hole covers. One day walking across Powis Square I spotted a poem etched onto the face of a coal hole cover. 'This Streetwise area is dedicated to all absolute beginners, signed the Napoleon of Notting Hill – Michael Holroyd, 2004.' After a little research I discovered this poem was one of seven scattered throughout the neighbourhood, part of a project called 'Pavement Poetry', undertaken by an enterprising local woman named Maria Vlotides. She had commissioned a group of local writers to submit a short haiku poem, 'distilling the essence of what they felt for the area in terms of the changes that have happened here'. She agreed to meet me and took me on a guided tour of some of the poems close to Portobello, explaining that the initial idea came from seeing some poetry scrawled onto the pavement while on holiday in San Francisco. 'Its simplicity really affected me.' Using coal hole covers was a stroke of genius. They were a Victorian invention that allowed the delivery of that dusty black stuff directly into the coal cellar beneath the pavement without having to tramp through the house. By using a piece of urban architecture that had long since lost its intended use, she not only highlighted a forgotten chapter of social and domestic history, but granted them a fresh layer of meaning and relevance. On Kensington Park Road, just west of Westbourne Grove, Maria points out John Heath-Stubbs' contribution, the lengthiest of the seven: 'Incline your head, passer-by, and peruse what you see, with some danger from passing perambulators, not to mention incontinent sparrows and pigeons. Here is a long, thin, coiling around, It isn't a centipede, but an unrhymed poem – free verse at that! What is it there for – only to prove what a cultured place this town of ours is, isn't it?' Another local writer, Sebastian Faulks, is direct and to the point: 'A word in

Michael Holroyd's contribution to the Pavement Poetry project, 2004

your eye, don't worry or push, a step in the gate, is worth two in the bush.'

Heathcote Williams and the Ruff, Tuff, Cream Puff Squatting Agency

The revered playwright, poet, sculptor and occasional actor Heathcote Williams is one of the most colourful and subversive characters to have lived in the neighbourhood, setting up home here in the late 1960s and staying for most of the 1970s. For much of this time he squatted, founding the brilliantly titled Ruff, Tuff, Cream Puff Squatting Agency that provided regular bulletins listing empty properties ripe for new occupants. He was also a gifted graffiti artist and anyone visiting the area would have seen his political slogans daubed up on walls and buildings long before Banksy made a multi-million pound empire out of it. Following the huge success of his trilogy of book-length poems centred on environmental themes – *Whale Nation* (1988), *Sacred Elephant* (1989) and *Autogedden* (1991) – he has proven something of an enigma. He has been living in rural Cornwall and more recently in Oxfordshire, never giving interviews and only occasionally publishing new work via small presses.

He tells me that he first visited Portobello as a twelve-year-old, coming up from Fulham to buy records. He moved into a flat on Lancaster Road in 1968, but was forced out soon afterwards when he failed to pay the rent, moving into a squatted house in Westbourne Park Road, signalling the start of his adventures in squatting.

He was part of the 1960s wave of squatters who took their cue from the radicals of the past like Wat Tyler – the leader of the Peasants' Revolt of 1381 – and the Diggers of the seventeenth century, who rejected the rights of landlords to charge rent and saw seizing property as a political act. Heathcote explains: 'In accordance with anarchism's basic tenets, property is theft. We stole property and gave it away.' This radical agenda stood in stark contrast to the Family Squatting Movement of the immediate post-war years, which had seen ex-servicemen and their families move into derelict army camps and empty properties, spurred on by need rather than political motivation.

Moving on from Westbourne Park Road, he squatted 'the old Bingo Hall in Lancaster Road to put on free concerts'.

I forged a letter from the estate agents to the effect that they would appreciate nothing better than that we used their empty property to promote local Notting Hill Gate charities. The police were miraculously taken in by it. We rechristened the bingo hall the Albion Meat Roxy. It was popular with proto-punk bands. The house in Westbourne Park Road was pretty primitive. Jonathan Marconi from the BIT information service came by and doctored the payphone so you could ring up for free. We lived off 'rubbish risotto' – food left in the street from vegetable stalls in the market and stewed up. We started feeding homeless people. The place filled up. Anyone could stay the night until we found them a place.

He soon realised that there were many people in his position, in need of somewhere to live and in search of a squat. There was no organisation or structure in place to help them, and with this in mind he founded the Ruff, Tuff, Cream Puff squatters' estate agency, which ran from 1974 to 1977, producing over twenty-five bulletins throughout that period. Looking at them today they offer a remarkable insight into the squatting community. Their bulletins would feature black and white photos of the houses in question with descriptions such as, 'There's a six storey block of flats which would suit an Astronomers Collective (the roof is very leaky at the top) on the corner of Cleveland Gardens and Leinster Terrace, just off Queensway and Gloucester Terrace. All empty and unsaleable. IS THIS YOUR PLACE? REMEMBER WILFUL WASTE BREEDS WOEFUL WANT.' Another one reads, '69 Talbot Road, W11 needs a lot of work. 71 next door has been squatted. For further information contact Malcolm therein, a poet, formerly of Newton Road. The house (69) has a garden and strange trapdoors leading from floor to floor, which would suit a thieves kitchen, or compulsive levitators.' And so they go on: description after description of houses, police stations, former embassies and terraces awaiting demolition. 'Keep away from the low numbers they are coming down first' warns one ad, and another advises caution: 'Don't jump the gun, or they might jump your gun.'

Heathcote explains his thinking:

The idea for a mock estate agency that charged nothing for handing someone the keys to an empty property grew from this situation. I was quite influenced by Abbie Hoffman, whom I'd met in New York. I remembered a stroppy character in a Robert Crumb cartoon called the Ruff, Tuff, Cream Puff and I adopted this name for the agency, which we fraudulently claimed to have been founded by Wat Tyler in 1381. We started listing the empty properties that people told us about, or which we were cracking open ourselves, and we duplicated the bulletins to give to anyone who came by looking for a place to live.

The operation worked by having at least a dozen people who would constantly feed information back to him about empty houses, along with 'people from the BIT information service in Westbourne Park Road, started by "Hoppy" John Hopkins, and Nicholas Albery, and people who'd been housed by RuffTuff and would happily become part of the network of squatters feeding information back into the system.' A huge map was laid out in one room of Heathcote's squat, with labelled pins stating whether a property was 'squatted' or 'ripe for squatting'. This was a revolutionary idea and certainly the first of its kind in this country, predating a similar move in the mid-1990s by a group calling themselves 'Justice?', who established a squatters' estate agency in 1996 and received international media coverage. I ask how many people he thinks they housed in this manner.

Hard to say, but people got housed. Its purpose was to put homeless people into empty properties, often kept deliberately empty by speculators. The properties had to be jemmied open and the locks changed. Or, more simply, a visit to a straight estate agent such as Foxtons or Savills with a suit and tie and an interest in viewing one of their flats could secure the keys, which were then copied for future use. We only once squatted a house that was in use. We burst into somewhere in Clarendon Road that we thought was empty and found a couple eating their dinner on the top floor. We apologised for interrupting them and legged it. Someone did make a death threat – the owner of a number of properties who felt threatened. He sent round his minders. The newspapers were also unsympathetic. 'He Jemmies Way in for Squatters' was a front-page headline in the *Sunday People*. This was inconvenient, as we were also reviving the Windsor Free Festival, in breach of a High Court injunction, preventing us holding a festival in Windsor Great Park, the Queen's back yard. It now meant the house was watched, and an informant stole a draft of the latest

Ruff Tuff bulletin and took it to the *Evening Standard*, with
the result that they came out with a front page story: 'Squatters Plan to Take over London'. That was an inflated view of
my organizational skills. Being told that I'd soon face charges
of incitement, I thought that discretion was the better part
of valour and disappeared.

Running alongside this, Heathcote was busy daubing slogans
and artwork on walls throughout the neighbourhood.

There were about fifty or sixty slogans, and a big mural: the
Albion Free State Declaration of Independence in Lancaster
Road. Many were done with Tony Allen; Mike Lesser and I
did Buckingham Palace – a lengthy graffiti taking exception
to the imminent hanging of Michael X, whom both of us
knew. The Judicial Committee of the Privy Council in the
UK was retained as Trinidad's highest court of appeal. On
referral of Michael's case to this committee and the refusal
of his final appeal, the Queen personally signed his death
warrant. Mike and I thought this was objectionable since
there was no death penalty in this country. It had been abolished in the UK in 1964. Michael's execution was therefore
an act of wilful hypocrisy. Afterwards, I wrote Michael's
name all over the place, but with a Christian cross this time,
rather than an X. I climbed up onto the Ladbroke Grove
railway bridge to spray his name from the parapet so that it
could be seen on the bridge by passing traffic.

I ask him what he makes of the current property prices and
the way the bankers have moved in and built their underground
swimming pools in the same properties he once squatted.

Wat Tyler, John Ball and Gerrard Winstanley ('There is no

my thing, there is no your thing. The world is a common treasure house to all.') trump the number-crunching nerds of JP Morgan Chase. Bankers lower the tone, and steal an area's vibrancy. Likewise, plutocratic, coke-sniffing celebrities create the same imbalance. Ever since seamen, pirates possibly, came to Portobello Farm to sell their booty – as legend has it – Portobello has always had a faintly criminal atmosphere. It's still to be savoured. When I see that the encroachment of the wealthy is being corrected by crime, i.e. their houses are broken into and adjustments are made to their economic apartheid – such as their Ferraris and Lamborghinis being vandalised – then what can I do but rejoice? Blake's proverb, which was written up (not by me) in Basing Street, summed up something of Portobello's radical spirit: 'The tigers of wrath are wiser than the horses of instruction.'

One of Heathcote and Co.'s regular bulletins

Frestonia

Frestonia shot into the public consciousness in 1977, when a group of squatters living in vacant properties on Freston Road were threatened with eviction by the GLC ahead of its redevelopment. The street is located close to Latimer Road and at the time was in the borough of Hammersmith and Fulham, it has since been incorporated into Kensington and Chelsea. The community of around 120 squatters gathered together under the leadership of Nick Albery and Heathcote Williams, and came up with an audacious plan – they would declare the street an independent state separate from the UK. Heathcote recalled: 'It was Nicholas who first had the idea of declaring independence from Hammersmith Council and then from London itself.' A referendum was duly held, finding 94 per cent in favour of this action, and so on 31 October 1977 the free state of Frestonia was declared. An appeal was lodged with the UN for assistance with their struggle against the GLC.

'We wrote to the UN to apply for a tank to defend ourselves from the Greater London Council. I don't recall them replying but I do remember we had a visit from an organization called the Micro-Patrological Society of Chicago, which specialized in small nations, and also from someone in Vienna who'd declared his house an independent country.' The world's media descended on the street, with film crews from as far afield as Japan and New Zealand among those eager to cover the story. The residents changed their surname by Deed Poll *en masse* to Bramley, the idea being that the council would then be forced to rehouse them collectively. The state adopted the Latin motto 'Nos Sumus Una Familia' – We Are All One Family. Border controls were introduced, and a daily newspaper called *The Messenger* was set up, along with a national theatre, postage stamps. There were even plans for a currency.

We established the National Theatre of Frestonia in the People's Hall and it premiered a play called *The Immortalist* with David Rappaport (from *Illuminatus!* and *Time Bandits*). It was a course in 'how to live for ever with no expensive props'. David played the Interviewer and Neil Cunningham played the 278-year-old man – the Immortalist of the title. All the gardens in Freston Road were joined together. Open Head Press – an anarchist publisher, in Blenheim Crescent, off Portobello, which I ran with Richard Adams and John Angus Mackay – was used as the Frestonian Embassy to the UK. We issued passports and postage stamps.

I ask Heathcote if he was surprised at the level of interest in Frestonia. 'I just saw it as a way of embarrassing Hammersmith Council when they'd set their heart on evicting people in Freston Road. Essentially Frestonia was a piece of filibustering – buying time to delay eviction. But miraculously there are still people there, in Freston Road, from that time now living in protected housing, i.e. Hammersmith Council caved in, not wanting egg on their face. So, yes it worked.' An unlikely champion was found in the Shadow Chancellor of the Exchequer Geoffrey Howe, who penned them a letter of support saying, 'As one who had childhood enthusiasm for *The Napoleon of Notting Hill*, I can hardly fail to be moved by your aspirations.' In the end, the residents formed into the Bramley Housing Co-operative and negotiated with the Notting Hill Housing Association over the planned redevelopment of the site, securing their continued residence.

Colossal basement excavations bring chaos to the neighbourhood, 2014

Basement Bedlam and
The Rise of The Super Rich

Over the last ten years the super rich have signalled their arrival in Notting Hill by building ever more elaborate basement extensions to their homes, incorporating swimming pools, cinemas, wine cellars, gyms and car parks. It seems it is no longer enough to have the latest model Range Rover parked outside for the school run, or to be seen at the right ski resort during the half term holiday – nothing says it quite like a megabasement. Kensington and Chelsea have seen applications for these so-called 'iceberg homes' rocket from 13 in 2001 to 307 in 2012, leading the Press to dub the phenomenon a 'subterranean land grab'.

Strolling around the neighbourhood it is not difficult to spot these developments in progress. The house in question usually resembles a building site and, depending on how far into the development they are, you will likely hear the ear-shattering sound of a high-powered drill boring its way through the ground below. A conveyor belt set up in the front garden rolls endlessly around, depositing its cargo of soil and rock into a waiting skip as lorries come and go all day long. These developments take on average two years to complete, during which time the owners usually decamp to one of the other properties in their portfolio, only returning when the work is complete. A successfully dug basement extension can add 15–20 per cent to the value of a property, and with increasingly restrictive planning regulations making building upwards a tougher proposition, it is easy to see why their popularity has so quickly caught on.

But it seems local disquiet at these developments is growing, with news in late 2013 that plans to build a vast extension beneath a financier's home on Elgin Crescent were thrown out by councillors following a storm of protest from a group of local residents, including such celebrities as Ruby Wax and Rachel Johnson. This comes after new rules were published in early 2013 limiting basement extensions to a single storey. But this is all too late for distinguished writer and foreign correspondent Ed Vulliamy, a long-time resident of the neighbourhood who found himself and his eighty-six-year-old mother caught in the midst of several of these developments at their home on Lansdowne Road.

The drilling starts at around 8AM each day, he explains, 'until the walls crack, and you become progressively more deranged and turn into a nervous wreck. You cannot think or speak, let alone work.' We are sitting in the studio flat that occupies the (regular) basement of the house where Ed resides when he is up in London during the week. The drilling goes on all day, making it impossible for anyone in the house to work, more than an inconvenience for both him and his mother, who is the revered children's book illustrator Shirley Hughes. Shirley is adored by generations who grew up on her books like *Alfie* and *Dogger*. 'There is the rub, actually, because now everyone says, "Oh your lovely mother, oh how wonderful," but she can't fucking work because of the noise. So there is some kind of repulsive irony within all of that.'

Ed is in no doubt that these developments, with their 'I don't give a fuck about my neighbour' attitude, signal the end of sharing space in a community that has become dominated by a group of very wealthy bankers and hedge fund managers. He describes them as 'uneducated people. They don't have any soul with a capital S, in the James Brown sense of the word. They are as unfunky as you can get. If you have made your money by looting the economy, gorging on the bail out when the poor were robbed to keep the rich afloat, by definition you are not a very nice person.'

Things were very different when his parents bought the house in 1954, shortly after he was born. He and his brother grew up here on the border between salubrious Holland Park to the south and the more rough and ready environs of Ladbroke Grove to the north. 'Politically, back then the constituency was called North Kensington, and it was red, absolutely solid Labour, and south of Holland Park Avenue was Conservative and that was the border. My earliest memories are of the race riots and my mother at Holland Park station accosting two Teddy Boys who were beating up a black kid, saying, "What on earth do you think you are doing?" and she was only in her late twenties at the time.'

Ironically, his parents moved here because it was relatively cheap, and they managed to scrabble together the £3,000 to buy the house. They were typical of the kind of people who populated the street back then. While they were by no means poor, they were nowhere near as wealthy as the yuppies of the 1980s or the more recent breed of super rich. 'Mostly arty-farty, cash-poor, book-rich types, for example our best friends who lived across the garden – he was a painter – and next to them was a scientist, and a mixture of minor academics. My father was an architect who gave it up in his fifties to become an etcher working down here in the basement, and my mother was a then struggling children's book illustrator. It wasn't a poor area but we didn't have a car until the 1960s or a television until the 1966 World Cup, and yet we had a house this size. But it was always full because the family economy here was lodgers and I think a lot of people did that.'

A steady parade of lodgers would occupy the basement flat and a spare room upstairs. 'My brother was asked once at school what his mother did for a living and he said, "Landlady".' The people lodging with them over the years ranged from a retired merchant sea captain, who would occasionally appear in his full military regalia before he headed out for an evening function, to a hip young designer working for Mary Quant, who gave the teenage Ed a prototype leather jacket.

He describes nearby Clarendon Cross, now one of the most expensive parts of the neighbourhood as 'really rough. It was chewing gum and cigarettes, very seedy sweet shops, a betting shop, a building works and the kiln. I can just about remember people trying to keep warm by the kiln opposite Avondale Park, huddled up against the wall. There was a pub there called the Zeckland, which was all tinkling pianos and prostitutes. There was an unofficial red light area just behind the Zeckland, and my brother and I used to ride out and look at them.'

Their house backs on to a beautifully maintained garden square. I took a turn around it before our interview, and I could see how the majority of houses either side of them had been given the minimalist open-plan treatment. One in particular, a few doors down, was literally a bright white cube. The only thing that remained from the original house was the façade; everything else had been entirely rebuilt. That is one of the mysteries that Ed cannot fathom. Why do these super rich bankers want to buy these characterful properties in the first place? 'Why do they want to live in a nice quiet green area, when actually all they want to do is create bedlam. Why do they want nice early Victorian stucco architecture when they want to trash it? If you want a minimalist Japanese coconut grove house, why don't you buy one?'

He tells me that at one point a couple of years ago, five out of the seven houses to the east of theirs were being gutted or having a basement extension dug out. It is not as if he hasn't voiced his opposition to these developments, going along to council meetings where the plans are discussed, but it seems that money wins out in the end. This fact is borne out by a recent example of a hedge fund manager who was ordered to pay £825,000 towards affordable housing in the area in order to gain the necessary permission to dig out a basement extension eight times the size of the average London home underneath the two Victorian villas that he owned in Notting Hill. The 9,160 square foot, two-storey development, complete with swimming pool, whirlpool spa and cinema, represents the biggest development yet.

I ask Ed when he thinks the area started to shift and lose this community focus. 'Everyone looks back at the film as the beginning of the end, the start of the ravaging of the rich, but it actually started before then. The film was at the end of the 1990s and by then the worst was well under way. But the real rich vandals, the rich thugs, came in the last ten years, in the 2000s.'

One of the most noticeable changes over the last twenty years has been the lack of any life in the garden square behind the house. He tells me that it has become 'a waste of space, because it is just that, literally and figuratively. I mean it always used to be packed at weekends with football, people messing about making a nuisance of themselves, being naughty. But now on the weekends it is empty, because they are all up in the Cotswolds and in the summer it is deserted because they are all in Tuscany.'

When he was growing up they would regularly have community parties there, describing the mayhem of Bonfire Night. 'It was chaos, no health, no safety. We had some quite dysfunctional families living here. There was one particularly tough Scottish family and I remember one of the kids lobbing a firework in the box of fireworks so they would all go up. There were always a lot of drunk people falling into the fire clutching the girl they had been trying to kiss for months and months. It was funny and chaotic.' Nowadays 'it's all men in fluorescent coats with roped off displays. It costs thousands and thousands of pounds to put on. It is now completely boring as people go "ooh" and "ahh", as yet another thousand pounds goes up in smoke.'

The midsummer party too has turned into a display of wealth and ostentation. Ed can remember organizing the 'sports day' for the occasion in 1970 that included a sack race and egg and spoon race. The Mangrove Steelband played and the guests would bop around to their tin pan melodies. 'Now it's utterly sterile and a very expensive affair. They have a sit down marquee dinner with ridiculous speeches. You couldn't make it up. You gradually start to feel like Jacques Tati – sort of bewildered by it all.' He tells me that the dinner parties are the same huge productions, with thousands of pounds lavished on outside catering and flowers, but missing one vital ingredient – interesting conversation. 'It is mind-bogglingly banal, it really is. It is personal trainers for half an hour, then it's clothes. I am sure that thirty years ago we didn't talk about Kierkegaard all night, but we did go to the Bush Theatre or the Riverside and we might discuss the play. These people talk loudly about nothing. The wives are quite a species; they all have a little blonde pony tail tied up and they have their Starbucks coffee and tracksuit on. I see them out at the back with their personal trainers.'

Ed has a train to catch to his home in the West Country. 'We live in Glastonbury now, not least because it was the drummer from Hawkwind, Richard Armitage, who said something to the effect of: "If you grew up in Notting Hill, you gotta be down here to stay with the neighbours. It's Portobello Road in a field, man!" And it is. It is ironic that in 2013 we have had to move to Somerset to stay with the neighbours.' And hopefully to get some peace and quiet.

Behind the Blue Door
with Richard Curtis

280 Westbourne Park Road is far and away the most famous and the most popular address in the neighbourhood. People flock from all corners of the globe in search of this mythical house that they refer to as the Blue Door. Located a few feet from Portobello Road, opposite Nu-Line the builders' merchants, and a few doors down from Starbucks, this nondescript doorway sandwiched between two pillars was the fictional home of William Thacker, the floppy-haired bookshop owner played by Hugh Grant in the film *Notting Hill*. Released in 1999 the film charts the love affair between Thacker and film star Anna Scott, played by Julia Roberts, that blossoms when she walks unexpectedly into his shop one day.

On Saturdays, you will see a constant stream of people approaching the door, some shaking their heads in wonder or pumping their fists to the sky. They have found it! It exists! Posing for photographs outside, they flick the V-for-victory sign, documenting the successful conclusion of their quest. Everyone in the neighbourhood has been asked for directions to the Blue Door at one time or another including Richard Curtis, the man who wrote the film.

About once or twice a year someone will come up to me and say, 'Do you know the way to the Blue Door?' and most times I'll say, 'Yes, it's along there and to the left,' but sometimes, if I'm feeling insecure, I'll say, 'Actually, I wrote it,' and they always just look at me and say, 'no', shaking their heads. The concept that it wasn't Hugh who wrote the film, or that it isn't a documentary, is just unthinkable.

The house in question was in fact Richard Curtis's own home at the time of the film's production in 1998, but it was never his intention to use it as a location, as he explained when we meet at his office, a short walk from the Blue Door on Portobello Road. He tells me that the decision was made by production designer Stuart Craig, who went out on a scouting mission in the neighbourhood:

He came back a little while later and said, 'I have absolutely found the place and I won't have any argument about it.' He then showed us a picture of my own front door. I said. 'You must be joking. This must be a prank, this is *my* house,' and he said, 'No it's just perfect – it's got these wonderful pillars and a blue door and it's just ten yards to the left from Portobello so it's perfect, so when you shoot the scene when they bump into each other, he can just point to his house. It was uncanny the fact that, without any input, he picked my own house! It really was spooky.

Richard had bought the house in the early 1990s, telling me that it is in fact a former chapel – there was even a font tucked away somewhere beneath the floorboards. Shortly after buying the property, when they were poised to have some building work done, the house was squatted. The squatters, Richard explains, 'set up an art gallery in our house and we had to wait the traditional three weeks or three months – whatever it is – before we were allowed to evict them. We got to know them quite well and worried that they weren't selling enough stuff, so we ended up buying a painting from them. So I have a photograph of the former German leader Helmut Kohl and John Major with a speech bubble saying above Kohl saying, "Smell my poo". I think we paid a tenner for that.'

This is a typically Curtis-style story; he is the ultimate nice guy. Who else would worry that whether the squatters holding up work on your house were selling enough of their art? I find myself being slowly charmed by the man who has carved out reputation for making hugely popular films that tap into a certain strain of English sentimentality that belies his Australian lineage.

He has lived in the area since the late 1980s. 'We settled in Ledbury Mews, and then Westbourne Park Road and now Ladbroke Grove, so I have just lived in a very tight circle around here.' He clearly loves the place: 'You never know what is going to happen when you turn around a corner.' To illustrate this point he tells me the story of a Saturday morning, when he came into his office to get some work done. 'There was a busker down there', he says, gesturing to the window and the street below. 'He played literally three of my favourite songs: one Waterboys song, an Oasis song and a Beatles song. And I went downstairs and I said, "This is brilliant, you know you are making my day," and I gave him a fiver to thank him. But it turned out that those were the only three songs he knew, and he played those same fucking three songs all day long. It quickly turned into the worst day! I eventually went back down and said, "I want my money back!"'

He wrote *Notting Hill* looking out at the market, and in his self-deprecating manner tells me, 'It was a classic example of my lack of imagination. When I was living in Camden Town I wrote a film called *Camden Town Boy*, which eventually got called *The Tall Guy*.' I have encountered many people over the course of writing this book who have described *Notting Hill* as the tipping point after which house prices went up and the area became

Richard Curtis at his studio close to Portobello Road

popular with a new breed of super rich residents. When I
mention this, Richard replies, 'I hope that, on the other side of
the balance book, it is responsible for bringing a lot more money
to the traders and people who work along this road.' The main
criticism levelled at the film is the lack of black people in it – it
must be the whitest depiction of the street in cinematic history.
Before I can mention this, Richard addresses this point:

I have always been slightly frustrated at the criticism that is
levelled at the movie not being representative of the area,
because I wasn't making a movie about the area, and I didn't
plan on calling it *Notting Hill*. It was known as 'The Notting
Hill Film' during production, but I always assumed we
would think of another title. I wanted to call it *The Famous
Girl* but Roger [Michell], the director, told me it never

occurred to him that it wouldn't be called *Notting Hill*, and because he didn't like *The Famous Girl* he won that argument. I don't think that *Manhattan* by Woody Allen takes into account the different socioeconomic groups involved in Manhattan, so I have always been a bit sensitive about that.

As I try to imagine the film called *The Famous Girl* Richard qualifies what he has just said. 'Since all my early career at *Not the Nine O'Clock News* was about coming up with unfair charges about people that weren't true for humour, I don't see why other people shouldn't do that to me.'

He explains that the majority of the film was shot in a studio, an irony not lost on him. 'I set it in my own street so that I wouldn't have to get up early in the mornings, and what they did was simply recreate it in a studio fifty miles away.' But they did do some location work in and around Portobello, including the famous 'four seasons in one shot' sequence that sees Hugh Grant walking along Portobello as the seasons change around him.

Shooting the film on location came with its own set of challenges, not least the fact that they had to work around the businesses and residents who were going about their daily lives when shooting kicked off on 17 April 1998. 'We were filming a scene where all the friends were walking along – so we had Hugh Grant, Tim McInnerny and Hugh Bonneville, and someone came out from one of the shops and chucked eggs at us and accused us of depriving them of a few hours of business, because we had blocked off the street. I thought that was absolutely excellent and quite symptomatic of the fact that it's not a gentrified street. It is a place where everyone sticks up for their own rights – a working street.'

The funniest story connected with the film concerns the establishing shots of the bookshop. The exterior was shot at 142

That blue door

Portobello Road, at the time an antiques shop that was transformed to resemble the Travel Book Company:

> We ended up with only about twelve frames of the shop without Hugh or someone else walking into it. And consequently if you watch the film very carefully on the three occasions when you see the outside of the bookshop, there is a woman tying her shoelace. So it seems like a great tragedy for the woman, who has been caught perpetually tying up the same shoelace. But we didn't have an alternative because we didn't have any other shots.

Richard clearly thrives on being part of the community, and remains as in love with the area as when he first moved here twenty-five years ago. Walking through his office to collect my coat he says, 'There is no doubt that it has the advantages of feeling very much like a village. Our children go to school just along the road, and a lot of the parents at those schools live around here. I would say it is impossible for me to walk from Ladbroke Grove down to Westbourne Park Road without meeting at least one person I know, and that is a real luxury in London.'

On that note I leave him and head out onto Portobello Road. Turning left onto Westbourne Park Road I go past the Blue Door, which has now been restored to its signature blue after being painted black for a number of years.

Rhys Ifans

Rhys Ifans was the break-out star of *Notting Hill*. Playing the part of Spike, the eccentric Welsh flatmate of William Thacker (played by Hugh Grant), he stole the show with his hilarious antics and *that* famous scene where he confronts the paparazzi camped outside their front door wearing only his dirty grey Y-fronts. Rhys lives nearby, and I caught up with him over a pint to quiz him about how he landed the part, and to hear about his initial impressions of Notting Hill.

I wasn't actually living in Notting Hill then; I was living in a squat in New Cross, so it was like manna from heaven getting that gig. I had visited Notting Hill before that, in the late 1980s when I first moved to London. I was doing something for the Royal Court who had a rehearsal space at the top of Portobello Road. When I first came down to the market I couldn't believe it – it was like this bohemian idyll, it was heaven! Coming from North Wales this was what you imagined, the halcyon image you have of London, deeply multicultural, absolutely joyous. Then I went to my first Carnival, took acid, invited friends down from Wales. It was so liberating, just absolutely fucking brilliant!

When I ask him if he could have guessed that the film would be so successful and would have such a long lasting legacy he says: 'I had absolutely no idea. Previously to *Notting Hill* there had been *Four Weddings*, which I thought was great. I thought, "Right, I'm in a film with Hugh Grant and Julia Roberts!" but I didn't think that my character would become messianic! It got to the point that, when the film was released, the character of Spike was so popular they added me to the poster!' He has fond memories of the shoot. 'I remember there were moments on set where the crew would be pissing themselves laughing

Rhys stealing the show as Spike in *Notting Hill*, 1999

as Hugh would be talking, while I was being quiet in the background. And he would go, "All right, what's he fucking doing now then?" and I'd be filling my goggles with smoke or whatever.'

He tells me he feels connected to the area: 'I have only great gratitude to Richard Curtis and *Notting Hill*. I have great affection for this place. Earlier on I got a taxi here from Soho. I got in the car and said, "Notting Hill, please", and it was only when we arrived here that the driver said to me, "Sorry mate, I gotta say, I just rang my mate to tell him I can't believe I am taking you back to Notting Hill! Do you still live in that house?"'

Despite the influx of wealthy bankers Rhys believes that the area retains a unique atmosphere: 'I'll sit here in The Cow [pub] some days in the summer and I will see swarms of bankers outside that pub over there [gesturing to The Westbourne] and I wanna fucking firebomb them. I have got very close several times – I just haven't found the right mix yet. Ultimately I am optimistic about the future of this area, I have to be. I can see the argument that it has been overrun by bankers – but the whole world has been overrun by bankers. Ultimately the human spirit will always be the victor.'

Afterword

After talking to more than sixty people, across ninety hours of interviews over the last two and a half years, my journey has come to an end. I have met some truly inspirational characters, made new friends and discovered much about the neighbourhood I have lived in for the last decade. Were it not for my publisher's deadline, I could go on interviewing and writing for another two and a half years and still be no closer to finishing. As I said at the start, this book was conceived as a series of snapshots, and I have endeavoured to cover the main threads that have helped to bind the neighbourhood together over the last sixty years. For those of you who live in the area or who were already familiar with some of these stories and events, I hope I have helped to shed new light on them or added some fresh insight. And for those who have rarely set foot in this corner of the city then I hope that this book has prompted you to visit again and look our for some of the characters I have met and introduced you to here.

At the outset I discussed my concern that the street was in danger of disappearing, its origins stripped away and phased out, replaced by chain shops and invaded by wealthy bankers. While I have seen much to support this, I feel far more optimistic, having unearthed a layer of creativity and individuality that exists in spite of these changes, proof that the bohemian, non-conformist spirit of the place can never be completely rubbed out. In the words of the protagonist of G. K. Chesterton's novel

The Napoleon of Notting Hill: 'There has never been anything in the world absolutely like Notting Hill. There will never be anything quite like it to the crack of doom. I cannot believe anything but that God loved it as He must surely love anything that is itself and unreplaceable.'

The author enjoying a coffee
at his favourite haunt

NOTES

1. Zukin, Sharon, *Naked City: The Death and Life of Authentic Urban Places* (Oxford University Press, 2011), p.6

2. Jacobs, Jane, *The Death and Life of Great American Cities* (Jonathan Cape, 1961), p.56

3. http://www.vaguerants.org.uk/wp-content/uploads/2010/06/fiftyeightweb2.pdf

4. Pilkington, Edward, *Beyond Mother Country: West Indians and the Notting Hill White Riots* (I. B. Taurus & Co., 1988), p.31

5. http://www.vaguerants.org.uk/wp-content/uploads/2010/06/fiftyeightweb2.pdf

6. http://www.vaguerants.org.uk/wp-content/uploads/2010/06/fiftyeightweb2.pdf

7. http://www.vaguerants.org.uk/wp-content/uploads/2010/06/fiftyeightweb2.pdf

8. Pilkington (1988), p.9

9. Phillips, Mike and Trevor, *Windrush: The Irresistible Rise of Multi-Racial Britain* (HarperCollins, 1998)

10. Letter from Hoppy, Flat 5, 115 Queensway, 9/3/1966

11. Minutes from 5th LFS meeting, 25/1/1966

12. Minutes from 6th LFS meeting, 8/2/1966

13. *The Gate*, issue 1, 4/4/1966

14. Green, Jonathon, *Days in the Life: Voices from the English Underground* (Pimlico, 1988), p.96

15. *Ibid.*, p.96

16. *The Grove*, 23/5/1966

17. Farquharson, Robin, *Drop Out!* (Anthony Blond, 1968), p.91–2

18. *Touch*, 199, interview with Bill Tuckey, p.20

19. Younge, Gary, 'The Politics of Partying', *Guardian*, 17 August 2002

20. Raban, Jonathan, *Soft City* (Harvill Press, 1974), pp.195–6

21. Palacios, Julian, *Syd Barrett and Pink Floyd: Dark Globe* (Plexus, 2010), p.98

22. *EVO*, quoted in Palacios (2010), p.100

23. Andrew King, quoted in Rob Chapman, *Syd Barrett: A Very Irregular Head* (Faber & Faber, 2010), p.114

24. *Melody Maker*, quoted in Nick Mason, *Inside Out: A Personal History of Pink Floyd* (Weidenfeld & Nicolson, 2005), p.49

25. *Ibid.*, p.48

26. Taylor, Neil, *Document and Eyewitness: An Intimate History of Rough Trade* (Orion Books, 2010) p.5

27. Steve Montgomery, quoted in Taylor (2010), p.53

28. Ari Up, quoted in Rob Young, *Rough Trade* (Black Dog Publishing Ltd, 2006), p.18

29. Taylor (2010), p.58

30. Vivien Goldman, quoted in Young (2006), p.19

31. Repsch, John, *The Legendary Joe Meek: The Telstar Man* (Woodford House, 1989), p.54

32. Lancaster, Osbert, *All Done from Memory* (John Murray, 1963), p.77

33. http://www.theguardian.com/commentisfree/2013/jun/04/justice-at-risk-law-centre-legal-aid

34. http://www.nklc.co.uk/userfiles/annual%20reports/Annual%20Review%202011.pdf

INDEX

Entries in *italics* refer to illustrations

ACKNOWLEDGEMENTS

I owe an enormous debt of gratitude to my agent Jane Turnbull, who believed in this book from the outset and has consistently gone above and beyond the call of duty. Without her boundless enthusiasm and steady editorial eye the book would not be in existence. I would like to thank Alice Smith for making the book look so wonderful and her partner Christian Brett for his typesetting; Andrew Dunn and his team at Frances Lincoln for their help and support; Alice Brett for her keen editorial eye and proofreading skills; Joseph Perman Turnbull and Leonard Neumann for their generosity in donating their wonderful photographs; Tom Hodgkinson and Victoria Hull for being so understanding and allowing me time away from the Idler Academy to complete the book; the Royal Society of Literature and Jerwood Foundation for their support in awarding me a Jerwood Award for Non-Fiction. Above all, I thank my girlfriend Gudrun Kloepsch for her constant love and support. And of course I am hugely grateful to all those I have interviewed. They were all without exception incredibly generous with their time: Damon Albarn, Rose Alfred, Sarah Anderson, Michael Barham, Nicola Beauman, Joe Boyd, Gill Bradley, Paul Breuer, Nick Brown, Cleo and Mark Butterfield, Peter Cain, Cheryl Collins, Caroline Coon, Richard Curtis, Laura Del-Rivo, Duncan Fallowell, Bill and Anne Forsyth, Pepe Francis, Muhammed Fuheid, Simon Godley, Fiona Hawthorne, Sasha Hawthorne, Ian Hensall, Delia Holt, Nigel House, Dave Hucker, Mustafa Idris, Rhys Ifans, Peter Jenner, Mike Laslett-O'Brien, Sandy Lieberson, Jessica Mann, Gaz Mayall, Brian Nevill, Jerome O'Connell, Robert Orbach, Leslie Palmer, Alex Paterson, Matthew Phillip, Richard Russell, Richard landlord of the Cock and Bottle, Nicolas Roeg, Felicity Rubenstein, Chris Salewicz, Greg Sams, Bob Stanley, N.J. Stevenson, Dudley Sutton, Barbara Thomson, Geoff Travis, Nik Turner, Tom Vague, Maria Vlotides, Ed Vulliamy, Gladdy Wax, Nigel Waymouth, Heathcote Williams, Emily Young, Youth.

PICTURE ACKNOWLEDGEMENTS

Into the Market
Brian Perman: 2, 40, 45
Leonard Neumann: 4–6
Getty: 12, 83
Joseph Perman Turnbull: 17–21, 31, 73, 78
Bill Forsyth: 25–28
Johnny Millar: 32
Lutyens and Rubinstein: 39
Julian Mash: 44–49, 63, 74, 86–87
Gregory Sams: 53–61
Cleo Butterfield: 64–68
Gill Bradley: 91

Lord, Don't Stop The Carnival
Joseph Perman Turnbull: 94, 122, 146, 156
Tony Withers: 97
Getty: 98–105, 136
Emily Young: 120
Gaz Mayall: 134, 140–142
Fiona Hawthorne: 158–159

In Love With Rock'n'Roll
Joseph Perman Turnbull: 164, 229
Getty: 172, 211
Nigel Waymouth: 181
Barney Bubbles / UA: 182
Nik Turner: 189
TEL Bough: 195
Geoff Travis: 201
Rosław Szaybo / Rocco Macauly: 205
Frank Jenkinson: 206
Louise Butterly / RMP: 216
Rex: 223

Bricks and Mortar
Joseph Perman Turnbull: 232, 261
Julian Mash: 236–247, 280, 292
Private collection: 250
Getty: 253
Private collection: 254
Duncan Fallowell: 265–268
Maria Vlotides: 271
Ruff Tuff Crème Puff Bulletin: 277
Rich Hardcastle: 290
MCA / Everett / Rex: 295
Jane Turnbull: 297